Dinner Menus
with
Wine

Introducing Emily Chase

We persuaded Emily Chase, who has worked with the winemakers of California as a consultant to the Wine Institute, to enlarge her delightful volume, DINNER WITH EMILY, for publication by The Wine Appreciation Guild.

This new edition, DINNER MENUS WITH WINE, contains additional menus and recipes, suggestions for wines to accompany the dinners, and tips on serving, storing, and enjoying wine.

Knowing that daily menu-planning can become a chore for many people, Emily had gathered together menus and recipes for the sort of uncomplicated dinners she enjoys serving to her family and friends. Three thousand copies of DINNER WITH EMILY were privately published by Emily Chase and her husband, George Leistner, and were quickly sold out. It is our hope that the DINNER MENUS WITH WINE, with its many additions will be received with even greater enthusiasm.

It is a small wonder that Emily's recipes produced delicious meals — she has a wealth of background in the food field. A native California, Emily graduated from Stanford University and received degrees in Home Economics from Simmons College and the University of Washington. As Home Economics Editor of SUNSET Magazine for six years, she tested and presented hundreds of recipes highlighting Western ingredients, including California wines. For SUNSET she edited *Sunset Salad Book* and *Sunset Cook Book of Favorite Recipes*. Later as a freelance foods consultant, she spent six years creating and testing wine recipes for the Home Advisory Service of the Wine Institute. She is the author of the *Pleasures of Cooking with Wine* (Prentice-Hall, Inc.).

We believe that those who enjoy meals from this book will agree with Emily that "Wine makes the dish and the dinner!"

> WINE ADVISORY BOARD
> D.C. Turrentine, Manager

Over the past year we have received a number of inquires from homemakers and wine lovers for Emily Chases' "Wine Cookbook". In this age of increased wine awareness, the popularity of a totally planned gourmet meal with matching wines is well apparent. We at The Wine Appreciation Guild are delighted to again publish this useful and timely cookbook.

> Donna Bottrell
> THE WINE APPRECIATION GUILD

Dinner Menus
with
Wine

By Emily Chase

Other books published by The Wine Appreciation Guild:
THE CHAMPAGNE COOKBOOK
NEW ADVENTURES IN WINE COOKERY
EPICUREAN RECIPES OF CALIFORNIA WINEMAKERS
GOURMET WINE COOKING THE EASY WAY
FAVORITE RECIPES OF CALIFORNIA WINEMAKERS
WINE COOKBOOK OF DINNER MENUS
EASY RECIPES OF CALIFORNIA WINEMAKERS
THE POCKET ENCYCLOPEDIA OF CALIFORNIA WINE
IN CELEBRATION OF WINE AND LIFE
WINE CELLAR RECORD BOOK
WINE COOKING FOR EVERYDAY
CORKSCREWS: AN INTRODUCTION TO THEIR APPRECIATION
THE CALIFORNIA WINE DRINK BOOK
THE VINTAGE IMAGE SERIES:
NAPA VALLEY WINE TOUR
NAPA VALLEY WINE BOOK
SONOMA MENDOCINO WINE TOUR
SONOMA MENDOCINO WINE BOOK
CENTRAL COAST WINE TOUR
CENTRAL COAST WINE BOOK

Production Editor
Frances W. Hewlett
Editor
Marjorie Kent Jacobs
Assistant Editor
Elizabeth Bannerman
Illustrator
Nancy J. Kennedy
Cover Design
Caldewey & Nelson
Cover Photographer
Bill Miller
Food Stylist
Olivia Erschen

CONTENTS

Items in menus not marked by asterisks are simple accompaniments for which no recipes are included in this book.

Aperitif

Have you ever started to plan dinner and suddenly had the feeling that you were going around in circles, serving the same familiar dishes week after week? I guess you'd call this acute menu-itis, and lucky is the cook who doesn't suffer from it once in a while!

Of course, there are people who really like an unvaried menu routine. I have a friend to whom Monday night for years has been synonymous with broiled lamb chops, frozen peas, and baked potatoes. But if, like me, you consider variety the spice of good eating, you'll enjoy giving your old standbys a rest and perking things up with some new ideas now and then.

Gathered here are menus for dinners designed to make the eaters happy without exhausting the cook. Except for the menus in the chapter, "Something A Little Special," these are two-course affairs, because I belong to the short-menu, plenty-of-it school of thought. You'll notice I've left the choice of what bread to serve up to you, except where a special recipe is involved. Thanks to the neighborhood bakery, packaged mixes, and such temptations as refrigerated *croissants* and frozen *brioches,* interesting breadstuffs are no problem at all.

An asterisk after a dish in the menu means you'll find the recipe on that page, or the next. On some pages, where space permits, I have also included another main-dish recipe that isn't in the menu. These "extras" are other favorites of mine that I want you to try. A dotted line separates these from the menu recipes.

A number of my menu suggestions don't require recipes and therefore aren't marked with an asterisk. These are things like *Lemon Sherbet* or *Eclairs* that are easy to buy ready-made, and *Buttered Noodles* or *Sliced Tomato Salad* that are very simple to prepare.

Naturally you won't want to follow every one of my suggestions to the letter. What your family likes, what's left in the larder from last night, and various other "whats" are bound to make a difference in your dinner plans. But you can always tailor these menus to fit your needs, mixing and matching, adding and subtracting as you wish. I hope my ideas will serve as a source of culinary inspiration, and will lead to the enjoyment of many happy meals.

I. Simmer Gently Until Tender

Stews and other good meat-in-gravy dishes

When it comes to soul-satisfying main dishes, it's hard to beat the meat-in-gravy family. A good stew, a succulent pork chop braised with wine, or a tender, well-sauced lamb shank make wonderful eating. What's more, these dishes are delightfully undemanding from the cook's standpoint. Any preliminary flouring and browning of the meat takes but a few minutes, then the rest of the ingredients go into the pot, and slow simmering, with an occasional stirring, is all that's required. A stew or any of its relatives is even better made ahead of time...in the morning for dinner, or even the day before.

Many meat-in-gravy recipes are amply proportioned, a blessing in disguise for the small family. Change the accompaniments the second time around, and you'll have the effect of a different dish without any of the preparation.

DINNER

Beef San Joaquin*
Buttered Shell Macaroni
Broccoli Polonaise*
Lemon or Pineapple Sherbet
(dash a little California Sherry over each serving)
Mystery Chocolate Balls*

With this menu we enjoy:

California Cabernet Sauvignon

Beef San Joaquin

2 pounds round steak, cut ½ inch thick
½ cup flour
3 tablespoons butter or bacon drippings
1 (1-lb.) can stewed tomatoes
½ cup California Dry or Medium Sherry or
   Dry Vermouth
½ cup canned consommé or bouillon-cube broth
3 carrots, thinly sliced
1 cup diced celery
1 medium-sized onion, diced
   Bit of chopped or pressed garlic
1 bay leaf, crumbled
2 tablespoons parsley flakes
   Salt and pepper to taste

Trim excess fat from meat. Pound flour into both sides of meat with a meat tenderizer or the edge of a heavy saucer. Cut meat across grain into narrow strips about 2 inches long. Heat butter in a large, heavy skillet or a Dutch oven; add meat and brown nicely on all sides. Add all remaining ingredients. Bring to a boil, then cover and simmer very gently for 1½ hours, or until meat is fork-tender. Stir occasionally, and add a little consommé or water if gravy becomes too thick. Before serving, taste and add salt and pepper, if necessary. Serves 4 to 6.

Broccoli Polonaise

Melt ¼ cup butter in a small skillet. Add ½ cup packaged fine bread crumbs; stir over low heat until crumbs are golden brown. Add 1 teaspoon lemon juice and a generous sprinkling of dry shredded green onions; lightly mix in 1 shredded, hard-cooked egg. Drain hot, cooked broccoli and arrange in serving dish or on dinner plates; sprinkle with crumb mixture. Enough crumb mixture for 6 servings. This is also a good treatment for cauliflower, green beans, and asparagus.

I really never thought I'd give this recipe away! I've had fun mystifying people with it for years, and so far no one has been able to guess the ingredients. These are rich-flavored, handsome little cooky balls that I can't recommend too heartily.

Mystery Chocolate Balls

1 (6-oz.) package semi-sweet chocolate morsels
1 (9¼ or 11-oz.) package pie crust (2 sticks)
2 teaspoons vanilla
½ cup finely chopped walnuts or pecans
¾ cup cocoa
¾ cup confectioners' sugar

Melt chocolate morsels in top of double boiler over *hot* (not boiling) water. Remove pan from water. Gradually blend in pie crust mix, stirring until smooth after each addition. Add vanilla, then nuts, mixing until well blended. At this point, if dough is soft and sticky, let it stand at room temperature until it can be handled easily without sticking to your hands. (You can chill it *briefly* in the refrigerator, but don't let it get too hard!) Shape dough into marble-sized balls (a scant 1 inch in diameter, no bigger) and place on ungreased baking sheets. Bake the cookies in a hot oven (400° F.) for 10 minutes. Meantime, mix cocoa and confectioners' sugar; sift into a large mixing bowl. Remove baked cookies from oven and let stand 5 minutes, then roll carefully in the cocoa-sugar mixture. When thoroughly cold, roll again. (Store any unused cocoa-sugar mixture in a covered jar for your next batch of cookies.) Makes about 6 dozen cookies.

DINNER

Baked Swiss Steak with Rice*
Green Beans with Pine Nuts*
Pimiento-Stuffed Olives and Carrot Sticks
Bananas Tropical with Coconut Cream*

With this menu we enjoy:

California Burgundy

Baked Swiss Steak with Rice

1½ pounds round steak, cut 1 inch thick
    Flour, salt, and pepper
¼ cup bacon drippings or other fat
1 large onion, thinly sliced
    Bit of chopped or pressed garlic
1 green pepper, slivered
½ cup uncooked rice
2 cups well-drained canned tomatoes
1½ cups canned consommé or bouillon-cube broth
½ cup California Red Table Wine
    Pinch each of thyme and marjoram

Trim excess fat from meat. Mix ½ cup flour, 1½ teaspoons salt, and ½ teaspoon pepper. Pound mixture into both sides of meat, using a meat tenderizer or the edge of a heavy saucer. Cut meat into 4 pieces. Heat bacon drippings in a large, heavy skillet; add meat, onion, garlic, and green pepper; cook until meat is nicely browned, turning to brown both sides. Transfer meat and vegetables to a baking dish. Sprinkle rice over meat; arrange tomatoes over the top. Add 2 tablespoons flour to drippings in skillet and blend well; add consommé and wine; cook, stirring constantly, until mixture boils and thickens; season to taste with salt, pepper, thyme, and marjoram. Pour over contents of casserole. Cover and bake in a moderate oven (350° F.) for about 1¾ to 2 hours, or until meat is very tender. Serves 4.

Green Beans with Pine Nuts

Use cooked fresh or frozen French-style green beans, or canned ones, if you prefer. For 4 to 6 servings of beans, melt 2 tablespoons butter in a small skillet; add ½ cup pine nuts; toast over low heat just until nuts are a light golden brown. Stir often and watch carefully lest the nuts burn! Add toasted nuts to the well-drained beans, along with additional butter to taste. Toss gently and heat thoroughly before serving.

Bananas Tropical with Coconut Cream

Peel 4 firm bananas; arrange in a greased, shallow baking dish; brush with melted butter. Sprinkle generously with brown sugar and sparingly with rum or California Sweet Sherry. Bake in a moderately hot oven (375° F.) for 15 to 20 minutes, or until tender. Serve warm with *Coconut Cream:* Whip ⅔ cup heavy cream; sweeten with 1 tablespoon confectioners' sugar; fold in ⅔ cup flaked coconut and ½ teaspoon vanilla. Serves 4.

....

Mushroom Braised Beef

Have 2 pounds round steak cut 1 inch thick; trim off excess fat. Pound ⅓ cup flour into both sides of meat; cut into strips about ½ inch wide and 2 inches long. Heat ¼ cup bacon drippings or salad oil in a large, heavy skillet; brown meat nicely. Add 1 (10½-oz.) can condensed cream of mushroom soup; ½ cup California Dry or Medium Sherry or Dry Vermouth; 1 (8-oz.) can mushrooms, drained; 1 large onion, chopped; bit of chopped garlic; 2 tablespoons parsley flakes; ½ teaspoon *each* paprika and Worcestershire sauce; salt and pepper to taste. Cover; simmer gently about 1½ hours, or until meat is tender, stirring often. Before serving, add 1 cup dairy sour cream; taste and correct seasoning. Serves 4 to 6. Wine choice: California Gamay. P. S. If gravy seems too thick at any time, add a little of the mushroom liquid. Serve with noodles and spinach soufflé.

DINNER

Braised Beef with Olives*
Buttered Spaghetti with Parmesan Cheese
Zucchini Sauté*
Upside-Down Boysenberry Pudding*

With this menu we enjoy:

California Red Chianti

Braised Beef with Olives

4 slices bacon, diced
1 large onion, diced
2 pounds lean beef stew meat, cut in small cubes
  Flour
½ cup California Red Table Wine
½ cup canned consommé or bouillon-cube broth
1 (8-oz.) can tomato sauce
  Bit of chopped or pressed garlic
1 bay leaf, crumbled
¼ teaspoon marjoram
  Salt and pepper to taste
1 cup pitted ripe olives, halved
2 tablespoons parsley flakes

Cook bacon and onion together slowly in a Dutch oven or other heavy kettle until bacon begins to brown. Dredge meat with flour; add to kettle and brown slowly on all sides. (If bacon is lean, 1 to 2 tablespoons fat may be added for browning meat.) Add wine, consommé, tomato sauce, garlic, and seasonings. Cover and simmer very gently for about 2½ hours, or until meat is fork-tender. Stir frequently and add water as needed during cooking to keep gravy from becoming too thick. Shortly before serving, add olives and parsley. Correct seasoning as necessary. Serves 4 to 6.

Zucchini Sauté

2 pounds small zucchini (or 1 pound each: zucchini and crookneck squash)
2 tablespoons each: salad oil and butter
1 tablespoon instant minced onion
1 tablespoon parsley flakes
¼ cup water
  Pinch each of thyme and rosemary
  Salt, garlic salt, and pepper to taste

Wash zucchini and trim off ends (do not peel); slice crosswise paper-thin. Heat oil and butter in a large skillet; add zucchini and sauté gently, stirring fre-

quently, until zucchini is lightly browned. Add remaining ingredients. Cover and cook gently for 5 to 10 minutes, or just until zucchini is tender, stirring occasionally. Serves 6.

Upside-Down Boysenberry Pudding

Mix 1¼ cups prepared biscuit mix with 2 tablespoons sugar; stir in ½ cup milk. Spread in bottom of greased 2-quart casserole. Drain 1 (1-lb.) can boysenberries (or youngberries), reserving syrup. Arrange berries over dough; sprinkle with ½ cup sugar. Heat 1 cup boysenberry syrup and 2 tablespoons butter to boiling; pour over berries. Bake in a moderately hot oven (375° F.) 45 to 50 minutes. (As the pudding bakes, the crust will rise to the top.) Serve warm with cream. Serves 6.

•••••••••••••••••••••

Mexican Beef and Bean Stew

This would also be good in the menu. Dredge 2 pounds cubed beef stew meat with flour. Heat ¼ cup salad oil in a heavy kettle; brown meat slowly. Add 1 large onion, 1 clove garlic, and 1 green pepper, chopped; 1 (10½-oz.) can condensed consommé; 1 cup *each* California Red Table Wine and water; 1 (6-oz.) can tomato paste; 1 teaspoon chili powder; ½ teaspoon *each* cumin seed and oregano; salt and pepper to taste. Cover; simmer 2½ hours, or until meat is tender. Add 2 (1-lb.) cans red kidney beans, drained, and 1 cup pitted ripe olives; heat thoroughly. If gravy needs thinning, add a little bean liquid. Serves 6 to 8. Wine choice: California Charbono.

DINNER

Beef and Pork Ragoût*
Rice and Spinach Torta*
Sliced Tomato or Tomato Aspic Salad
(with French dressing)
Lemon Velvet Pie*

With this menu we enjoy:
California Claret

Beef and Pork Ragoût

2 tablespoons butter or bacon drippings
1 pound lean beef stew meat, cubed
1 pound lean pork, cubed
1 large onion, chopped
1 clove garlic, chopped or pressed
½ teaspoon paprika
2 tablespoons flour
¾ cup canned consommé or bouillon-cube broth
½ cup California Red Table Wine
1 (6-oz.) can sliced broiled mushrooms (undrained)
1 tablespoon parsley flakes
1 teaspoon Worcestershire sauce
Salt and pepper to taste
1 cup dairy sour cream

Heat butter in a large, heavy skillet or a Dutch oven. Add beef, pork, onion, and garlic; sprinkle with paprika; sauté, stirring frequently, until meat is nicely browned. Sprinkle flour over meat and stir well; add consommé, wine, mushrooms (including liquid), parsley, Worcestershire sauce, salt and pepper; cook, stirring constantly, until gravy boils and thickens. Cover and simmer very gently for about 2½ hours, or until meat is fork-tender. Stir frequently and add a little consommé or water if gravy seems too thick. Just before serving, stir in sour cream; taste and add additional salt and pepper if necessary. Serves 4 to 6.

Rice and Spinach Torta

1 (10-oz.) package frozen chopped spinach
⅔ cup uncooked rice (2 cups cooked)
1 cup grated Cheddar cheese
3 eggs, well beaten
1 cup milk
1 tablespoon instant minced onion
3 tablespoons salad oil or melted butter
½ teaspoon Worcestershire sauce
Seasoned salt and pepper to taste
Paprika

Cook spinach according to directions on carton; drain *thoroughly*. Boil or steam rice until tender; drain, if necessary. With a fork, lightly mix spinach, rice, and cheese. Blend eggs and milk; add to spinach mixture; add all remaining ingredients except paprika. Turn into a well-greased 10 by 6 by 2-inch baking dish; bake in a moderate oven (350° F.) about 45 minutes, or until firm in the center. Remove from oven and sprinkle with paprika. Let stand 5 to 10 minutes to settle before serving. Serves 6.

Lemon Velvet Pie

Prepare 1 (3¾-oz.) package instant lemon pudding according to package directions for pie, using 1 cup milk and 1 cup dairy sour cream as the liquids. Pour into 8-inch graham cracker pie shell (available packaged); chill at least one hour. Before serving, spread with thin layer of your favorite preserves. Serves 6. Luscious!

....

Easy-Do Beef Stew

Dredge 2 pounds cubed beef stew meat with flour. Heat 2 tablespoons butter or bacon drippings in a large, heavy skillet or a Dutch oven; brown meat nicely. Add 1 (10½-oz.) can condensed onion soup, 1 cup water, ½ cup California Dry or Medium Sherry or Dry Vermouth, and salt and pepper to taste. Cover; simmer gently, stirring frequently, about 2½ hours, or until meat is fork-tender. Add a little water if gravy thickens too much. Before serving, add 1 (10-oz.) package frozen peas and celery (cooked and drained) and, if you like, some cooked or canned sliced or julienne carrots. Serves 4 to 6. Wine choice: California Burgundy. Good with buttered noodles or spaghetti sprinkled with grated Parmesan cheese, or with rice.

DINNER

Braised Beef Italienne*
Polenta*
Hot Asparagus or Asparagus Salad
Fresh Pears and/or Apples
Monterey Jack Cheese

With this menu we enjoy:

California Barbera

Braised Beef Italienne

2 pounds lean beef stew meat, cubed
   Flour
2 tablespoons olive oil
1 medium-sized onion, chopped
1 clove garlic, chopped or pressed
1 ounce dried mushrooms
1 cup water
1 (15-oz.) can marinara sauce (or two 7¾-oz. cans)
½ cup California Dry or Medium Sherry or
   Red Table Wine
½ teaspoon mixed Italian seasoning
   Salt and pepper to taste

Dredge meat with flour. Heat oil in a large, heavy skillet or a Dutch oven; sauté meat, onion, and garlic until meat is nicely browned. Combine mushrooms and water in a small saucepan; heat to boiling. Remove from heat; drain mushrooms, reserving liquid. Cut mushrooms fairly fine with scissors; add with their liquid to the meat. Add remaining ingredients. Cover and simmer gently, stirring frequently, for about 2½ hours, or until meat is fork-tender. Add a little more water if needed as gravy cooks down. Serves 4 to 6.

Polenta

1½ cups corn meal
1½ teaspoons salt
4½ cups water
  ¼ to ½ pound process Cheddar cheese, shredded
    (the more the better!)
  3 tablespoons butter

In top of a double boiler mix corn meal, salt, and 1½ cups cold water; stir until smooth; stir in 3 cups boiling water. Place over low heat and cook, stir-

ring, until mixture boils and thickens. Cover; cook over boiling water for 1 hour, stirring occasionally. Add cheese and butter; stir until melted and blended with the polenta mixture. Taste and add more salt, if needed. To serve, spoon polenta in a ring on a heated platter; fill center with *Braised Beef Italienne*. Serves 6.

••••••••••••••••••••••••••

Stew à la Grecque

2 tablespoons butter or bacon drippings
2 pounds lean beef stew meat, cubed
2 tablespoons flour
1 (8-oz.) can tomato sauce
1 cup California Red Table Wine
1 large onion, diced
2 carrots, scraped and diced
2 tablespoons parsley flakes
1 teaspoon powdered cinnamon
¼ teaspoon powdered cloves
1 (2-in.) strip each: orange peel and lemon peel
   Salt and pepper to taste

Heat butter in a Dutch oven or a large, heavy skillet; brown meat slowly. Stir in flour; add tomato sauce and wine; cook, stirring, until mixture boils. Add remaining ingredients. Cover; simmer gently about 2½ hours, or until meat is fork-tender. Stir often; add a little water if needed to thin gravy. Serves 4 to 6. Wine choice: California Red Chianti. The spices and peels give this stew a delightful flavor. Macaroni mixed with butter and Parmesan cheese is a "must" with it.

DINNER

Lazy Bones* or Lazy Stew*
with Vegetables
Mashed Potatoes, Noodles, or Rice
Crisp Celery Hearts
Chocolate Moussette*

With this menu we enjoy:

California Zinfandel

Lazy Bones

3 pounds beef shortribs, cut in pieces for serving
1 (10¾-oz.) can beef gravy
1 (10½-oz.) can condensed cream of mushroom
  soup
½ cup California Red Table Wine
2 tablespoons instant minced onion
  Bit of chopped or pressed garlic
2 tablespoons parsley flakes
1 (1-lb.) can small whole onions, drained
1 (1-lb.) can small whole carrots, drained
1 (10-oz.) package frozen peas, cooked and drained
  Salt and pepper to taste

Arrange shortribs in a single layer in a large casserole or in a Dutch oven or roaster. Mix gravy, soup, wine, onion, garlic, and parsley; pour over meat. Cover and bake in a moderate oven (350° F.) for 2½ to 3 hours, or until meat is tender, turning and basting meat occasionally. Before serving, check the gravy (see *Gravy Notes* below) and add drained vegetables. Serves 4.

Lazy Stew

Follow the recipe above for Lazy Bones, but substitute 3 pounds lean beef stew meat, cubed, for the shortribs. (I use a 4-quart casserole for cooking.) Serves 6 to 8. This is one of the best (and simplest!) stews I know. We often serve it to company. Sometimes I substitute canned sliced mushrooms for the onions, and serve the carrots and peas separately on the plate rather than in the gravy with the meat.

Gravy Notes: A few minutes before you are ready to add the vegetables to *Lazy Bones* or *Lazy Stew,* check the gravy for consistency. If it is thinner than you like it, shake about ½ cup water and 2 table-spoons or so of flour together in a pint jar until smooth, stir this mixture into the hot stew, and return the pot to the oven for a few minutes, to let the gravy simmer and thicken.

If you want fat-free gravy, cook the meat a day ahead. Cool it, then chill it overnight. Before serving, remove the solid layer of fat from the top of the meat, reheat the dish and check the gravy for consistency as above.

If you want more gravy for either of these dishes, just add another can of beef gravy to the finished dish.

In any case, before serving, be sure the gravy is properly seasoned with salt and pepper, and, if you like, add a spoonful or two of California Sherry for a good flavor touch.

Chocolate Moussette

1 pint chocolate ice cream
½ cup milk (or sour cream, for a richer dessert)
1 (4½-oz.) package instant chocolate pudding
  Whipped cream

Stir ice cream to soften it slightly; blend in milk. Add pudding mix and beat *just* until well blended, about 1 minute. Spoon into sherbet glasses or dessert dishes; chill at least 1 hour. Serve topped with whipped cream. For an added touch of truly ambrosial flavor, trickle a little coffee-flavored wine or liqueur or crème de menthe over the cream. Serves 5 or 6. This is a wonderful dessert, and so simple to make.

P. S. To make *Mocha Moussette,* substitute coffee ice cream for the chocolate ice cream. Trickle a little chocolate or coffee-flavored wine or liqueur over the whipped cream. Delectable!

DINNER

Stuffed Flank Steak Bohemia*
Buttered Wide Noodles
Baked Spinach-Topped Tomatoes*
Swedish Applesauce Torte*

With this menu we enjoy:

California Claret

Stuffed Flank Steak Bohemia

1 flank steak (1½ to 2 lbs.)
1 (4-oz.) can mushroom stems and pieces
⅓ cup butter
2 cups packaged herb-seasoned bread stuffing
¼ cup grated Parmesan cheese
2 tablespoons parsley flakes
Salt and pepper to taste
Flour
3 tablespoons bacon drippings or salad oil
1 (10½-oz.) can condensed onion soup
½ cup California Red Table Wine

Have meat dealer score flank steak. Drain mushrooms, reserving liquid; chop mushrooms coarsely. Measure mushroom liquid and add water to make ⅔ cup; combine with butter in a saucepan. Heat mixture until butter melts; add stuffing crumbs; toss lightly with a fork to moisten crumbs. Add cheese, parsley, salt, and pepper. Spread this mixture evenly over steak; roll up, from one wide side to the other, tucking in ends as you roll. Fasten roll with skewers or string. Dredge with flour. Heat bacon drippings in a large, heavy skillet; brown steak nicely on all sides. Add soup and wine; cover and simmer gently for 1½ to 2 hours, or until meat is very tender. Turn steak frequently and add a little water as needed during cooking to keep gravy from becoming too thick. To serve, remove skewers or string and place steak on heated platter. Slice, cutting across fibres. Pass gravy separately. (If you like *lots* of gravy, you may want to add all or part of a can of beef gravy to the pan gravy before serving.) Serves 5 or 6.

Baked Spinach-Topped Tomatoes

Cook and drain *thoroughly* 1 (10-oz.) package frozen chopped spinach. Mix spinach, 2 tablespoons mayonnaise, 2 tablespoons grated Parmesan cheese, 1 teaspoon dry shredded green onions, and salt and pepper to taste. Cut 3 medium-sized tomatoes crosswise in halves; place cut side up in a shallow baking dish. Spread spinach mixture on top of tomatoes; sprinkle with cornflake crumbs, more Parmesan cheese, and paprika. Bake in a very hot oven (450° F.) for 15 minutes, or until crumbs are golden. Serves 6.

Swedish Applesauce Torte

Mix 1½ (1-lb.) cans applesauce (3 cups) and 1 teaspoon cinnamon; spread in a 9-inch pie plate. Mix 1 cup packaged graham cracker crumbs, ½ cup (firmly packed) brown sugar, and ¼ cup melted butter; sprinkle evenly over applesauce and pat down gently but firmly. Bake in a moderately hot oven (375° F.) for 30 to 35 minutes. Serve warm or chilled, with plain or whipped cream, sour cream, or vanilla ice cream. Serves 6. Incidentally, this is an excellent dessert for a large gathering, since it's almost as easy to make several tortes as it is one.

. . . .

London Broil à la Emily

This isn't a "simmer gently" dish, but it's too good to omit. With tip of a sharp knife, score an untenderized flank steak (1½ pounds or more) on both sides in 1½-inch diamonds; rub with garlic. Lay it in a shallow glass dish. Brush with salad oil; sprinkle with California red wine vinegar, seasoned salt, and coarse black pepper; turn and repeat on other side. Cover dish with foil; refrigerate several hours. Bring meat to room temperature before cooking. Broil 3 to 4 inches from heat, 5 minutes to a side. (No more!) To serve, slice *thinly* on diagonal across grain. Pass this sauce: Melt ¼ pound butter; add ⅓ cup canned consommé, ¼ cup California Red Table Wine, 1 to 2 teaspoons Worcestershire sauce, 1 tablespoon parsley flakes, 1 teaspoon dry shredded green onions, salt to taste; heat to simmering. Serves 4 or more. Wine choice: California Zinfandel.

DINNER

Pot Roast Monterey*
with Vegetables
Baked Potatoes Caliente*
Ripe Olives and Radishes
Toasted Pound Cake*

With this menu we enjoy:

California Burgundy

Pot Roast Monterey

4 to 5 pounds beef chuck, rolled and tied
2 tablespoons bacon drippings or salad oil
1 (10¾-oz.) can condensed tomato soup
½ cup canned consommé or bouillon-cube broth
½ cup California Red Table Wine
2 tablespoons instant minced onion
1 clove garlic, chopped
2 tablespoons parsley flakes
   Dash of thyme
1 bay leaf, crumbled
6 whole peppercorns
3 whole allspice
   Salt and pepper to taste

Heat fat in a Dutch oven or other heavy kettle; brown meat slowly on all sides. Add remaining ingredients. Cover and simmer very, very gently for 3 to 4 hours, or until meat is tender, turning meat occasionally. Remove meat from kettle and make gravy (below). If necessary, reheat pot roast gently in the gravy before serving. Serves 8 or more.

Gravy for Pot Roast: Strain broth and skim off as much of the fat as possible. Measure 3 cups broth, adding consommé or water as needed to make that amount; pour back into kettle and heat to simmering. In a covered jar, shake together ⅓ cup flour and ½ cup consommé or water until smooth; stir slowly into simmering broth; continue cooking and stirring until mixture is thickened and smooth, then simmer about 5 minutes longer. Add 2 tablespoons California Sherry and salt and pepper to taste. Serve piping hot.

Vegetables for Pot Roast: Carrots, peas, and little whole onions are a "must" with this roast. You can cook fresh ones if you like, but I usually use canned baby carrots, canned small whole onions, and frozen peas. Arrange the hot vegetables around the roast on the platter, and you'll have a picture pretty enough to paint (*and* eat)!

More Thoughts About Pot Roast

Substitute cream of mushroom soup for the tomato soup in *Pot Roast Monterey* and you'll have another flavorful dish. Canned or sautéed fresh mushrooms are a good addition to the gravy in either case.

Pot roast left over? Heat slices in the gravy and serve on buttered, toasted English muffins for an excellent hot sandwich. Or, flavor the gravy with curry powder, heat slices in it, and serve with rice. Canned beef gravy is handy if you run short of the "original."

Baked Potatoes Caliente

Bake 1 good-sized potato for each person to be served. When done, remove from oven and cut a slice from the flat side. Scoop out the inside with a teaspoon and mash well. For each potato add:

2 tablespoons dairy sour cream
2 tablespoons grated Cheddar cheese
1 tablespoon finely chopped canned peeled green
   chili pepper
   Salt to taste

Beat mixture well; pile lightly in potato shells. Sprinkle each potato with another 1 tablespoon grated Cheddar cheese and dust with paprika. Bake in a hot oven (450° F.) for 10 minutes, or until hot and delicately browned.

Toasted Pound Cake

Toast thick slices of pound cake lightly. Brush with melted butter. Serve at once accompanied by a bowl of whipped cream cheese (cream cheese beaten till light with a little milk) and a bowl of your favorite jam or jelly, so that each person can create an open-faced cake "sandwich." (Store-bought pound cake is excellent for this.)

DINNER

Veal Cream Stew*
Peas with Carrots*
Noodles O'Brien*
Warm Gingerbread
with Whipped Cream Cheese
(blend cream cheese with a little milk)

With this menu we enjoy:

California Chablis

Veal Cream Stew

2 pounds veal stew meat, cubed
3 cups boiling water
1 cup California White Table Wine
1 each: large onion, carrot, and celery stalk, sliced
1 bay leaf, pinch of thyme, and 5 or 6 whole peppercorns
  Salt to taste
6 tablespoons butter
6 tablespoons flour
1 cup cream
2 tablespoons parsley flakes
2 tablespoons drained capers (if you like)
1 teaspoon Worcestershire sauce
½ teaspoon grated lemon peel
¼ teaspoon paprika
  Pepper to taste

Place veal in a Dutch oven or other heavy kettle. Add water, wine, onion, carrot, celery, bay leaf, thyme, peppercorns, and salt. Cover and simmer very gently for about 1½ to 2 hours, or until veal is very tender. Remove veal from stock. Strain stock; measure 2 cups. Melt butter and stir in flour; add reserved 2 cups stock and cream; cook, stirring constantly, until mixture boils and thickens. Add remaining ingredients and the veal. Season with salt to taste. Heat thoroughly before serving. Serves 4 to 6.

P. S. Mushrooms may be added to the veal, if desired. Add canned ones to the sauce as is; sauté fresh ones in the butter for a few minutes before adding the flour.

Peas with Carrots

Use frozen peas and carrots, or combine cooked peas with canned baby carrots or cooked fresh carrots.

In any case, add a generous pat of butter to the hot vegetables, and season with celery salt and a dash of pepper.

Noodles O'Brien

Cook 8 oz. wide noodles in boiling salted water until tender; drain. Melt ¼ cup butter in the same pot, add noodles and stir gently over low heat until thoroughly heated. Add 2 tablespoons chopped pimiento, 2 tablespoons grated green pepper and 2 teaspoons dry shredded green onions; stir until well mixed. Salt to taste. Serves 5 or 6.

. . . .

Curried Veal Stew

2 pounds boneless veal shoulder, cut in 1-inch cubes
⅓ cup flour
4 tablespoons bacon drippings or salad oil
1 cup California White Table Wine
1 (1-lb.) can stewed tomatoes
2 large onions, chopped
1 clove garlic, chopped or pressed
2 teaspoons curry powder (or to taste)
  Salt and pepper to taste
6 carrots, scraped and thinly sliced
1 cup diced celery

Dredge veal with flour by shaking cubes together in a paper bag. Heat bacon drippings in a Dutch oven or other heavy kettle; add veal and any flour remaining in bag; brown veal slowly on all sides. Add wine, tomatoes, onions, garlic, and seasonings; cover; simmer gently, stirring often, for 30 minutes. Add carrots and celery; continue cooking for 30 to 45 minutes, or until veal is tender. Add a little water if needed to thin gravy during cooking. Serves 4 to 6. Wine choice: California Rosé.

DINNER
Veal and Pork Drumsticks*
Special Mashed Potatoes*
Mimi's Succotash*
Strawberry Sundae   Cookies

With this menu we enjoy:

California Dry Sauterne

"Drumsticks," "City Chicken Legs," "Mock Chicken Legs"... by any name these are succulent morsels.

Veal and Pork Drumsticks

1 pound veal steak, cut in 1 to 1½-inch cubes
1 pound pork steak, cut in 1 to 1½-inch cubes
    Seasoned salt and pepper
    Flour
  2 eggs, slightly beaten
  2 tablespoons water
  1 cup packaged corn flake crumbs
  2 tablespoons each: bacon drippings and salad oil
1½ cups canned chicken broth (or make it with chicken-stock base or bouillon cubes)
 ¾ cup California White Table Wine or Dry Vermouth
  1 tablespoon instant minced onion
  2 tablespoons parsley flakes
    Dash of thyme and paprika

Sprinkle meat with seasoned salt and pepper. Thread veal and pork cubes alternately on 10 or 12 (4½ to 5-inch) wooden or metal skewers. Roll drumsticks in flour; dip in beaten eggs mixed with water; roll in corn flake crumbs. Heat bacon drippings and oil in a large, heavy skillet; add drumsticks and brown slowly on all sides. Remove drumsticks from pan. Add 2 tablespoons flour to drippings in pan and blend well. (If drippings are on the scant side add 1 to 2 tablespoons butter, also.) Add chicken broth and wine; cook, stirring constantly, until gravy boils and thickens; add onion, parsley, thyme, and paprika; season to taste with seasoned salt and pepper. Return drumsticks to skillet. Cover and simmer gently for about 1 hour, or until meat is tender. Turn and baste drumsticks occasionally, and add a little more chicken stock or water if gravy becomes too thick. Serves 5 or 6.

Special Mashed Potatoes

Prepare instant mashed potatoes as directed on the package, but substitute canned chicken broth for the required water. Taste before adding salt, since the broth is seasoned. Extra-special flavor!

Mimi's Succotash

5 slices bacon, cut fine with scissors
1 small onion, chopped
1 (1-lb.) can French-style green beans, drained, or about 2½ cups cooked green beans
1 (12-oz.) can vacuum-packed Mexican-style whole kernel corn, drained
1 tablespoon parsley flakes
    Dash each of marjoram and rosemary
    Salt and pepper to taste

Cook bacon slowly until crisp. Remove bacon bits from pan. Add onion to bacon drippings; sauté gently 5 minutes. Add beans, corn, parsley, and seasonings; cover; simmer gently for 5 minutes. Turn into a heated serving dish and sprinkle bacon bits on top. Serves 6.

Braised Veal Chops Amelia

Flour 4 *thick* veal rib chops; brown slowly in 3 tablespoons bacon drippings in a heavy skillet; pour off most of drippings. Add 1 (10½-oz.) can condensed onion soup, ⅓ cup California Dry Vermouth or Sherry, 2 tablespoons tomato paste, 1 tablespoon parsley flakes, dash of thyme and marjoram. Cover; simmer gently 1 hour, or until chops are tender; turn and baste occasionally. Serves 4. Wine choice: California Rosé.

SUMMER DINNER

Jellied Veal and Ham Loaf*   Dilly Potato Salad*
Tossed Green Salad with Wedges
of Tomato & Avocado
Fresh Peach-Strawberry Bowl*
Macaroons

With this menu we enjoy:

California Grey Riesling

Jellied Veal and Ham Loaf

Have 1 veal shank (2½ to 3 lbs.) sawed in pieces. Place in large kettle. Add 2½ quarts water and 2 cups California White Table Wine. Add 1 large onion, 1 stalk celery, 1 carrot and 1 clove garlic, all sliced, several sprigs parsley, 3 bay leaves, ¼ teaspoon thyme, several whole peppercorns and salt to taste. Bring to a boil, cover and simmer 2 to 2½ hours, or until meat is tender enough to fall from the bones. Remove meat from kettle. Strain broth; boil rapidly until reduced to 1 quart. Separate meat from bone; remove fat and gristle; put through food grinder, using coarse blade. Proceed as follows:

1 envelope (1 tablespoon) unflavored gelatin
¼ cup cold water
½ pound boiled or baked ham, ground
3 hard-cooked eggs, coarsely shredded
2 tablespoons chopped parsley
1 tablespoon finely chopped onion
2 teaspoons Worcestershire sauce
 Seasoned salt to taste

Soften gelatin in cold water; dissolve in a little of the hot veal broth; add to remaining broth. Let cool for 15 minutes or so. Mix veal, ham, eggs, parsley and onion; stir in gelatin-broth mixture; season with Worcestershire and seasoned salt. Pour into a loaf pan (10 by 5 by 3 inches) that has been rinsed with cold water; chill until firm. Unmold and garnish with sprigs of parsley or watercress. Slice with a very sharp knife and serve as you would any cold meat. Serves 8 or more. Dijon-style prepared mustard is a must with this.

Dilly Potato Salad

6 medium-sized potatoes (about 3 lbs.)
1 medium-sized onion, chopped
1 pimiento, chopped
½ cup chopped dill pickle
½ cup dill pickle liquid
4 strips bacon, cooked crisp and crumbled
2 hard-cooked eggs, shredded
½ cup salad dressing**
1 teaspoon prepared mustard
¾ cup mayonnaise (approximately)
1 teaspoon celery seed
 Seasoned salt and pepper to taste

Boil potatoes in their jackets just until tender; drain. When cool, peel and dice into mixing bowl. (Bowl may be rubbed with garlic, if you like.) Add onion, pimiento, dill pickle, dill pickle liquid, bacon, and eggs; toss gently until ingredients are well mixed. Blend salad dressing and mustard together; add to salad; add just enough mayonnaise to moisten mixture nicely. Add celery seed, salt, and pepper. (Remember: A light touch is needed in mixing to avoid mashing the potatoes!) Cover; chill thoroughly before serving. Serves 6.

**I use Miracle Whip for it gives just the flavor this dish requires.

Fresh Peach-Strawberry Bowl

2 cups crushed strawberries
¼ cup California Port
1 tablespoon lemon juice
 Sugar to taste
6 fresh peaches
2 (3-oz.) packages cream cheese
¼ cup cream

Mix strawberries, Port, lemon juice, and sugar. Peel and halve peaches; arrange in a serving bowl; pour strawberry mixture over them; chill thoroughly. Mash cream cheese with a fork; gradually add cream, beating until mixture is smooth; heap in a bowl and serve as a topping for the fruit. Serves 6 or more, depending on size of peaches. (Drained canned peach halves may be substituted for fresh.)

DINNER

Lamb Shanks Marino*
or Lamb Shanks in Mushroom Sauce*
Scalloped Potatoes
Mixed Green Salad with Herb French Dressing*
(add canned artichoke hearts to the greens)
Your Favorite Cake

With this menu we enjoy the indicated
California Wines

Lamb Shanks Marino

4 tablespoons bacon drippings or salad oil
4 lamb shanks
1 cup California Red Table Wine
1 cup diced celery
1 medium-sized onion, chopped
1 clove garlic, chopped or put through garlic press
   Salt and pepper to taste
   Canned consommé or water
3 tablespoons flour
2 tablespoons California Dry or Medium Sherry
1½ teaspoons Worcestershire sauce
   Dash of thyme
1 (10-oz.) package frozen peas and onions,
   cooked and drained
2 tablespoons parsley flakes

Heat bacon drippings or oil in a large, heavy skillet or Dutch oven; brown lamb shanks *slowly* on all sides. Add red wine, celery, onion, garlic, salt, and pepper. Cover and simmer gently (or bake at 350° F.) for 1½ to 2 hours, or until shanks are very tender, turning and basting shanks occasionally. Remove shanks from pan. Measure liquid and add consommé or water to make 2 cups; return mixture to pan. Mix flour to a smooth paste with ½ cup cold consommé or water; add to liquid in pan; cook, stirring, until smoothly thickened, then continue cooking 2 or 3 minutes longer. Add Sherry and Worcestershire sauce; season with thyme, salt, and pepper. Return shanks to pan; add peas and onions and parsley. Heat thoroughly before serving. Serves 4. Wine choice: California Claret.

Lamb Shanks in Mushroom Sauce

Dust 4 lamb shanks with salt and pepper. Heat 4 tablespoons salad oil or bacon drippings in a large, heavy skillet or a Dutch oven; brown shanks slowly on all sides. Remove shanks from pan. Add 3 tablespoons flour to drippings; blend well. Add 1 (10½-oz.) can golden mushroom soup and ¾ cup *each* California Red Table Wine and canned consommé; cook, stirring, until thickened and smooth. Add 1 tablespoon instant minced onion, bit of chopped or pressed garlic, 2 tablespoons parsley flakes, and salt and pepper to taste. Cover; simmer gently (or bake at 350° F.) 1½ to 2 hours, or until shanks are very tender. Turn and baste occasionally; add more consommé if gravy needs thinning. Serve gravy over shanks or separately. Serves 4. Wine choice: California Gamay.

Herb French Dressing

1 cup salad oil (preferably part olive oil)
¼ cup California red wine vinegar
¼ cup California Red Table Wine
1½ teaspoons salt
½ teaspoon coarse black pepper
½ teaspoon Worcestershire sauce
1 thick slice onion
½ clove garlic
1 small, tender stalk celery
¼ cup (firmly packed) parsley sprigs
   Pinch each: rosemary, marjoram, and sweet basil

Combine oil, vinegar, wine, salt, pepper, and Worcestershire sauce in a pint jar; shake vigorously to blend. Chop onion, garlic, celery, and parsley together until *very, very* fine; add this mixture and the herbs to the dressing; shake again. Chill several hours. Makes about 1⅔ cups dressing. Good with any green or vegetable salad.

DINNER

Savory Braised Lamb*
Kasha*   **Eggplant Armenian***
Applesauce Topped with Sour Cream
(and a dash of cinnamon)
Cookies

With this menu we enjoy:

California Cabernet Sauvignon

Savory Braised Lamb

2 tablespoons butter or bacon drippings
2 pounds boneless lamb shoulder, cubed
3 tablespoons flour
¾ cup California Red Table Wine
1 (10½-oz.) can condensed consommé
1 (7¾-oz.) can marinara sauce
½ teaspoon Worcestershire sauce
Pinch of rosemary and thyme
Salt and pepper to taste
1 cup finely cut celery
½ cup chopped onion
Bit of chopped or pressed garlic
1 (4-oz.) can sliced mushrooms, drained
2 tablespoons parsley flakes

Heat butter in a Dutch oven or other heavy kettle; brown lamb slowly on all sides. Sprinkle flour over meat and stir well; add wine, consommé, and marinara sauce; cook, stirring, until mixture boils and thickens. Add Worcestershire sauce, rosemary, thyme, salt, pepper, celery, onion, and garlic. Cover and simmer very gently for 1¼ to 1½ hours, or until meat is fork-tender, stirring occasionally. If gravy thickens down toward end of cooking time, thin it with a little of the liquid drained from the mushrooms. Before serving, add mushrooms and parsley. Serves 5 or 6.

Kasha *(Buckwheat Groats)*

Despite their non-palate-tickling name, buckwheat groats make a delicious alternate for potatoes, especially with lamb. To serve 5 or 6, you'll need 1½ cups whole buckwheat groats (be sure they are *whole*) and 3 cups boiling chicken or beef stock, or water. Put the groats in a large skillet and toast them *lightly* over very low heat, stirring often. (Don't let them burn!) Add the boiling stock or water (there will be quite a sizzling and sputtering when you pour in the liquid), then quickly put on the lid. Cook as *slowly* as possible for 15 to 20 minutes, or until groats are tender and liquid is absorbed. Gently stir in a generous lump of butter and salt to taste before serving.

Eggplant Armenian

2 medium-sized eggplants (about 2 lbs.)
½ cup packaged fine, dry bread crumbs
½ cup grated Parmesan cheese
3 tablespoons salad oil (preferably olive oil)
2 eggs, slightly beaten
½ green pepper, grated
1 tablespoon instant minced onion
1 clove garlic, chopped or pressed (if you like)
1 teaspoon Worcestershire sauce
½ teaspoon oregano
Seasoned salt and pepper to taste
Paprika

Pare eggplant and cut in 1-inch cubes; cook, covered, in boiling salted water about 10 minutes, or just until tender. Drain thoroughly. Add all remaining ingredients except paprika; mix well. Spread mixture evenly in a greased 9-inch pie plate; sprinkle with paprika. Bake in a moderate oven (350° F.) about 45 minutes, or until firm in the center. Serves 5 or 6.

P. S. Sometimes I vary *Eggplant Armenian* thusly: Before baking, top with thin slices of tomato; spread tomato thinly with anchovy paste; sprinkle with capers, grated Parmesan cheese, paprika.

DINNER

Lamb Curry Calcutta*
(with condiments)
Raisin Rice*   Buttered Spinach
Raspberry or Strawberry Sherbet
Filled Ladyfingers*

With this menu we enjoy:

California Rosé

Lamb Curry Calcutta

2 pounds boneless lamb shoulder, cubed
3 cups boiling water
1 cup California White Table Wine
2 medium-sized carrots, sliced
2 tablespoons instant minced onion
1 clove garlic, chopped or pressed
    Salt to taste
1 apple, pared, cored, and chopped
½ green pepper, chopped
3 stalks celery, cut fine
¼ cup butter
⅓ cup flour
1 tablespoon curry powder (or to taste)
2 tablespoons California Dry or Medium Sherry
2 tablespoons chutney (mince any large pieces)
2 tablespoons parsley flakes

Place lamb in a Dutch oven or other heavy kettle; add water, white wine, carrots, onion, garlic, and salt. Bring to a boil; cover and simmer gently 1 hour. Remove lamb from stock and set aside. Strain stock; measure 3½ cups, adding water, if needed, to make that amount. Sauté apple, green pepper, and celery gently in the butter for 5 minutes; blend in flour and curry powder. Add the reserved 3½ cups stock and cook, stirring constantly, until mixture boils and thickens. Add remaining ingredients; taste and add salt, if needed; add lamb. Cover and simmer for 30 minutes, or until lamb is very tender, stirring frequently. Serve with rice and any desired curry condiments (chutney, chopped crisp bacon, canned French-fried onions, chopped salted peanuts, flaked coconut, grated hard-cooked egg, diced banana, etc.). Serves 5 or 6.

P. S. Individual soufflé dishes, arranged on a tray, make attractive containers for the curry condi-ments. These little dishes are also useful for refrigerator desserts such as Chocolate Moussette (page 15), and I often use them to hold juicy or "saucy" vegetables on the dinner plate.

Raisin Rice

1½ cups long-grain white rice
3 cups chicken stock (use canned or make it with bouillon cubes or chicken stock base)
3 tablespoons butter
2 tablespoons instant minced onion
    Salt to taste
1 cup seedless raisins (preferably the golden ones)
2 tablespoons parsley flakes

In a saucepan, combine rice, stock, butter, onion, and salt. Bring just to a boil, then stir well and pour into a 2-quart casserole. Cover tightly; bake in a moderately hot oven (375° F.) for 30 minutes. Uncover; with a fork, gently stir in raisins and parsley. Cover and continue baking another 10 minutes. Stir gently again before serving. Serves 5 or 6.

Filled Ladyfingers

Packaged ladyfingers are fine for this. Simply split the halves apart, spread with your favorite jam, jelly, or marmalade, and put back together again. What could be simpler? Another good idea: Use thin slices of frozen or bakery pound cake in place of the ladyfingers. Put two slices together with a filling of jam, jelly, or marmalade; cut in strips to make finger sandwiches.

DINNER

Baked Pork Chops with Rice*
Hot Artichokes
(fresh ones or frozen hearts)
Apricot-Pineapple Compote
(canned apricots and pineapple chunks)
Hungarian Tea Cakes*

With this menu we enjoy:
California Grey Riesling

Baked Pork Chops with Rice

4 pork chops, cut about 1¼ inches thick
1 cup uncooked white rice
1 cup diced celery
1 medium-sized onion, chopped
½ green pepper, chopped
2 pimientos, chopped
1 (10½-oz.) can condensed consommé
½ cup California White Table Wine
¼ cup water
    Pinch each of thyme and marjoram
    Salt and pepper to taste

Heat a large, heavy skillet; grease it with a bit of fat trimmed from the chops; brown chops slowly on both sides. While chops are browning, mix rice, celery, onion, green pepper, and pimientos; spread in the bottom of a 2-quart casserole. Arrange browned chops on top of rice mixture. Mix consommé, wine, and water; season with thyme, marjoram, salt, and pepper. Heat this liquid to boiling; pour over chops and rice. Cover and bake in a moderately hot oven (375° F.) for 30 minutes. Uncover; remove chops and stir rice mixture gently with a fork; replace chops. Cover and continue baking about 30 minutes longer, or until chops are tender and rice has absorbed all the liquid, turning chops occasionally. Serves 4.

Hungarian Tea Cakes

⅓ cup butter
1 cup granulated sugar
2 eggs, yolks and whites separated
1 teaspoon vanilla
1½ cups sifted all-purpose flour
1 teaspoon baking powder
⅛ teaspoon salt
½ cup (firmly packed) brown sugar
1 cup chopped walnuts or pecans
⅓ to ½ cup quartered candied cherries

Cream the butter; gradually cream in the granulated sugar, beating until light and fluffy. Beat in the unbeaten egg yolks, then the vanilla. Mix and sift flour, baking power, and salt; blend into first mixture. Pat into a well-greased 9-inch square pan. Beat egg whites stiff; gradually beat in brown sugar; add nuts and cherries; spread over dough in pan. Bake in a moderate oven (350° F.) for 45 minutes. Let cool in pan, then cut in 1½-inch squares. Makes 36 squares.

. . . .

Favorite Braised Pork Chops

Have 4 pork chops cut 1¼ to 1½ inches thick. Brown slowly on both sides in a large, heavy skillet, using a little fat trimmed from the chops. Pour off excess fat. Mix 1 (10½-oz.) can condensed cream of chicken soup; ⅓ cup California Dry or Medium Sherry or Dry Vermouth; 1 teaspoon instant minced onion; bit of garlic (if you like); 1 tablespoon parsley flakes; thyme, paprika, seasoned salt, and pepper to taste. Pour mixture over chops. Cover; simmer 1 hour or until chops are tender; turn and baste occasionally. Serves 4. Wine choice: California Dry Semillon. With these we like bread stuffing in place of potatoes. Broccoli and side dishes of applesauce can complete the main course.

II. Hamburger's What You Make It

Delicious ways to feature the ever-faithful ground beef

Imagine the culinary scene without ground beef! No hamburgers, no meat balls, no fun! Here indeed is the cook's most faithful main-dish ingredient.

With a little kitchen sorcery, and *saucery,* ground beef dishes can be transformed from old standbys into the "glamour girls" of the kitchen. A delectable red wine sauce, a buttery-smooth Hollandaise, or a spoonful of flavorful creamed mushrooms can transform a simple hamburger patty or a slice of meat loaf into a dinnertime treat. Simmer tender meat balls in a savory gravy, baste hamburger-stuffed peppers or mushrooms with a tasty sauce, and you forget that the main ingredient is the Cinderella of the meat department.

Featured in this chapter are some of my favorite ground-beef dishes, equally enjoyed by my family and our guests.

DINNER

Elegant Hamburgers*
with Sauce Diablo* or Red Wine Sauce*
French Fried Potatoes
(I'd use frozen ones)
Zucchini Parmesan*
Minted Lemon Jelly*

With this menu we enjoy:

California Gamay

Elegant Hamburgers

    2 pounds lean ground beef (I use chuck)
1½ teaspoons seasoned salt
    ½ teaspoon coarse black pepper
        Sauce Diablo or Red Wine Sauce (below)
    4 slices buttered toast
    1 (3-oz.) can liver pâté
        Parsley or watercress for garnishing

Mix beef, seasoned salt, and pepper lightly with a fork. Shape into 4 nice fat steaks. Broil or panbroil until they're done to your liking. While they're cooking, prepare *Sauce Diablo* or *Red Wine Sauce* (below). Spread each slice of toast with some of the liver pâté; place in a slow oven to warm slightly. To serve, place toast on heated dinner plates; top each slice with a hamburger steak; spoon a little of the sauce over the meat. Garnish with sprigs of parsley or watercress. Pass remaining sauce at the table. Serves 4.

Sauce Diablo: In a saucepan combine 1 (10¾-oz.) can beef gravy, ¼ cup catsup, 2 tablespoons California Dry or Medium Sherry or Dry Vermouth, 2 tablespoons butter, 1 tablespoon parsley flakes, 1½ teaspoons prepared mustard (the brown variety), and 1½ teaspoons Worcestershire sauce. Heat to simmering. Add seasoned salt to taste.

Red Wine Sauce: In a saucepan melt 2 tablespoons butter and stir in 2 tablespoons flour; add 1 (10½-oz.) can condensed consommé and ⅓ cup California Red Table Wine; cook, stirring, until mixture boils and thickens. Add 2 teaspoons dry shredded green onions, bit of chopped or pressed garlic, 1 tablespoon parsley flakes, ½ teaspoon Worcestershire sauce, dash of thyme, and salt and pepper to taste. Simmer gently, uncovered, for 10 minutes, stirring frequently.

Zucchini Parmesan

Scrub small zucchini and trim off ends. Cook whole in boiling salted water for about 10 minutes, or *just* until tender. Drain. When cool enough to handle, cut lengthwise in halves. Arrange halves, cut side up, in a greased shallow baking dish. Brush with melted butter; sprinkle *generously* with grated Parmesan cheese; dust with paprika. Bake in a hot oven (450° F.) about 10 minutes, just long enough to melt the cheese. This can be prepared ahead and baked just before serving.

Minted Lemon Jelly

To serve 4, dissolve 1 (3-oz.) package lemon-flavored gelatin in 1 cup hot water. Add ⅔ cup cold water, ¼ cup green crème de menthe, and 1 tablespoon lemon juice. Pour into stemmed glasses. Chill until firm. Before serving, top with whipped cream. Very refreshing!

• •

Hamburger Mignon

This looks and tastes (well, *almost*) like a fancy steak. To serve 4, *lightly* mix 2 pounds ground chuck with ¼ cup California Red Table Wine and 2 tablespoons meat sauce**; shape into a big oval patty about 2 inches thick. Place on a rack in a shallow pan. Broil 5 minutes to brown the top; reduce heat to 425° F. and bake 5 to 10 minutes, depending on rareness desired. Sprinkle with salt and pepper. Spread with soft butter or serve with *Red Wine Sauce.* Wine choice: California Burgundy.

**I use A-1 sauce for it gives just the flavor this dish requires.

DINNER

Pepper Steak Patties*
Cheesey Mashed Potatoes*
Corn on the Cob or Whole-Kernel Corn
Butterscotch Pecan Pudding*

With this menu we enjoy:
California Zinfandel

Pepper Steak Patties

2 green peppers
4 tablespoons bacon drippings or salad oil
1 large onion, chopped
1 clove garlic, chopped or put through garlic press
2 tablespoons flour
1 (8-oz.) can tomato sauce
¾ cup canned consommé or bouillon-cube broth
¼ cup California Dry or Medium Sherry or
    Dry Vermouth
    Pinch of thyme
    Salt and pepper
1½ pounds of ground beef

Cut a thin slice from the stem end of each pepper; remove seeds and fibrous white portion; wash under running water. With a sharp knife, cut peppers in thin strips. Heat 2 tablespoons of the bacon drippings in a saucepan; add peppers, onion, and garlic; sauté gently, stirring frequently, for 20 minutes. Sprinkle flour over peppers and onion; mix well. Add tomato sauce, consommé, and wine; cook, stirring constantly, until mixture boils and thickens. Season with thyme, salt, and pepper. Cover and simmer gently, stirring occasionally, for 10 minutes. Meantime, mix ground beef lightly with 1 teaspoon salt and ¼ teaspoon pepper; shape into 4 thick patties. Heat remaining 2 tablespoons bacon drippings in a large skillet; brown patties on both sides. Pour off all fat from skillet; pour green pepper sauce over meat. Cover and simmer until meat is as done as desired, 5 minutes or so for rare, longer if you like it medium or well done.

Cheesey Mashed Potatoes

Prepare 6 servings instant mashed potatoes as usual, then to the hot potatoes add ½ cup shredded process Cheddar cheese and 2 tablespoons chopped pimiento. Whip lightly with a fork until cheese melts. Delectable!

Butterscotch Pecan Pudding

1 (3¾-oz.) package butterscotch pudding and pie filling (*not* instant)
1½ cups milk
3 tablespoons California Medium or Sweet Sherry
1 cup miniature marshmallows
½ cup chopped pecans
½ cup heavy cream, whipped
    Additional whipped cream for topping

Prepare pudding according to package directions, using the milk and Sherry as the liquid. Cool, stirring occasionally. Stir in marshmallows and nuts; fold in whipped cream. Spoon into sherbet glasses; chill. Just before serving, garnish with whipped cream. Serves 5 or 6.

•••••••••••••••••••••

Hamburgers Hollandaise

Mix 1½ pounds ground beef, ⅓ cup California Red Table Wine, a bit of grated onion, 1½ teaspoons seasoned salt, ¼ teaspoon coarse black pepper. Shape into 4 patties; broil or panbroil. Serve on buttered, toasted English muffins. Top with this sauce: Mix and heat gently 1 (6-oz.) can Hollandaise sauce, 2 tablespoons water, 1 tablespoon butter, 1 teaspoon lemon juice, ½ teaspoon dry shredded green onions, and salt to taste. Serves 4. Wine choice: California Gamay.

DINNER

Hambolognas* or Steakies*
(on toast or toasted buns)
Waffle Potato Chips   Olives & Pickles
Avocado Green Salad
French Dressing Aurora*
Apple Strudel*

With this menu we enjoy the indicated
California Wines

Hambolognas

  1 pound ground beef
½ pound bologna, skinned and ground
½ cup (firmly packed) soft bread crumbs
¼ cup milk
  1 tablespoon instant minced onion
½ teaspoon salt
¼ teaspoon pepper
  2 tablespoons butter or bacon drippings
  1 tablespoon flour
  1 (8-oz.) can tomato sauce
⅓ cup California Dry or Medium Sherry or
    Dry Vermouth

Mix beef, bologna, bread crumbs, milk, onion, salt, and pepper together lightly but thoroughly. Shape into 6 thick patties (about ½ cup meat mixture per patty). Heat butter in a large skillet; brown patties nicely on both sides. Remove patties from skillet. Pour off all but about 1 tablespoon drippings from skillet. Add flour to drippings in skillet and blend well; add tomato sauce and wine; cook, stirring constantly, until sauce boils and thickens. Return patties to sauce. Cover and simmer gently for 20 minutes, basting several times. Serve on toast or toasted hamburger buns, with rice or mashed potatoes. Serves 6. Wine choice: California Rosé.

Steakies

1½ pounds ground beef
  1 cup (firmly packed) soft bread crumbs
  2 eggs, slightly beaten
½ cup cream
  1 tablespoon instant minced onion
    Salt and pepper
  3 tablespoons butter or bacon drippings
  2 (10¾-oz.) cans beef gravy
¼ cup California Red Table Wine
  2 tablespoons parsley flakes

In a mixing bowl combine beef, bread crumbs, eggs, cream, onion, 1 teaspoon salt, and ¼ teaspoon pepper; mix lightly but thoroughly. Shape mixture into 6 fat patties. Heat butter in a large, heavy skillet; brown patties slowly on both sides. Pour off fat from skillet. Pour gravy and wine over the patties; cover and simmer very gently for 45 minutes, turning and basting patties several times. Taste and add salt and pepper to gravy, if needed; add parsley. Serve on toast or toasted hamburger buns, or with mashed or baked potatoes. Serves 6. Wine choice: California Zinfandel.

French Dressing Aurora

In a pint jar combine 1 cup salad oil (I like part olive oil), 2 tablespoons *each* California red wine vinegar and tarragon wine vinegar, 1 teaspoon Worcestershire sauce, 1 tablespoon brown sugar, ½ teaspoon paprika, 1½ teaspoons salt, ¼ teaspoon coarse black pepper, 1½ teaspoons dry shredded green onions, and a bit of chopped or pressed garlic. Shake vigorously to blend. Chill before using. Makes about 1¼ cups.

Apple Strudel

To serve 6, you will need 2 (14-oz.) packages frozen apple strudel. Bake as directed on carton; serve topped with hard sauce or with sour cream and a dusting of cinnamon.

28

DINNER

Mariposa Meat Balls*   Perfect Pilaf*
Artichoke Hearts & Mushrooms*
Pickled Beets
Honey-Walnut Sundae
*(drizzle honey over vanilla ice cream;
sprinkle with chopped walnuts)*

With this menu we enjoy:
California Burgundy

Mariposa Meat Balls

1½ pounds ground beef
½ cup fine cheese-cracker crumbs
½ cup milk
1 tablespoon instant minced onion
2 tablespoons parsley flakes
   Salt and pepper
2 tablespoons butter or bacon drippings
2 tablespoons flour
1 (10¾-oz.) can beef gravy
½ cup California Red Table Wine

Combine beef, cheese-cracker crumbs, milk, onion, parsley, 1 teaspoon salt, and ¼ teaspoon pepper, mixing lightly but thoroughly. Shape into about 36 balls, using 1 tablespoon mixture per ball. Heat butter in a large, heavy skillet; brown balls nicely on all sides. Remove balls from skillet and pour off all but 2 tablespoons of the drippings. Blend flour with drippings in skillet; add beef gravy and wine; cook, stirring, until mixture boils and thickens. Season with salt and pepper, if needed. Return balls to skillet. Cover and simmer gently for 20 minutes, shaking pan gently several times to turn balls. Serves 6.

Perfect Pilaf

6 tablespoons butter
½ cup broken uncooked vermicelli
1½ cups uncooked long-grain white rice
3½ cups chicken stock (use canned or make it
   with bouillon cubes or chicken stock base)
   Salt to taste
1 cup finely diced celery
½ cup chopped onion
1 tablespoon parsley flakes

Melt 3 tablespoons butter in a large, heavy skillet; add vermicelli and sauté very gently, stirring frequently, just until a pale golden color. (Watch it *carefully!*) Stir in rice. Add chicken stock; stir well

and season with salt. Bring to a boil, then cover and cook over *very* low heat for 25 minutes, or until liquid is absorbed. Meantime, sauté celery and onion gently in remaining 3 tablespoons butter for 10 minutes. Remove cooked vermicelli and rice from heat; with a fork gently stir in celery-onion-butter mixture, then parsley. Cover and let stand in a warm place 5 to 10 minutes before serving. Serves 6.

Artichoke Hearts and Mushrooms

Cook and drain frozen artichoke hearts; combine with sliced canned mushrooms. Add butter, dry shredded green onions, salt, and pepper to taste. Heat gently before serving. Canned artichoke hearts may also be used here. Drain and rinse them; cut in halves or leave whole. Combine with the other ingredients as directed.

• •

Hamburger Stroganoff

Sauté 1½ pounds lean ground beef and 1 medium onion, chopped, in 2 tablespoons butter until meat is no longer red, stirring with a fork to separate it into bits. Stir in 3 tablespoons flour. Add 1 (10½-oz.) can condensed consommé, 1 cup evaporated milk, ¼ cup California Sherry or Dry Vermouth, 3 tablespoons tomato paste, 1 (4-oz.) can mushrooms (drained), 1 tablespoon parsley flakes, bit of garlic, 2 teaspoons Worcestershire sauce, and salt and pepper to taste. Simmer 10 minutes, stirring frequently. Serve with baked potatoes, noodles, or rice. Serves 4 or 5. Wine choice: California Rosé.

DINNER

Beef Mousse* with Mushroom Sauce*
Green Beans   French Fried Onions
Shoestring Potatoes
(canned ones, heated briefly in the oven)
Graham Cracker Torte*

With this menu we enjoy the indicated
California Wines

Beef Mousse? It's that old standby, meat loaf, with a new name, a new shape, and an excellent flavor.

Beef Mousse

  2 eggs, slightly beaten
1⅔ cups evaporated milk
  2 cups (firmly packed) soft bread crumbs
  2 pounds ground beef
½ cup shredded process Cheddar cheese
  2 tablespoons instant minced onion
  2 tablespoons parsley flakes
  2 tablespoons grated green pepper (if you like)
  2 teaspoons salt
¼ teaspoon pepper
  3 strips bacon, halved crosswise

In a large mixing bowl combine the eggs, milk, and bread crumbs; let stand 5 minutes or so. Add meat, cheese, onion, parsley, green pepper, salt, and pepper; beat with a wooden spoon until thoroughly mixed (or use your hands!). Pack mixture into an 8 by 8 by 2-inch baking dish; arrange bacon over the top. Bake in a moderate oven (350° F.) for 1 hour. Pour off juices, then let stand 5 minutes or so before cutting. Serve with *Mushroom Sauce* (below). Plenty for 6, with leftovers for sandwiches. Wine choice: California Claret.

Mushroom Sauce

Scrub ½ pound fresh mushrooms (don't peel unless skin is very tough); remove tough portion of stems; slice mushrooms thinly. Cover and sauté gently in 2 tablespoons butter for 5 minutes, stirring occasionally. Add 1 (10½-oz.) can condensed cream of mushroom soup, 3 tablespoons cream, 2 tablespoons California Sherry, 1 tablespoon parsley flakes, and a dash of pepper; mix well; heat gently until piping hot. Makes about 2 cups.

Graham Cracker Torte

  3 eggs
  1 cup packaged graham cracker crumbs
½ cup finely chopped walnuts or pecans
  1 cup sugar
¼ teaspoon cinnamon
      Dash of salt
  1 cup heavy cream, whipped
¼ teaspoon almond extract

Beat eggs well; stir in crumbs, nuts, sugar, cinnamon, and salt. Pour into a well-greased 9-inch pie plate. Bake in a slow oven (325° F.) for 40 minutes. When cold, spread with whipped cream flavored with almond extract; chill several hours. A dot of currant jelly, or strawberry or raspberry jam, atop each serving makes a nice-but-not-necessary garnish for this torte. Serves 6. Wine choice: California Cream Sherry.

• •

Chili-Beef Muffins

Mix 1 pound ground beef, 1 cup finely crushed corn chips, ½ cup milk, 1 slightly beaten egg, 1 tablespoon instant minced onion, ¾ teaspoon salt, ¼ teaspoon pepper. Pack mixture into 8 muffin tins. Bake in a moderately hot oven (375° F.) for 30 minutes. Let stand 2 or 3 minutes before removing from tins. Serve with this sauce: Heat 2 (15-oz.) cans chili con carne (with beans) to simmering; stir in ½ cup California Red Table Wine. Pass a bowl of grated Parmesan cheese. Serves 4. Wine choice: California Barbera. Good with a salad and hot cornbread.

DINNER

Stuffed Meat Loaf* & Scalloped Potatoes
or Tomato Meat Loaf* & Celery Stuffing*
Buttered Cauliflower or Broccoli
*(sprinkle generously with
Parmesan cheese and paprika)*
Strawberry Shortcake

With this menu we enjoy the indicated
California Wines

Stuffed Meat Loaf

1 (8-oz.) package herb-seasoned bread stuffing
2 pounds lean ground beef
1 cup milk
2 eggs, slightly beaten
1 tablespoon instant minced onion
2 tablespoons parsley flakes
1½ teaspoons salt
¼ teaspoon pepper
1 (4-oz.) can mushroom stems and pieces
  California Dry Vermouth
⅓ cup butter
  Catsup

Measure 1 cup of the stuffing crumbs into a mixing bowl; add meat, milk, eggs, onion, parsley, salt, and pepper; mix well. Spread half of this mixture evenly over the bottom of an 8 by 8 by 2-inch baking dish. Drain mushrooms, reserving liquid. Measure mushroom liquid; add Vermouth to make ⅔ cup. Combine this ⅔ cup liquid with butter in a saucepan; heat until butter melts; add remaining stuffing crumbs and mushrooms; toss lightly with a fork to moisten crumbs. Pat this prepared stuffing evenly over meat mixture in baking dish; cover evenly with remaining meat mixture; spread catsup thinly over top. Bake in a moderate oven (350° F.) for 1 hour. Remove from oven and let stand 5 minutes or so before cutting. Serves 6. Wine choice: California Zinfandel. If you'd like gravy with the meat loaf, season canned beef gravy with a spoonful of California Sherry and a generous shake of dry shredded green onions; heat piping hot.

Tomato Meat Loaf

1 (8-oz.) package herb-seasoned bread stuffing
1 pound lean ground beef
1 (1-lb.) can stewed tomatoes (dice any large
  pieces of tomato with scissors)

2 eggs, slightly beaten
¾ teaspoon salt
¼ teaspoon pepper
3 strips bacon, halved crosswise

Measure 1 cup of the dry stuffing into a mixing bowl; add meat, tomatoes, eggs, salt, and pepper; mix well. Spread mixture in a 9-inch pie plate. Arrange bacon strips over the top. Bake in a moderate oven (350° F.) for 1 hour. Remove from oven, pour off drippings, and let stand a few minutes before cutting in wedges. If you want the bacon crisper, lay it in a pie pan and put it back in the oven for a few minutes. Watch *carefully* lest it burn! Serves 4. Wine choice: California Gamay. Canned beef gravy, heated and seasoned with a dash of California Sherry, is good with this meat loaf.

Celery Stuffing: While the meat loaf is baking, sauté 1 cup finely cut celery gently in ¼ cup butter for 5 minutes. Add ½ cup water, ¼ cup California Dry Vermouth and 2 tablespoons parsley flakes; cover and simmer 5 minutes. Remove from heat. Add remaining dry stuffing; toss gently with a fork until well mixed. Cover and let stand in a warm place until time to serve, then toss gently again. Serve stuffing as a side dish with the meat loaf. Serves 4.

Hamburger-Spinach Special

Sauté 1 pound ground beef and 1 tablespoon grated onion in 3 tablespoons butter until meat is no longer red, stirrring with a fork to separate it into bits. Add 1 (10-oz.) pkg. frozen chopped spinach (cooked and *well* drained), 5 slightly beaten eggs, ½ teaspoon Worcestershire sauce, and seasoned salt and pepper to taste. Stir over low heat *just* until eggs are set. Serve at once. Pass Parmesan cheese. Serves 4. Wine choice: California Rosé.

DINNER

Crusty French Meat Loaf*
(pass catsup and pickle relish)
Buttered Lima Beans
Sliced Tomatoes with Watercress Dressing*
Angel Dream Cake*

With this menu we enjoy:

California Cabernet Sauvignon

Crusty French Meat Loaf

  1 long (15-oz.) loaf French bread (preferably
      with rounded, not pointed, ends)
  ¾ cup evaporated milk
  2 eggs
1½ pounds *lean* ground beef
  ½ cup shredded Cheddar cheese
  ¼ cup California Red Table Wine
  ½ green pepper, shredded
  1 tablespoon instant minced onion
  1 tablespoon parsley flakes
  1 teaspoon Worcestershire sauce
1½ teaspoons seasoned salt
  ½ teaspoon pepper
      Soft or melted butter

With a very sharp knife, cut a thin lengthwise slice
from the top of the loaf of French bread. (Reserve
this lid.) With your fingers, scoop out as much of
the inside of the loaf as possible. Shred enough of
this bread to make 1½ cups (firmly packed) crumbs;
set aside. In a large mixing bowl, beat milk and eggs
together until blended. Add reserved crumbs; beat
until moistened. Add meat, cheese, wine, green pepper, onion, parsley, and seasonings; mix thoroughly.
Fill hollowed-out loaf with the meat mixture, pack-
ing it in firmly. Meat mixture should be just level
with the top of the loaf; if there's any extra, bake it
separately for a sandwich. Set filled loaf on a baking
sheet; brush sides of crust with soft or melted butter. Bake in a moderate oven (350° F.) for 1 hour.
Brush reserved lid with butter; set it in place on
the loaf; cover top of loaf *loosely* with a piece of
aluminum foil. Continue baking at 350° F. for 15
minutes. Remove from oven and cool on a wire rack
for 15 minutes or so before serving. To serve, cut the
loaf crosswise in thick slices with a sharp knife. The
traditional hamburger accompaniments (catsup,
pickles, mustard) go well with this. Serves 6 or
more. Leftovers are good cold, or sliced and reheated in the oven.

Sliced Tomatoes with Watercress Dressing

Peel and core tomatoes; cut crosswise in *thick* slices.
(To serve 6, allow 4 large or 6 medium-sized tomatoes.) Arrange slices on a lettuce-lined platter; top
each with a spoonful of *Watercress Dressing* (below).
Chill 1 hour or so before serving.

Watercress Dressing: Chop 1 cup (firmly packed)
sprigs of watercress and several sprigs parsley very
fine; add 1 tablespoon snipped fresh chives (or use
frozen ones). Blend 1½ cups well seasoned oil-vinegar
French dressing (bottled Italian-style dressing is
good) with ½ cup chili sauce; add watercress mixture; mix well. If dressing is not to be used at once,
cover and store in the refrigerator. Mix again before
using. Makes about 2¼ cups. (P. S. If you have a
blender, put the watercress sprigs in the container
with all the other ingredients and whirl the mixture
until the watercress is sufficiently chopped.)

This Watercress Dressing is also excellent over
canned celery hearts. It's good, too, with fresh or
canned pear halves, and with avocado and grapefruit salad.

Angel Dream Cake

Slice a loaf-shaped store-bought angel food cake
(about 12 oz.) lengthwise into 3 layers. Whip 1½
cups heavy cream; fold in ½ cup butterscotch topping and ½ teaspoon rum extract. Fill and frost the
cake with the cream mixture. Chill. (This can be
done as long as a day ahead of time.) Shortly (not
more than 1 hour) before serving time, sprinkle top
with crushed English toffee (or peanut brittle). Slice
as you would any loaf cake.

DINNER
Hamburger-Mushroom Casserole*
Buttered Noodles
(add a sprinkling of poppy seeds)
Peas with Celery
(the frozen combination)
Peach Supreme*

With this menu we enjoy:
California Burgundy

Hamburger-Mushroom Casserole

1 pound fresh mushrooms
2 tablespoons butter
2 pounds lean ground beef
2 tablespoons flour
1 (10¾-oz.) can beef gravy
2 tablespoons California Sherry
1 tablespoon instant minced onion
2 tablespoons parsley flakes
2 teaspoons Worcestershire sauce
   Salt and pepper to taste
½ cup packaged corn flake crumbs, mixed with
   1 tablespoon melted butter
   Dairy sour cream

Scrub mushrooms gently (don't peel unless skin is very tough); remove tough portion of stems; slice mushrooms thinly. Melt butter in a large skillet; sauté mushrooms gently for 5 minutes, stirring frequently. Add meat; sauté until it is no longer red, stirring with a fork to separate into bits. Sprinkle flour over meat and mushrooms; stir well. Add gravy and Sherry; cook, stirring, until mixture boils and thickens. Add onion, parsley, and seasonings. Turn mixture into a 2-quart casserole; sprinkle with the crumbs. Bake in a moderately hot oven (375° F.) for 25 minutes. Pass a bowl of sour cream to be spooned atop each serving. Serves 5 or 6.

Peach Supreme

For each person to be served, place a well-drained canned freestone peach half, cut side up, in a sherbet glass or dessert dish. Top with a scoop of vanilla or lemon custard ice cream. Over the ice cream spoon some of this sauce: Melt 1 (10-oz.) glass red currant jelly over low heat; stir in ⅓ cup California Port and 1 teaspoon *each* lemon juice, grated lemon peel, and grated orange peel. Cool thoroughly, then chill. Plenty of sauce for 6 servings.

• •

Hamburger-Stuffed Mushrooms

16 to 18 fresh mushrooms, about 2½ inches
   in diameter (approximately 1 pound)
1 pound lean ground beef
¼ cup packaged corn flake crumbs
1 egg, slightly beaten
½ cup milk
2 teaspoons meat sauce**
1 teaspoon seasoned salt
¼ teaspoon pepper
1 cup canned consommé
4 tablespoons butter
⅓ cup California Dry or Medium Sherry or
   Dry Vermouth
1 teaspoon dry shredded green onions

Scrub mushrooms gently; remove stems. Lightly but thoroughly mix beef, crumbs, egg, milk, meat sauce, seasoned salt and pepper. Fill mushrooms with meat mixture, patting in firmly and rounding tops. Place mushrooms, meat side up, in baking dish. (Two 8 by 8 by 2-inch dishes are just right.) Heat consommé, butter, wine and onions to simmering; pour over mushrooms. Cover with aluminum foil; bake in a 350° F. oven 25 minutes. Uncover; continue baking for 20 minutes, basting often. Serve on toast or on mounds of steamed rice. Serves 4 or 5. Wine choice: California Claret. For flavor variation, I cut 2 slices bacon in small pieces and top each mushroom with one before baking. Also, if sour cream is your "dish", pass a bowl of it to be spooned over the mushrooms.

**I use A-1 sauce for it gives just the flavor this dish requires.

DINNER

Stuffed Peppers Lomita*
Panned Carrots with Mushrooms*
Bacon Cornbread
*(use a mix; add 4 or 5 slices crumbled
crisp bacon to the batter)*
Pumpkin Chiffon Pie*

With this menu we enjoy the indicated
California Wines

Stuffed Peppers Lomita

6 large or 8 medium-sized green peppers
1 pound lean ground beef
2 tablespoons bacon drippings or butter
1½ cups cooked rice
1 cup drained canned Mexican-style
   whole-kernel corn
1½ cups grated Cheddar cheese
1 tablespoon instant minced onion
1 teaspoon celery seed
1 teaspoon Worcestershire sauce
   Salt and pepper to taste
1 (10¾-oz.) can condensed tomato soup
½ cup California Red Table Wine
¼ cup water

Cut a thin slice from the stem end of each pepper; remove all seeds. Place peppers in a saucepan; cover with boiling water; boil 5 minutes. Remove peppers and turn upside down to drain. Sauté beef in bacon drippings until meat is no longer red, stirring with a fork to separate it into small bits. Add rice, corn, 1 cup of the cheese, onion, celery seed, Worcestershire sauce, salt, and pepper. Stuff peppers with this mixture. Arrange peppers upright in a greased baking dish. Mix tomato soup, wine, water, and remaining ½ cup cheese; pour over and around peppers. Bake, uncovered, in a moderate oven (350°F.) for 45 minutes, basting peppers several times with the sauce. Serves 6 to 8. Wine choice: California Burgundy.

Panned Carrots with Mushrooms

1½ pounds carrots, scraped and sliced in
   very thin rounds
3 tablespoons butter

1 (4-oz.) can sliced mushrooms
   Water
2 teaspoons instant minced onion
1 tablespoon parsley flakes
   Salt and pepper to taste

Heat butter in a large, heavy skillet; add carrots; sauté gently, stirring frequently, for 5 minutes. Drain mushrooms, reserving liquid; measure liquid and add water, if needed, to make ½ cup; add to carrots. Add mushrooms and remaining ingredients; cover and simmer gently, stirring occasionally, for 15 minutes, or just until carrots are tender. Serves 6.

Pumpkin Chiffon Pie

1 envelope (1 tablespoon) unflavored gelatin
¼ cup California Sweet Sherry
3 eggs, separated
1 cup canned pumpkin
½ cup milk
1 cup sugar
¼ teaspoon salt
½ teaspoon each: cinnamon and nutmeg
1 (9-inch) baked pastry shell or chilled
   graham-cracker shell
1 cup heavy cream, whipped

Soften gelatin in the wine. Beat egg yolks slightly in the top of a double boiler; stir in pumpkin, milk, ½ cup of the sugar, salt, and spices; cook over boiling water, stirring constantly, for 5 minutes. Remove from heat; add softened gelatin and stir until dissolved; chill. When mixture begins to thicken, fold in the egg whites which have been beaten until stiff with the remaining ½ cup sugar. Pour into pie shell; chill several hours. Top with whipped cream before serving. Wine choice: California Cream Sherry.

DINNER

Mexican Beef Pancakes*
Buffet Vegetable Salad*
Marinated Garbanzos   Corn Chips
Fruit in Season
(apples, pears, bananas, grapes)
Port Salut & Blue Cheese   Crackers

With this menu we enjoy:

California Red Chianti

Mexican Beef Pancakes

Pancakes:
¾ cup sifted all-purpose flour
½ cup white corn meal
1½ teaspoons salt
3 eggs, slightly beaten
1½ cups milk

Mix flour, corn meal, and salt; gradually add combined eggs and milk, stirring until smooth. Bake pancakes, one at a time, in a greased skillet measuring 6½ inches across the bottom. Use about ¼ cup batter per pancake, and tilt skillet as you pour in batter so that bottom of skillet is completely covered. Turn pancakes once. Stack cooked pancakes on a pie plate. If they are to be used at once, cover and keep them warm in a slow oven. If you prepare them ahead of time, let them cool, then store them, covered, in the refrigerator. Be sure to reheat them in the oven before using. Makes 12.

Filling:
1½ pounds lean ground beef
1 large onion, chopped
1 clove garlic, chopped or put through garlic press
1 green pepper, chopped
2 tablespoons bacon drippings or butter
2 teaspoons Worcestershire sauce
Salt and pepper to taste

Sauté beef, onion, garlic, and green pepper gently in bacon drippings for 10 minutes, stirring often with a fork to separate meat into bits. Drain off any excess fat. Add seasonings.

Sauce:
2 tablespoons butter
2 tablespoons flour
2 (8-oz.) cans tomato sauce
1 (10½-oz.) can condensed consommé

¼ cup California Dry or Medium Sherry or Red Table Wine
½ teaspoon each: oregano and cumin seed
Salt to taste

Melt butter and stir in flour; add tomato sauce and consommé; cook, stirring, until mixture boils and thickens a bit. Add wine and seasonings; simmer gently for 5 minutes or so.

To assemble the dish:
Put about ¼ cup of the hot meat mixture down the center of each warm pancake; roll up loosely. Place 2 of the filled pancakes on a heated dinner plate. Spoon piping hot sauce over them and sprinkle generously with grated Parmesan cheese. Garnish with ripe olives, radish roses, and small lettuce leaves. Serve at once. Pass additional Parmesan cheese. Serves 6.

Buffet Vegetable Salad

Line a platter with crisp lettuce leaves and on the lettuce arrange in groups: sliced tomatoes or tomato aspic, green beans (I like canned vertical-pack beans for this), and canned or cooked frozen artichoke hearts; sprinkle vegetables with French dressing, then with grated hard-cooked egg and paprika. With the salad serve a bowl of guacamole, to be used both as dressing for the vegetables and dip for the corn chips. The frozen guacamole (avocado dip) is excellent! Sometimes I use it as is, and sometimes, if I want a little less nippy flavor, I add a tablespoon or two of mayonnaise and a squeeze of lemon juice. When it's to be used just as a dip, a bit of chopped, seeded and peeled tomato is a good addition.

III. Chickens in Various Pots

Serve forth the favorite bird in gourmet style

When I was a youngster, my idea of heavenly eating was chicken fricassee with hot biscuits. I can still see it (and almost taste it!)...a big platter of tender chicken in a golden, rich-flavored gravy, with plenty of feather-light biscuits to catch every drop. It was always so hard to make my biscuits and gravy come out even. By the time perfect balance was achieved, I had usually more than "reached capacity."

Over the years my tastes have changed, as tastes have a way of doing. I still like chicken fricassee, but chicken baked with crisp corn flake crust, chicken sautéed in wine, and chicken simmered in a savory tomato sauce are all favorites, too.

You'll note that most of the recipes in this chapter call for one 2½ to 3-pound frying chicken to serve three or four. Obviously someone at the table is going to have to be fond of wings and backs. (In our house, I'm it.) If you prefer, you can buy only the choice pieces...breasts, legs, and thighs...in whatever amounts you need to satisfy three or four appetites.

A note about the chicken stock called for in many of these recipes: You can, of course, make your own, or you can use canned or bouillon-cube broth, or make it with chicken-stock base.

DINNER

Chicken Mascotte*
or Chicken Jerusalem*
Noodles or Rice
Hot Asparagus or Asparagus Salad
Rum-Butterscotch Ice Cream Sandwich*

With this menu we enjoy the indicated

California Wines

Chicken Mascotte

1 (2½ to 3-lb.) frying chicken, cut up
   Flour
2 tablespoons each: butter and salad oil
1 tablespoon instant minced onion
1 clove garlic, chopped or pressed
1 tablespoon parsley flakes
   Sprinkling of thyme and paprika
   Salt and pepper to taste
½ cup California White Table Wine
1 (4-oz.) can sliced mushrooms (undrained)
1 (10¾-oz.) can beef gravy
2 tablespoons California Dry or Medium Sherry
1 (9-oz.) package frozen artichoke hearts,
   cooked and drained, or
1 (14-oz.) can artichoke hearts, drained,
   rinsed and halved

Dredge pieces of chicken with flour. Heat butter and oil in a large, heavy skillet; add chicken and sauté slowly until golden brown. Add onion, garlic, parsley, thyme, paprika, salt, pepper, white wine, and mushrooms with their liquid. Cover tightly and simmer very gently for 30 to 45 minutes, or until chicken is tender, turning pieces occasionally. Remove chicken from pan. Add gravy and Sherry to juices in pan; taste and add salt and pepper, if needed. Return chicken to pan; add artichoke hearts. Cover and heat gently before serving. Serves 3 or 4. Wine choice: California Claret.

Chicken Jerusalem

1 (2½ to 3-lb.) frying chicken, cut up
   Flour
2 tablespoons each: butter and salad oil
1 tablespoon instant minced onion
   Chopped or pressed garlic to taste
1 tablespoon parsley flakes
   Sprinkling of thyme and paprika
   Salt and pepper to taste

⅔ cup California Dry or Medium Sherry or
   Dry Vermouth
1 (10½-oz.) can white sauce
   Milk or cream
   Nutmeg
1 (9-oz.) package frozen artichoke hearts,
   cooked and drained, or
1 (14-oz.) can artichoke hearts, drained,
   rinsed and halved
1 (4-oz.) can sliced mushrooms, drained

Dredge chicken with flour. Heat butter and oil in a large skillet; brown chicken nicely on all sides. Add onion, garlic, parsley, thyme, paprika, salt, pepper, and wine. Cover; simmer very gently for 30 to 45 minutes, or until chicken is tender, turning pieces occasionally. Remove chicken from pan. Add white sauce to drippings; heat and stir until smooth. Thin gravy as desired with milk or cream; season with nutmeg, salt, and pepper. Return chicken to pan; add artichoke hearts and mushrooms. Heat gently before serving. Serves 3 or 4. Wine choice: California Chablis.

Rum-Butterscotch Ice Cream Sandwich

For each serving, top a thick slice of angel food, sponge, or chiffon cake with a scoop of vanilla or butter brickle ice cream. Serve with *Rum-Butterscotch Sauce:* Melt 1 cup (firmly packed) brown sugar and ½ cup butter together in a double boiler. Beat 1 egg and ¼ cup milk together until blended; stir gradually into sugar-butter mixture. Cook over boiling water, stirring frequently, for 10 minutes. Add ½ teaspoon rum extract. Serve warm. Makes about 1½ cups sauce. Store leftover sauce in a covered jar in the refrigerator.

DINNER

Italian Chicken Sauté*
Polenta Parmesan*
Spinach with Mushrooms*
Sabayon Pudding*   Macaroons

With this menu we enjoy the indicated

California Wines

Italian Chicken Sauté

1 (2½ to 3-lb.) frying chicken, cut up
  Flour
2 tablespoons butter
3 tablespoons olive oil
1 cup chicken stock
½ cup California White Table Wine
1 tablespoon instant minced onion
2 cloves garlic, chopped or pressed
1 tablespoon parsley flakes
  Pinch of rosemary
  Generous dash each of thyme and paprika
  Salt and pepper to taste

Dredge pieces of chicken with flour. Heat butter and oil in a large, heavy skillet; brown chicken slowly on all sides. Add remaining ingredients. Cover and simmer very, very gently for 30 to 45 minutes, or until chicken is tender, turning and basting pieces occasionally. Before serving, taste and add more salt, if needed. Serves 3 or 4. Wine choice: California Burgundy.

P. S. Canned or sautéed fresh mushrooms may be added to the chicken during the last few minutes of cooking. In this case, serve plain spinach (or other green vegetable) with it.

Polenta Parmesan

1 cup corn meal
  Salt
1 cup cold water
2 cups chicken stock
2 tablespoons butter
1 cup grated Cheddar cheese (or diced
  Monterey Jack)
¼ cup grated Parmesan cheese

Mix corn meal, ½ teaspoon salt, and the cold water. In top of a double boiler, heat chicken stock to boiling over direct heat; add moistened corn meal, stirring constantly. Cook, stirring, over direct heat for 2 minutes. Cover and cook over boiling water for 1 hour, stirring occasionally. Just before serving, add butter and cheeses; stir until cheeses are melted. Taste and add more salt, if needed. Spoon polenta into a heated serving dish. Pass additional grated Parmesan cheese at the table. Serves 4. Polenta is also wonderful with stews and many other "gravied" meat dishes.

Spinach with Mushrooms

Cook and chop fresh spinach, or use frozen chopped spinach. Combine it with canned or sautéed fresh mushrooms, plus butter, salt, and pepper to taste.

Sabayon Pudding

1 (3¼-oz.) package vanilla pudding and pie
  filling mix (*not* instant)
1½ cups milk
¼ cup California Medium or Sweet Sherry
½ cup heavy cream, whipped

Combine pudding mix with milk and Sherry; cook according to package directions. Cool, stirring occasionally. Gently fold in whipped cream. Spoon into 4 sherbet glasses or dessert dishes; chill. Serve topped with additional whipped cream, if desired. Serves 4. Wine choice: California Cream Sherry.

DINNER

Chicken Provence* or Chicken Brittany*
Gnocchi*   **Green Beans with Bacon***
Mandarin Orange Sundae*   **Cookies**

With this menu we enjoy the indicated
California Wines

Chicken Provence

2 tablespoons each: butter and salad oil
1 (2½ to 3-lb.) frying chicken, cut up
    Liver and heart of the chicken
3 green onions (including 1 inch of tops)
1 clove garlic
    Several sprigs parsley
3 tablespoons flour
1 teaspoon prepared mustard (the brown variety)
1 (10½-oz.) can condensed consommé
1 cup California White or Red Table Wine
    (either is excellent here)
    Dash of thyme and paprika
    Salt and pepper to taste
2 tablespoons California Dry or Medium Sherry

Heat butter and oil in a large, heavy skillet; sauté chicken gently until golden brown on all sides. Remove chicken from skillet. Put liver and heart, onions, garlic and parsley through the food grinder or chop them very fine. Blend flour into drippings in skillet, then mustard; add consommé and table wine; cook, stirring, until mixture is smooth and slightly thickened. Add thyme, paprika, salt and pepper. Return chicken to pan; add ground giblet mixture. Cover and simmer gently for 30 to 45 minutes, or until chicken is tender, turning and basting chicken occasionally. Before serving, add Sherry and more salt, if needed. Serves 3 or 4. Wine choice: California Claret or Chablis.

Chicken Brittany

Have 1 (2½ to 3-lb.) frying chicken cut up. Dredge with flour; brown nicely in 2 tablespoons *each* butter and salad oil. Add 1 (10½-oz.) can condensed onion soup, ½ cup California Dry Vermouth or White Table Wine, 2 tablespoons parsley flakes, and salt and pepper to taste. Cover; simmer 30 to 45 minutes, or until tender, turning and basting occasionally. Serves 3 or 4. Wine choice: California Chablis.

Gnocchi

¼ cup butter
¼ cup flour
¼ cup cornstarch
2 cups milk, scalded
2 unbeaten egg yolks
¾ cup grated Cheddar cheese
½ teaspoon salt
¼ cup melted butter
⅓ cup grated Parmesan cheese
    Paprika

Melt ¼ cup butter in a saucepan; blend in flour and cornstarch. Add milk gradually and cook, stirring constantly, until mixture boils and thickens. Continue cooking and stirring over low heat for 2 or 3 minutes. Stir in egg yolks, one at a time. Add Cheddar cheese; stir until melted. Remove from heat. Add salt. Pour into a well-greased 10 by 6 by 2-inch baking dish. Cool, then chill several hours or overnight. Cut in 2-inch squares; lift out squares with a spatula and arrange, with edges overlapping, in a greased 9-inch pie plate. Sprinkle with the melted butter, Parmesan cheese, and paprika. Bake in a hot oven (400° F.) about 20 minutes, or until delicately browned. Serves 4.

Green Beans with Bacon

To hot cooked (or canned) green beans add butter, salt, and pepper to taste. Turn into a heated serving dish; sprinkle generously with crumbled crisp bacon.

Mandarin Orange Sundae

Drain canned mandarin oranges; sprinkle *generously* with Cointreau or Grand Marnier; chill. Serve as a sauce over vanilla ice cream.

DINNER

Chicken Sauté Mayonnaise*
Buttered Spaghetti or Tagliarini
Corn-Stuffed Zucchini*
Radishes and Green Olives
Jelly-Filled Nut Balls* with Wine Jelly*

With this menu we enjoy:

California Chablis

Chicken Sauté Mayonnaise

1 (2½ to 3-lb.) frying chicken, cut up
  Flour, salt and pepper
2 tablespoons each: butter and salad oil
1 medium-sized onion, chopped
1 cup California Dry Vermouth or Dry or
  Medium Sherry
1 cup mayonnaise
1 tablespoon parsley flakes
  Generous dash of paprika

Dust pieces of chicken with flour seasoned with salt and pepper. Heat butter and oil in large, heavy skillet. Brown pieces of chicken nicely on all sides. Add onion and wine; cover and simmer gently for 30 to 45 minutes, or until chicken is tender, turning and basting chicken occasionally. Remove chicken to a platter and keep warm. Add mayonnaise to juices in skillet and blend well. (Use a wire whisk or rotary beater to achieve perfect smoothness.) If gravy seems a bit too thick, thin it with a little additional wine. Add parsley and paprika; taste and add salt and pepper if needed. Serves 3 or 4.

Corn-Stuffed Zucchini

4 medium-sized zucchini (about 1 lb.)
1 small (7-oz.) can Mexican-style whole-kernel
  corn, drained
2 tablespoons cornflake crumbs
1 egg, slightly beaten
½ teaspoon dry shredded green onions
  Seasoned salt and pepper to taste
  Grated Parmesan cheese and paprika

Wash zucchini; trim off ends. Parboil whole in salted water for 10 minutes; drain. Cut lengthwise in halves; scoop out insides. Drain scooped-out portion; combine with corn; chop until zucchini and corn are well mixed. Stir in cornflake crumbs, egg, onions, salt, and pepper. Place zucchini shells in a greased shallow baking dish; heap corn mixture in

shells; sprinkle with Parmesan cheese and paprika. Bake in a moderate oven (350° F.) for 30 minutes. Serves 4.

Jelly-Filled Nut Balls

1 cup soft butter
½ cup (firmly packed) brown sugar
2 eggs, separated
1 teaspoon vanilla
2 cups sifted all-purpose flour
½ teaspoon each: salt and cinnamon
1 cup finely chopped walnuts or pecans
  Wine Jelly (below) made with California Port

Cream butter and brown sugar together until thoroughly blended. Beat in unbeaten egg yolks, one at a time; add vanilla. Mix and sift flour, salt and cinnamon; add to creamed mixture, blending well. Shape dough into balls about 1 inch in diameter. Dip balls in the slightly beaten egg whites, then roll in the nuts. Place on ungreased baking sheet. Using the end of a wooden spoon handle or a thimble, make a depression in the center of each cookie ball. Bake in a moderately hot oven (375° F.) for 10 to 12 minutes. When cookies are almost cool, put a dab of *Wine Jelly* (below) in hollow of each one. Makes about 4 dozen.

Wine Jelly

2 cups California Dessert or Table Wine
  (any kind you like)
3 cups sugar
½ bottle fruit pectin

Measure wine into top part of double boiler. Add sugar and mix well. Place over rapidly boiling water and stir until sugar is dissolved (about 2 minutes). Remove from heat and at once stir in pectin. Skim and pour quickly into glasses. Paraffin at once. Makes about 5 (6-oz.) glasses. A flavorful way to add the "wine touch" to a meal.

DINNER

Chicken Castillo with Saffron Rice*
French Peas*
Mincemeat Chiffon Pie*

With this menu we enjoy:

California Rosé

Chicken Castillo with Saffron Rice

1 (2½ to 3-lb.) frying chicken, cut up
    Flour
⅓ cup salad oil
1 (1-lb.) can stewed tomatoes (dice large pieces with scissors)
2 tablespoons instant minced onion
1 clove garlic, chopped or pressed
⅓ cup California Dry or Medium Sherry or Dry Vermouth
    Dash of thyme
    Salt and pepper to taste
2¼ cups chicken stock
    Pinch of Spanish saffron
1 cup uncooked long-grain white rice
½ green pepper, grated

Dredge pieces of chicken with flour. Heat oil in a large, heavy skillet; brown chicken slowly on all sides. Add tomatoes, onion, garlic, wine, thyme, salt, and pepper. Cover and simmer for 30 to 45 minutes, or until chicken is tender. Meantime, heat chicken stock to boiling in a saucepan. Dissolve saffron in a little of the stock; add to remaining stock; season with salt and pepper. Slowly sprinkle rice into boiling stock; stir well. Cover and cook over *very* low heat for 25 minutes, or until rice is tender and all liquid is absorbed. To serve, arrange rice in a ring on a heated platter; remove chicken from sauce and place in center. Add green pepper to sauce; taste and correct seasoning. Spoon a little sauce over the chicken; pass remainder separately. Serves 3 or 4.

P. S. You can omit the saffron and still have a good dish, albeit (to me) a less interesting one.

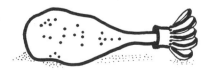

French Peas

No trick to these, and the extra flavor is delightful. Just cook frozen peas as usual (I like the "petite" ones), but before cooking, add a generous lump of butter and cover the peas with a large lettuce leaf or 2 or 3 smaller ones. Discard the lettuce before serving. Try this with frozen green beans, too.

Somehow we always think of mincemeat as synonymous with holiday fare. This pie is delectable any day of the year.

Mincemeat Chiffon Pie

1 envelope (1 tablespoon) unflavored gelatin
½ cup California Sweet Sherry or Muscatel
3 eggs, separated
1 tablespoon lemon juice
    Dash of salt
1 cup prepared mincemeat
¼ cup sugar
1 (9-inch) baked pastry shell
    Whipped cream

Soften gelatin in ¼ cup of the wine. Beat egg yolks slightly in the top of a double boiler; stir in remaining ¼ cup wine, lemon juice, and salt; cook over hot water for 4 or 5 minutes, or until mixture is thick and creamy, stirring constantly. Remove from heat. Add softened gelatin and stir until dissolved; add mincemeat. Chill until mixture begins to thicken. Beat egg whites stiff; gradually beat in the sugar; fold into partially thickened mincemeat mixture. Pour into pie shell. Chill until firm. Before serving, top with whipped cream. Makes 1 (9-inch) pie.

DINNER

Chicken Napoli* or Chicken à la Sophie*
Broccoli or Spinach Tart*
Buttered Noodles
Crisp Celery Hearts
Baked Marmalade Pears*

With this menu we enjoy the indicated
California Wines

Chicken Napoli

⅓ cup olive oil
1 (2½ to 3-lb.) frying chicken, cut up
1 large onion, chopped
1 clove garlic, chopped or put through garlic press
1 green pepper, chopped
½ cup slivered boiled or baked ham (meat only)
2 tablespoons flour
1 (7½-oz.) can Italian-style mushroom sauce
⅓ cup California Dry or Medium Sherry or
   Dry Vermouth
¼ cup water
   Salt and pepper to taste

Heat oil in a large, heavy skillet; brown pieces of chicken slowly on all sides. Remove chicken. Sauté onion, garlic, green pepper, and ham gently in the drippings for 5 minutes. Blend in flour, add mushroom sauce, wine, and water; cook, stirring, until mixture boils and thickens. Season with salt and pepper. Return chicken to pan. Cover and simmer gently for 30 to 45 minutes, or until chicken is tender, turning and basting occasionally. Serves 3 or 4. Wine choice: California Gamay.

Broccoli or Spinach Tart

Cook 1 (10-oz.) package frozen chopped broccoli or 2 (10-oz.) packages frozen chopped spinach according to package directions; drain *thoroughly*. Beat 3 eggs well; add 1 (10½-oz.) can cream of mushroom soup and beat until blended; stir in broccoli or spinach. Add 3 tablespoons grated Parmesan cheese, 1 tablespoon instant minced onion, ½ teaspoon Worcestershire sauce, and salt and pepper to taste. Turn into greased 9-inch pie plate. Bake in a moderate oven (350° F.) about 45 minutes, or until firm in the center. Serves 4 or 5.

Chicken à la Sophie

1 (2½ to 3-lb.) frying chicken, cut up
   Flour
2 tablespoons butter
3 tablespoons salad oil
1 cup cut-up, drained, canned tomatoes
2 tablespoons parsley flakes
1 clove garlic, chopped or put through garlic press
½ cup California Dry Vermouth or White
   Table Wine
   Pinch each of thyme and marjoram
   Salt and pepper to taste
1 (4-oz.) can sliced mushrooms, drained
1 cup pitted ripe olives
1½ cups cooked or canned peas

Dredge chicken with flour. Heat butter and oil in a heavy skillet; brown chicken slowly on all sides. Add tomatoes, parsley, garlic, and wine; season with thyme, marjoram, salt, and pepper. Cover tightly and simmer gently 30 to 45 minutes, or until chicken is tender. Before serving, add remaining ingredients; heat thoroughly. Serve with noodles or rice. Serves 3 or 4. Wine choice: California Zinfandel.

Baked Marmalade Pears

Drain 1 (1-lb. 13-oz.) can pear halves, reserving syrup. Arrange pear halves, cut side up, in a shallow baking dish. Place a heaping teaspoonful of orange marmalade in the center of each half. Mix ½ cup pear syrup, ½ cup California Medium or Sweet Sherry or Muscatel, and 1 tablespoon lemon juice; pour over pears. Bake in a moderately hot oven (375° F.) for 30 minutes, basting several times. Serve warm or chilled, topped with sour cream or vanilla ice cream. Serves 6.

DINNER

Baked Chicken with Red Wine*
Hominy Grits or Mashed Potatoes
Ada's Zucchini Pudding*
Brandied Coffee Jelly*
Ladyfingers

With this menu we enjoy:

California Burgundy

Baked Chicken with Red Wine

2 tablespoons butter
2 tablespoons salad oil
1 (2½ to 3-lb.) frying chicken, cut up
3 tablespoons flour
½ cup California Red Table Wine
½ cup chicken stock
1 (8-oz.) can mushroom stems and pieces
2 tender stalks celery, finely diced
2 medium-sized carrots, finely diced
1 small onion, chopped
1 clove garlic, chopped or put through garlic press
2 tablespoons parsley flakes
½ bay leaf, crumbled
   Dash of thyme and paprika
   Salt and pepper to taste

Heat butter and oil in a large, heavy skillet; sauté pieces of chicken slowly until golden on all sides. Transfer chicken to a large casserole or a baking pan. Add flour to drippings in skillet and blend well; add wine, chicken stock, and liquid from mushrooms; cook, stirring constantly, until mixture boils and thickens. Add all remaining ingredients including mushrooms; pour over chicken. Cover and bake in a moderate oven (350° F.) for 45 minutes to 1 hour, or until chicken is tender, turning and basting chicken occasionally. Taste for seasoning before serving. Serves 3 or 4.

Ada's Zucchini Pudding

2 pounds small zucchini
1 (4½-oz.) can chopped ripe olives
1 cup grated Cheddar cheese
1 tablespoon instant minced onion
   Bit of chopped or pressed garlic, if you like

2 eggs
½ cup milk
½ teaspoon Worcestershire sauce
   Dash of thyme
   Salt and pepper to taste
1 cup fine, soft bread crumbs
1 tablespoon melted butter
   Paprika

Wash zucchini and trim off ends. Cook whole in boiling salted water for 15 minutes, or just until tender. Drain; chop coarsely; drain again. Mix zucchini, olives, cheese, onion, and garlic. Beat eggs until light; blend in milk; add to zucchini. Season with Worcestershire sauce, thyme, salt, and pepper. Turn mixture into a greased 10 by 6 by 2-inch baking dish. Toss crumbs and melted butter together; sprinkle over pudding; dust with paprika. Bake in a moderate oven (350°F.) for 45 to 50 minutes, or until firm in the center. Serves 6. (To reheat leftover pudding, cover the baking dish tightly with aluminum foil, set it in a shallow pan of hot water, and bake in a moderate oven until piping hot.)

Brandied Coffee Jelly

1 envelope (1 tablespoon) unflavored gelatin
¼ cup cold water
¼ cup sugar
1½ cups hot, *strong* coffee
¼ cup California Brandy

Soften gelatin in the cold water 5 minutes. Add sugar and hot coffee; stir until gelatin and sugar are dissolved. Add Brandy. Pour into 4 sherbet dishes or stemmed glasses. Chill until firm. Serve topped with whipped cream. Serves 4.

DINNER

Oven-Barbecued Chicken*
Toasty Pilaf*
Buttered Carrots with Celery*
Pineapple de Menthe*
Brownies

With this menu we enjoy:

California Dry White or Red Table Wine

Oven-Barbecued Chicken

Have 1 (2½ to 3-lb.) frying chicken cut up. Dredge pieces of chicken with flour. Heat 2 tablespoons *each* butter and salad oil in a large, heavy skillet; sauté chicken slowly until nicely browned on all sides. Transfer chicken to a casserole or roasting pan. In the skillet combine the following ingredients:

1 cup catsup
½ cup California Dry or Medium Sherry or
　Dry Vermouth
⅓ cup water
2 tablespoons lemon juice
1 medium-sized onion, minced
1 tablespoon Worcestershire sauce
2 tablespoons brown sugar
　Salt and pepper to taste

Heat to simmering; pour sauce over chicken. Cover and bake in a moderate oven (350°F.) for 45 minutes to 1 hour, or until chicken is tender, turning and basting chicken occasionally. Serves 3 or 4.

Toasty Pilaf

Melt 2 tablespoons butter in a saucepan or skillet; add ⅔ cup uncooked long-grain white rice, ½ cup quick (15-minute) brown rice, and 2 tablespoons chopped onion; cook *gently,* stirring frequently, for 5 minutes. Stir in 2 cups boiling well-seasoned chicken or beef stock; cover and cook *very* slowly for 20 to 25 minutes, or until rice is tender and all liquid is absorbed. Before serving, fluff rice with a fork; taste and add salt, if needed. Serves 4.

Buttered Carrots with Celery

Wash and scrape 1 pound of carrots; cut crosswise in halves or in thirds; then lengthwise in quarters or halves. (The idea is to make strips as nearly uniform in size as possible.) Cook, covered, in a small amount of boiling salted water for 10 to 15 minutes, or until almost tender. Add 1 cup finely cut celery; cover and cook 5 to 10 minutes longer, or until both vegetables are tender. Drain. Add 2 tablespoons butter, 1 teaspoon dry shredded green onions, a sprinkling of celery seed, and salt and pepper to taste. Mix gently and serve piping hot. Serves 4.

Pineapple de Menthe

Drain canned pineapple chunks. Sprinkle liberally with green crème de menthe. Cover and chill thoroughly before serving.

....

Oven-Crisp Chicken

Cut up 1 (2½ to 3-lb.) frying chicken. Combine ½ cup melted butter and ¼ cup California White Table Wine in a pie plate or other shallow dish. Mix 1 cup packaged corn flake crumbs, ¾ teaspoon salt, ¼ teaspoon onion or garlic salt, ¼ teaspoon *each* thyme and paprika in a paper bag; shake to mix well. Dip pieces of chicken in butter-wine mixture, then shake 2 or 3 pieces at a time in the paper bag with the seasoned crumbs, coating chicken evenly. Place chicken, skin side up, in a shallow baking pan lined with aluminum foil. (Don't crowd the pieces.) Sprinkle with any remaining wine-butter mixture. Bake, uncovered, in a moderate oven (350°F.) about 1 hour, or until chicken is tender. (No turning necessary.) Serves 3 or 4. Wine choice: California Dry White or Red Table Wine. Best with creamy scalloped or au gratin potatoes and a green vegetable.

Note: One-half to ⅔ cup undiluted evaporated milk may replace the butter-wine mixture with excellent results. Good flavor variations: Add 2 tablespoons sesame seeds or ½ cup grated Parmesan cheese to the seasoned corn flake crumbs.

DINNER or LUNCHEON

Curried Chicken*   or Creamed Chicken & Ham Gourmet*
in Spinach Ring*
Rice   Chutney
Sliced Tomato & Artichoke Heart Salad
with French Dressing
Vanilla Ice Cream & Strawberry Sherbet   Cookies

With this menu we enjoy the indicated

California Wines

Curried Chicken

1 medium-sized onion, chopped
½ clove garlic, chopped or put through garlic press
¼ cup butter
⅓ cup flour
1 teaspoon curry powder (or to taste)
1 cup chicken stock
½ cup California White Table Wine
½ cup cream
1 tablespoon California Dry or Medium Sherry
  Salt and pepper to taste
2 cups coarsely diced, cooked chicken (or turkey)
1 (3-oz.) can chopped broiled mushrooms, drained
1 tablespoon parsley flakes

Sauté onion and garlic gently in butter for 5 minutes. Blend in flour and curry powder; add stock, white wine, and cream; cook, stirring constantly, until mixture boils and thickens. Stir in Sherry, salt, and pepper. Add chicken, mushrooms, and parsley. Heat gently but thoroughly. Serve in the center of *Spinach Ring.* Serves 5 or 6. Wine choice: California Sauterne.

P. S. Shrimp or crabmeat can be used here in place of the chicken with delicious results.

Creamed Chicken and Ham Gourmet

¼ cup butter
⅓ cup flour
1¼ cups light cream or rich milk
½ cup chicken stock
¼ cup California White Table Wine
½ teaspoon Worcestershire sauce
  Dash of mace or nutmeg
  Salt, celery salt, and pepper to taste
1 cup coarsely diced, cooked chicken (or turkey)
1 cup diced boiled or baked ham
1 (4-oz.) can sliced mushrooms, drained
2 tablespoons parsley flakes
1 tablespoon California Dry or Medium Sherry

Melt butter and stir in flour; add cream, stock, and white wine; cook, stirring, until mixture boils and thickens. Add seasonings; stir in remaining ingredients; heat *gently* until piping hot. Serve in the center of *Spinach Ring.* Serves 5 or 6. Wine choice: California Chablis. This is also good served in patty shells (frozen ones are fine), or in a noodle or rice ring.

Spinach Ring

Cook 1 (10-oz.) package frozen chopped spinach; drain *thoroughly.* Melt ¼ cup butter and stir in ¼ cup flour; add ¾ cup milk and cook, stirring, until mixture boils and becomes very thick. Add ½ cup grated Cheddar cheese and ¼ cup California Dry or Medium Sherry or White Table Wine; stir over low heat until cheese melts. Remove from heat. Add spinach; beat in 3 unbeaten egg yolks, one at a time. Season with salt, onion salt, and pepper to taste. Fold mixture into 3 stiffly beaten egg whites, blending gently. Pour into a well-greased 8½-inch (1¼-quart) ring mold; set in a shallow pan of hot water. Bake in a moderately hot oven (375°F.) about 45 minutes, or until firm. Remove mold from water and let stand a few minutes before turning ring out on a heated platter. Serves 5 or 6.

DINNER or LUNCHEON
Chicken Supreme*
in
Macaroni Ring*
Green Beans with Slivered Almonds
(the frozen combination)
Pickled Peaches
Cream Puffs or Eclairs
(from your favorite bakery)

With this menu we enjoy:

California Sauvignon Blanc

Chicken Supreme

4 tablespoons butter
1 medium-sized onion, minced
3 tablespoons flour
1 cup dairy sour cream
¾ cup chicken stock
¼ cup California Dry or Medium Sherry or
    White Table Wine
1 tablespoon parsley flakes
½ teaspoon Worcestershire sauce
¼ teaspoon paprika
    Salt and pepper to taste
2 cups coarsely diced, cooked chicken (or turkey)
1 (4-oz.) can sliced mushrooms, drained

Melt butter in top of a double boiler over direct heat; add onion and sauté gently for 5 minutes. Blend in flour; add sour cream and stock; cook, stirring constantly, until mixture boils and thickens. Place pan over hot water. Add remaining ingredients; heat thoroughly before serving. Serve in the center of *Macaroni Ring* (below). Serves 5 or 6.

P. S. Two cups of crabmeat or shrimp can replace the chicken here deliciously. Or, you can substitute 2 (7-oz.) cans solid-pack tuna. Drain, rinse, and flake the tuna before adding it to the sauce.

Macaroni Ring

Cook 1 cup elbow macaroni in boiling salted water *just* until tender; drain. In a saucepan, combine 1½ cups milk, 1 cup (firmly packed) soft bread crumbs, ¼ cup butter, and 1 cup grated Cheddar cheese; stir over very low heat until cheese is melted. Remove from heat. Add macaroni, 3 slightly beaten eggs, 1 chopped pimiento, 2 tablespoons grated green pepper, 1 tablespoon instant minced onion, ½ teaspoon Worcestershire sauce, and seasoned salt and pepper

to taste. Pour into a well-greased ring mold, set in a shallow pan of hot water, and bake in a moderate oven (350° F.) about 45 minutes, or until firm. Remove mold from water and let stand for 5 minutes or so before turning ring out on a heated platter. Serves 5 or 6.

••••••••••••••••••••••••

While it really isn't a dinner entrée, this chicken salad is so good that I can't resist including it here. I like to serve it in 4-inch baked tart shells, accompanied by a fruit or vegetable salad and hot cheese biscuits. I'm giving family and company-sized versions of the recipe.

Favorite Chicken Salad

	To serve 5 or 6	To serve 20-24
Diced, cooked chicken	2 cups	2 quarts
Diced heart of celery	1 cup	1 quart
French dressing (oil-wine vinegar or bottled Italian)	To moisten	To moisten
Fresh or canned seedless grapes	¾ cup	3 cups
Slivered, toasted almonds (available in cans)	¼ cup	1 cup
Mayonnaise	¾ to 1 cup	3 to 4 cups
Salt	To taste	To taste

Place chicken and celery in a bowl; sprinkle with *just* enough French dressing to moisten nicely, tossing with a fork to distribute the dressing. Cover; chill several hours or overnight. Drain chicken and celery if there's excess dressing in the bottom of the bowl. Add grapes and almonds; toss lightly to mix. Gently stir in enough mayonnaise to make salad creamy but not "over-dressed." Add salt to taste.

DINNER or LUNCHEON

Chicken Timbales Golden Gate*
Cranberry-Orange-Grapefruit Salad*
with Poppy Seed Dressing*
Brioches or Croissants
(frozen or from the bakery)
Chiffon or Angel Food Cake
with Toffee Topping*

With this menu we enjoy:

California Pinot Blanc

Chicken Timbales Golden Gate

½ cup (¼ pound) butter
½ cup plus 3 tablespoons flour
2½ cups cream or rich milk
2 cups chicken stock
½ cup California White Table Wine
3 cups ground, cooked or canned chicken
   (or turkey)
1¼ cups (firmly packed) soft bread crumbs
3 eggs, slightly beaten
   Seasoned salt and pepper to taste
1½ tablespoons parsley flakes
1 (8-oz.) can mushroom stems and pieces, drained
2 tablespoons California Dry or Medium Sherry
½ teaspoon Worcestershire sauce
   Dash of nutmeg
8 canned artichoke bottoms (at least 2 inches
   in diameter)
1 (4½-oz.) can deviled ham
   Paprika

Melt butter and stir in flour; add cream, stock, and white wine; cook, stirring constantly, until mixture is thickened and smooth. To 1½ cups of this sauce add the chicken, bread crumbs, eggs, seasoned salt, and pepper; blend well. Spoon mixture into 8 well-greased custard cups, set in a shallow pan of hot water, and bake in a moderate oven (350°F.) about 40 minutes, or until a knife inserted in the center comes out clean. Remove from oven and let stand 5 to 10 minutes before unmolding. To remaining sauce add parsley, mushrooms, and Sherry; season with Worcestershire sauce, nutmeg, seasoned salt, and pepper. To serve, have sauce piping hot. Rinse and drain artichoke bottoms; place, cup side up, in a shallow baking dish; spread each one with some of the deviled ham. Pour enough water into the dish to barely cover bottom; cover dish (with foil,

if necessary) and place in a 350° F. oven for a few minutes, to warm the artichokes through. Place artichoke bottoms in heated shallow individual casseroles or on plates; unmold timbales and place atop artichokes. Spoon a little of the hot mushroom sauce over each timbale; dust with paprika. Serve remaining sauce separately. Serves 8.

Cranberry-Orange-Grapefruit Salad

For each serving, place a ½-inch slice of canned jellied cranberry sauce in a crisp lettuce cup; top with 2 fresh or canned grapefruit sections and 3 canned mandarin orange sections. Spoon a little *Poppy Seed Dressing* (below) over the salad.

Poppy Seed Dressing: In a pint jar combine 1 teaspoon *each* dry mustard and salt, ½ teaspoon paprika, ¼ cup California red wine vinegar and 1 tablespoon lemon juice. Shake until dry ingredients are dissolved. Add 1 cup salad oil, ⅓ cup honey, 2 teaspoons grated onion, and 1½ tablespoons poppy seeds; shake until ingredients are well mixed. Makes about 1⅔ cups. Good on any fruit salad.

Toffee Topping for Cake

Whip 1⅓ cups heavy cream until quite stiff. Stir in ¼ teaspoon lemon extract and ¼ teaspoon rum flavoring. Gently fold in 1 cup crushed (not too fine) English toffee (or peanut brittle). Chill until time to serve. Heap on slices of angel food or chiffon cake before serving, or pass the topping for "self-service." Makes plenty of topping for 8 servings of cake. (It's best not to make this topping more than an hour ahead of serving time, lest the toffee or peanut brittle "melt" in the cream.)

DINNER or LUNCHEON

Chicken and Ham Delancey*
Shoestring Potatoes
Mixed Green Salad
(lettuces. sliced canned mushrooms, & avocado)
with Linden Dressing*
Crusty Baked Bananas*
With this menu we enjoy:
California Dry Sauterne

Chicken and Ham Delancey

  4 tablespoons butter
  4 tablespoons flour
  1 cup cream
  ¾ cup chicken stock
  1 tablespoon parsley flakes
  ¼ cup California Dry or Medium Sherry or
     White Table Wine
  ½ teaspoon Worcestershire sauce
     Salt and pepper to taste
16 to 20 cooked or canned asparagus tips
  4 serving-sized slices cooked ham
  4 serving-sized slices cooked chicken (or turkey)
  ¼ cup grated Parmesan cheese
     Paprika

Melt butter and stir in flour; add cream and chicken stock; cook, stirring constantly, until mixture boils and thickens. Add parsley, wine, Worcestershire sauce, salt, and pepper. Arrange 4 or 5 asparagus tips in the bottom of each of 4 greased shallow individual baking dishes; arrange ham and chicken slices over asparagus. Pour the hot cream sauce over all, then sprinkle with Parmesan cheese and paprika. Bake in a moderately hot oven (375°F.) for 10 to 15 minutes, or until bubbly. Serves 4.

    P. S. To vary this dish a bit, you can substitute 4 servings of cooked broccoli for the asparagus tips, and spread toast with deviled ham instead of using ham slices.

This is a robust-flavored dressing that is good with green, vegetable, and fruit salads. The horseradish is not perceptible in the finished dressing, but it does give it a good "nip."

Linden Dressing

  1 cup salad oil
  ½ cup California red wine vinegar
  1 (8-oz.) can tomato sauce
  1 tablespoon prepared horseradish
  1 clove garlic, chopped or put through garlic press
  1 tablespoon chopped onion
  ¼ cup sugar
  1 teaspoon Worcestershire sauce
  1 teaspoon salt
  ½ teaspoon each: celery salt and onion salt

Combine all ingredients in a jar or bowl; shake or beat until thoroughly blended. Cover and chill several hours to blend flavors. Shake or beat again just before using. Makes about 2⅓ cups.

Crusty Baked Bananas

  ¼ cup orange juice
  2 tablespoons melted butter
  ½ cup packaged corn flake crumbs
  2 tablespoons (firmly packed) brown sugar
  4 good-sized ripe bananas
     Whipped cream
     Cinnamon

Combine orange juice and melted butter. Mix corn flake crumbs and brown sugar. Peel bananas and cut crosswise in halves; roll in orange juice-butter mixture, then in the corn flake crumbs. Place bananas in a shallow baking pan lined with aluminum foil. Bake in a hot oven (400°F.) for 15 minutes. Serve hot, topped with whipped cream and a dusting of cinnamon. Serves 4.

DINNER

Duck with Cherry Sauce*
Chicken-Noodle Rice*
Peas with Mushrooms*
Chocolate Cloud Soufflé*

With this menu we enjoy:

California Pinot Noir

Duck with Cherry Sauce

1 (4 to 5-lb.) ready-to-cook duckling, quartered
  Seasoned salt and pepper
1 (1-lb.) can pitted dark, sweet cherries
2 tablespoons cornstarch
1 cup reduced Giblet Broth (below)
½ cup California Port
¼ cup orange marmalade
1 teaspoon Worcestershire sauce
  Salt to taste

Pat duck quarters dry with paper towels. Pull away surplus fat from the inside; trim off wing tips and cut off any excess skin to make quarters neat-looking. Sprinkle on all sides with seasoned salt and pepper; prick skin of each quarter in several places. Place, skin side up, on a rack in a shallow baking pan. Roast in a very hot oven (450°F.) for 15 minutes; reduce heat to 325°F. and continue roasting for about 40 minutes, or until duck is well browned and tender when tested with a fork. Pour off fat from pan two or three times during roasting. Transfer duck to a skillet, skin side down; set aside.

While duck is in the oven prepare sauce: Drain cherries, reserving syrup. Combine cornstarch and ½ cup cherry syrup in a saucepan; blend until smooth. Add the 1 cup reduced *Giblet Broth* (below) and Port; cook and stir over medium heat until mixture boils, thickens, and becomes clear. Stir in marmalade, Worcestershire sauce, and salt. Pour sauce over duck in skillet. Cover and heat ever so gently for 10 minutes or so, to give duck and sauce a chance to exchange flavors. Turn duck skin side up; add drained cherries; cover and heat briefly to warm the cherries. In serving, spoon a little of the sauce over each quarter and pass the rest of the sauce separately. Serves 3 or 4.

Duck Giblet Broth: Start this broth cooking before you put the duck in the oven, so it will be ready when you need it for the sauce. In a saucepan combine duck giblets, 1 (10½-oz.) can condensed consommé, and 1 cup water. Add 1 carrot, 1 medium-sized onion, 1 stalk celery, and 1 clove garlic, all sliced, several sprigs parsley, ½ bay leaf, dash of thyme, 3 peppercorns, and salt to taste. Bring to a boil; cover and simmer 1 hour. Strain. Boil rapidly until reduced to 1 cup.

Chicken-Noodle Rice

In a heavy saucepan cook noodles from 1 (2-oz.) envelope chicken-noodle soup mix in 3 tablespoons butter *just* until golden. Don't let them burn! Add 1 cup long-grain white rice; stir well. Add 2¼ cups boiling water, seasonings from soup mix, and salt to taste. Bring to a boil, stir well, then cover and simmer *very* gently about 25 minutes, or until liquid is absorbed. Uncover; stir gently with a fork. Cover; let stand in warm place 5 to 10 minutes before serving. Serves 4.

Peas with Mushrooms

Drain 1 (3-oz.) can sliced broiled mushrooms, reserving liquid. Use this liquid, plus water as needed, to cook 1 (10-oz.) package frozen petite peas according to package directions. Drain the cooked peas; combine with the drained mushrooms, 1 tablespoon butter, 1 teaspoon dry shredded green onions, and salt and pepper to taste. Heat just until butter melts and vegetables are piping hot. Serves 4.

Chocolate Cloud Soufflé

Have 5 egg whites at room temperature. Melt 3 (1-oz.) squares unsweetened chocolate over hot water. Beat egg whites until very stiff; gradually beat in ½ cup sugar and a dash of salt; fold in melted chocolate, blending gently but thoroughly. Spoon into a well-buttered 2-quart double boiler top; cover; cook over boiling water for 45 minutes. Do not lift lid or let water boil away. Turn out and serve with whipped cream lightly flavored with California Brandy or Sweet Sherry. Serves 4 or 5.

IV. A Pretty Kettle of Fish

Seafood specialties to tempt even non-fish-lovers

As far as I'm concerned, every day could be Fish Day! There are so many good fish dishes to enjoy, from the plain sautéed variety right up through company-fied creations involving delicious and delicate sauces. I hope you share my enthusiasm!

When you're planning to serve a baked fish-in-sauce dish for dinner, you can prepare the sauce early in the day, if you like. Let it cool, uncovered, then refrigerate it until shortly before baking time. Reheat it over very low heat or in a double boiler before pouring it over the fish. It's best to time the baking of a fish-in-sauce dish so that it can sit out of the oven for 5 to 10 minutes before serving. This gives the juices a chance to settle and makes the dish easier to serve. What's more, you're not so apt to burn your tongue!

If you use frozen fish fillets in any of these recipes, be sure to thaw and separate them before cooking.

DINNER

Sole Calypso*
or
Sole Sauté with Avocado Sauce*
Buttered Rice
(add chopped fresh parsley)
Baked Tomatoes au Gratin*
Quick Peach Melba*

With this menu we enjoy the indicated
California Wines

Sole Calypso

1 pound fillets of sole
1 cup California White Table Wine or
   Dry Vermouth
   Salt and pepper
   Flour
3 tablespoons butter
2 tablespoons salad oil
1 small to medium-sized ripe avocado
   Juice of 1 lime
2 teaspoons flour
½ cup heavy cream
   Toasted, slivered almonds
   Paprika

Arrange fillets of sole in a single layer in a shallow baking dish; pour wine over them; let stand an hour or so. Remove fillets from the dish. Measure ⅓ cup of the wine and set aside. Sprinkle fillets with salt and pepper; roll in flour. Heat 2 tablespoons of the butter and the oil in a large skillet; add floured fillets and sauté gently *just* until tender, about 4 minutes on each side. While fish cooks, peel avocado and cut in thin slices; sprinkle with lime juice; let stand at room temperature. Remove cooked fish from pan to a serving platter or shallow individual baking dishes; keep warm in a *very* slow oven. Melt remaining 1 tablespoon butter in the pan, stirring to scrape up any little browned bits; blend in flour; add cream and cook, stirring, until mixture boils and thickens. Stir in reserved ⅓ cup wine; season with salt and pepper to taste. (A dash of thyme and garlic salt may be added here, too, but the seasoning should be definitely "low key.") To serve, arrange avocado over sole; spoon piping hot cream sauce over all; sprinkle with almonds and dust with paprika. Serve pronto! Serves 2 or 3. Wine choice: California Chablis.

Sole Sauté with Avocado Sauce

Marinate, flour, and sauté 1 pound sole as directed above for *Sole Calypso*. While fish is cooking, prepare *Avocado Sauce:* Peel and mash 1 medium-sized ripe avocado; blend in 1 tablespoon lemon juice, 1 to 2 tablespoons mayonnaise, ¼ teaspoon Worcestershire sauce, and salt (or garlic salt) to taste. When sole is cooked, transfer it to a heated platter or dinner plates, garnish with bouquets of watercress or parsley, and serve with lemon wedges and the *Avocado Sauce*. Serves 2 or 3. Wine choice: California Dry Chenin Blanc. This sauce also makes a delicious dressing for sliced tomatoes or tomato aspic.

Baked Tomatoes au Gratin

Cut unpeeled tomatoes crosswise in halves. Spread cut sides thinly with mayonnaise; sprinkle with grated Parmesan cheese, then packaged fine, dry bread crumbs. Drizzle with a little melted butter; dust with salt, pepper, and paprika. Bake in a hot oven (450°F.) for 15 minutes.

Quick Peach Melba

For each serving, place a well-drained canned freestone peach half, cut side up, in a sherbet glass or dessert dish. Just before serving, top peach with a scoop of vanilla ice cream. Pass a pitcher of bottled berry pancake syrup to be poured over the ice cream. For a good variation on this dessert, omit the ice cream, pour the berry syrup over the peach half, and top with a dollop of sour cream or whipped cream cheese.

DINNER

Sole Angelique*
or Baked Sole in Oyster-Cheese Sauce*
Parsley-Buttered New Potatoes
Artichoke Hearts & Mushrooms Tarragon*
Canned Whole Peeled Apricots
(topped with sour cream)

With this menu we enjoy the indicated
California Wines

Sole Angelique

1½ pounds fillets of sole
  4 tablespoons each: butter and flour
1¼ cups milk (or part cream for a richer sauce)
  ½ cup California White Table Wine
  2 tablespoons mayonnaise
  2 tablespoons California Dry or Medium Sherry
  1 teaspoon lemon juice
  2 teaspoons anchovy paste
  ½ teaspoon prepared mustard (the brown variety)
  ½ teaspoon Worcestershire sauce
    Dash of thyme
    Seasoned salt and pepper to taste
  1 tablespoon parsley flakes
  1 teaspoon dry shredded green onions
  ¼ cup grated Parmesan cheese
    Paprika

Arrange fillets in a greased 12 by 8 by 2-inch baking dish, or in 4 shallow individual casseroles. Melt butter and stir in flour; add milk and white wine; cook, stirring constantly, until mixture boils and thickens. Add all remaining ingredients except cheese and paprika. Spoon sauce over fish, sprinkle with cheese and paprika. Bake in a hot oven (450°F.) for 10 to 15 minutes, or until fish flakes when tested with a fork. Serves 4. Wine choice: California Pinot Chardonnay.

Baked Sole in Oyster-Cheese Sauce

1½ pounds fillets of sole
  1 (10¼-oz.) can condensed (not frozen) oyster stew
  4 tablespoons each: butter and flour
  ¼ cup California White Table Wine or
    Dry Vermouth
  1 cup shredded Cheddar cheese
  1 tablespoon parsley flakes
  1 teaspoon dry shredded green onions
    Salt and pepper to taste
  ½ cup packaged corn flake crumbs, mixed with
    2 tablespoons melted butter

Arrange fillets in a greased 12 by 8 by 2-inch baking dish. Strain oysters out of stew; cut oysters coarsely with scissors. Melt butter and stir in flour; add strained oyster stew and wine; cook, stirring constantly, until mixture boils and thickens. Add cheese; stir over low heat until melted. Add cut-up oysters, parsley flakes, onions, salt, and pepper. Pour sauce over fish; sprinkle with buttered corn flake crumbs. Bake in a hot oven (450°F.) about 15 minutes, or until fish flakes when tested with a fork. Serves 4. Wine choice: California Johannisberg Riesling.

Artichoke Hearts & Mushrooms Tarragon

Cook 1 (9-oz.) package frozen artichoke hearts according to directions on carton; drain. Drain 1 (4-oz.) can sliced mushrooms. Melt ¼ cup butter; add 1 teaspoon lemon juice, ½ teaspoon dry shredded green onions, and a good pinch of dried tarragon. Combine this mixture with the artichoke hearts and mushrooms; season to taste with salt and pepper; reheat before serving. Serves 4.

. . . .

Sole with Shrimp Pronto

Divide 1 cup small shrimp among 3 individual baking dishes; top with 1 pound sole fillets. Thaw 1 (10-oz.) can frozen condensed cream of shrimp soup; add ¼ cup California Dry Vermouth, dash of pepper; spoon over sole; sprinkle with lots of Parmesan cheese. Bake at 375°F. about 25 minutes. Serves 3. Wine choice: California Dry Sauterne.

DINNER
Baked Sole with Clam Sauce*
or Baked Fish Louisiana*
Corn-Rice Pilaf*
Chilled Broccoli with French Dressing
(add a garnish of mayonnaise)
Warm Gingerbread with Whipped Cream

With this menu we enjoy the indicated
California Wines

Baked Sole with Clam Sauce

1½ pounds fillets of sole
1 cup finely diced celery
½ cup chopped onion
   Bit of chopped or pressed garlic
6 tablespoons each: butter and flour
1 cup chicken stock
½ cup California White Table Wine
1 (7-oz.) can minced clams (undrained)
1 tablespoon parsley flakes
1 tablespoon lemon juice
   Salt and pepper to taste
1 cup shredded Cheddar cheese
   Paprika

Arrange sole in a greased 12 by 8 by 2-inch baking dish. Sauté celery, onion, and garlic gently in butter about 5 minutes, stirring often. Blend in flour; add stock, wine, and undrained clams; cook, stirring, until mixture boils and thickens. Stir in parsley, lemon juice, salt, and pepper. Pour sauce over sole; sprinkle with grated cheese; dust with paprika. Bake in a hot oven (450°F.) about 15 minutes, or until fish flakes when tested with a fork. Serves 4 or 5. Wine choice: California Grey Riesling.

Baked Fish Louisiana

2 pounds fish fillets (or steaks)
1 cup finely diced celery
1 small onion, chopped
1 clove garlic, chopped or pressed
1 green pepper, chopped
3 tablespoons salad oil
3 tablespoons flour
1 (1-lb.) can stewed tomatoes (dice large
   pieces with scissors)
½ cup California Dry or Medium Sherry or
   Dry Vermouth

   Dash each of thyme and oregano
   Salt and pepper to taste
¼ cup grated Parmesan cheese

Arrange fish in a greased 12 by 8 by 2-inch baking dish. Sauté celery, onion, garlic, and green pepper gently in oil for 5 minutes. Blend in flour; add tomatoes and wine; cook, stirring, until mixture boils and thickens; add seasonings. Pour sauce over fish; sprinkle with Parmesan cheese. Bake in a hot oven (450°F.) about 15 minutes, or until fish flakes when tested with a fork. Serves 5 or 6. Wine choice: California Pinot Blanc.

Corn-Rice Pilaf

Melt 3 tablespoons butter in a large skillet; add ¼ cup chopped onion and 1½ cups uncooked long-grain white rice; sauté gently, stirring frequently, for 5 minutes. Add 3 cups chicken stock; stir well and bring to a boil. Cover; turn heat as low as possible; cook about 25 minutes, or until rice is tender and all liquid is absorbed. Drain 1 (12-oz.) can Mexican-style vacuum-packed whole-kernel corn; stir gently into rice with 1 tablespoon parsley flakes and salt to taste. Cover; heat thoroughly before serving. Serves 6.

....

Stuffed Sole New Orleans

Mix 2 cups soft bread crumbs, ¼ cup melted butter, 2 tablespoons *each* grated onion, parsley flakes, and lemon juice, 1 teaspoon grated lemon peel, salt and pepper. Spread on 1½ pounds sole fillets; roll up from one short side to other; place seam down in greased baking dish. Mix 1 (10½-oz.) can condensed chicken gumbo soup, ⅓ cup California Dry Vermouth; pour over sole. Bake at 375°F. 25 minutes; baste often. Serves 4. Wine choice: California Chablis.

DINNER

Fish Fillets Florentine*
Shoestring Potatoes
(canned ones)
**Sliced Tomato & Cucumber Salad
with Harlequin French Dressing***
Lemon Sherbet
Chocolate Graham-Nut Bars*

With this menu we enjoy:
California Dry Chenin Blanc

A bed of chopped spinach, a layer of fish fillets, and a creamy cheese-and-wine-flavored sauce add up to...

Fish Fillets Florentine

  4 tablespoons butter
  5 tablespoons flour
  1 cup light cream
  ¾ cup chicken stock
  ¼ cup California Dry or Medium Sherry or
    White Table Wine
  2 tablespoons mayonnaise
  ½ cup grated Parmesan cheese
  ½ teaspoon grated lemon peel
  ½ teaspoon Worcestershire sauce
    Salt, pepper, and paprika to taste
  3 (10-oz.) packages frozen chopped spinach,
    cooked and *thoroughly* drained
1½ pounds fish fillets (sole, perch, cod, or
    whatever you like)

Melt butter and stir in flour; add cream and stock; cook, stirring constantly, until mixture boils and thickens. Add wine, mayonnaise, ¼ cup of the cheese, lemon peel, Worcestershire sauce, salt, pepper, and paprika. Mix ½ cup or so of this sauce with the spinach; spread in bottom of a greased 12 by 8 by 2-inch baking dish. Arrange fish fillets over spinach; cover with remaining sauce. Sprinkle remaining ¼ cup cheese over the top; dust with paprika. Bake in a moderately hot oven (375°F.) for about 25 minutes, or until fish flakes when tested with a fork. Serves 4 or 5.

Harlequin French Dressing

  ¾ cup salad oil
  ¼ cup California red wine vinegar
1½ teaspoons Worcestershire sauce
  ¼ teaspoon sugar
  1 teaspoon salt
  ¼ teaspoon coarse black pepper
  2 tablespoons grated carrot
  2 tablespoons grated green pepper
  1 tablespoon grated onion
    Bit of chopped or pressed garlic

Combine all ingredients in a jar or bowl. Shake or beat well. Refrigerate until needed. Shake or beat again before using. Makes about 1 cup dressing. Very good with mixed green and vegetable salads.

Chocolate Graham-Nut Bars

  1 (15-oz.) can sweetened condensed milk
  2 cups packaged graham cracker crumbs
  1 (6-oz.) package semi-sweet chocolate morsels
  ½ cup chopped walnuts or pecans
  ¼ teaspoon cinnamon
    Dash of salt

Mix all ingredients together well. Spread evenly in a greased and floured 8-inch square baking pan. Bake in a moderate oven (350° F.) about 40 minutes. While still warm, cut in 2-inch squares and roll in confectioner's sugar. Makes 16 bars.

DINNER

Crisp Baked Fish Fillets*
with a Sauce*
or Walnut-Crusted Sole Meunière*
Stewed Tomatoes
(canned ones are good)
Waffle Potato Chips **Cole Slaw***
Surprise Marshmallow Sundae*

With this menu we enjoy the indicated
California Wines

Crisp Baked Fish Fillets

1½ pounds fish fillets
½ cup undiluted evaporated milk
1 cup packaged corn flake crumbs
1 teaspoon seasoned salt
¼ teaspoon each: pepper and paprika
3 tablespoons melted butter

Dip fish fillets in evaporated milk, then roll in a mixture of corn flake crumbs and seasonings. Place fillets in a shallow pan lined with aluminum foil. (Don't crowd them.) Sprinkle with melted butter. Bake in a moderately hot oven (375° F.) for 20 to 25 minutes, or until tender. Serve with *Caper-Sour Cream Sauce* or *Almond-Butter Sauce* (below), or with your favorite tartar sauce. Serves 3 or 4. Wine choice: California Chablis.

Caper-Sour Cream Sauce: Mix ½ cup dairy sour cream, ½ cup mayonnaise, and 2 tablespoons coarsely chopped, drained capers. Add salt to taste. Cover; chill an hour or more before serving. Makes 1 cup sauce.

Almond-Butter Sauce: Melt ½ cup butter; add ½ cup shaved or slivered unblanched almonds; sauté gently just until almonds are golden. Add 2 tablespoons California Dry Vermouth, 1 tablespoon lemon juice, and 1 tablespoon parsley flakes; heat to simmering. Serve at once. Serves 4.

Walnut-Crusted Sole Meunière

Follow the recipe for *Crisp Baked Fish Fillets* (above), using 1½ pounds fillets of sole and substituting a mixture of ½ cup packaged fine bread crumbs and ½ cup *very* finely chopped walnuts for the 1 cup corn flake crumbs. While fish cooks, heat ⅓ cup butter gently in a small saucepan until it is slightly brown; add 1 tablespoon *each* lemon juice and California Dry Vermouth and 2 tablespoons parsley flakes. Remove cooked fish to a heated platter or dinner plates; spoon sauce over it and serve at once. Serves 4. Wine choice: California Dry Semillon.

Cole Slaw

There are almost as many recipes for cole slaw as there are cooks! This is the way I usually make it, because I get good-tasting results with a minimum of effort. Shred the desired amount of cabbage and place in a bowl. Stir in enough oil-vinegar French dressing so that the cabbage is barely moistened. (Bottled Italian-style French dressing is good here.) Next mix in just enough mayonnaise to give the cole slaw a creamy effect. Add a generous sprinkling of celery seed; season to taste with onion salt, salt, and pepper. Cover and chill thoroughly before serving.

Surprise Marshmallow Sundae

Place a generous scoop of chocolate ice cream in a dessert dish. With a paring knife, make a little "well" down through the center of the ice cream, and into this pour a little coffee-flavored wine or liqueur. Cover ice cream with marshmallow sauce. Serve at once. Truly luscious! Another good combination: coffee ice cream, crème de cacao, and marshmallow sauce.

DINNER

Sole with Shrimp, Hollandaise*
or
Baked Salmon with Sour Cream*
Buttered Chopped Spinach
Potato Patties
(the frozen ones)
Jellied Orange Delight*

With this menu we enjoy the indicated
California Wines

Sole with Shrimp, Hollandaise

1 pound fillets of sole
2 teaspoons instant minced onion
1 bay leaf, crumbled
    Thyme, salt, and pepper
1 cup California White Table Wine or
    Dry Vermouth
2 tablespoons butter
1 (6-oz.) can hollandaise sauce
1 tablespoon lemon juice
2 teaspoons parsley flakes
¾ to 1 cup cooked or canned small shrimp
    Paprika

Arrange fish fillets in a single layer in a shallow baking dish. Sprinkle with onion, bay leaf, thyme, salt, and pepper. Pour wine over fish. Bake, uncovered, in a moderately hot oven (375°F.) for 15 minutes. Remove dish from oven and carefully transfer fillets onto paper towels to drain. Strain liquid from baking dish into a saucepan; boil rapidly until reduced to ¼ cup. Add butter; stir until melted. Remove from heat. Add hollandaise sauce, lemon juice, parsley, and salt to taste; blend well. Arrange fillets in 2 or 3 individual baking dishes (or put them back in the original baking dish). Scatter shrimp over fillets; spoon hollandaise sauce mixture over all; sprinkle with paprika. Return to a moderately hot oven (375°F.) for 10 minutes. Serves 2 or 3. Wine choice: California Chablis.

Baked Salmon with Sour Cream

Arrange 4 serving-sized salmon fillets or steaks in a single layer in a greased shallow baking dish. Sprinkle with 1 tablespoon instant minced onion, 1 tablespoon parsley flakes, and salt and pepper to taste. Pour 1 cup California White Table Wine over fish. Bake, uncovered, in a moderately hot oven (375°F.) for 15 minutes. Remove dish from oven; carefully pour off all liquid. Mix 1 cup dairy sour cream, ½ teaspoon dill weed, ½ teaspoon dry shredded green onions, and salt to taste; spread over salmon. Sprinkle with paprika. Return to a moderately hot oven (375°F.) for 10 minutes, or until fish is tender. Serves 4. Wine choice: California Grey Riesling. Easy and *very* tasty.

Jellied Orange Delight

Dissolve 1 (3-oz.) package of orange-flavored gelatin in 1 cup hot water; add ½ cup California White Table Wine, and ½ cup orange juice. Pour into stemmed glasses; chill until firm. Serve topped with a dollop of whipped cream or sour cream and a drizzle of Cointreau or other orange-flavored liqueur. Serves 4.

•••••••••••••••••••••

Baked Fish Fillets Tartar

Arrange 1 pound fish fillets in a single layer in a shallow baking dish. Mix 1 cup California White Table Wine and 2 teaspoons salt; pour over fish; let stand 30 minutes or so. Transfer fillets onto paper towels to drain. Pour off wine from dish; grease dish well; replace fillets in dish. Mix ¾ cup bottled tartar sauce, ½ cup grated Parmesan cheese, 2 teaspoons lemon juice, 1 teaspoon dry shredded green onions, and ½ teaspoon Worcestershire sauce; spread evenly over fillets; sprinkle with packaged corn flake crumbs and dust with paprika. Bake in a very hot oven (500°F.) for 10 to 12 minutes, or until fish is tender. Remove from oven; let stand a few minutes so juices can settle. Serve with lemon wedges. Serves 2 or 3. Wine choice: California Chablis.

DINNER

Sole Veronica*
Stuffed Potatoes au Gratin*
Hot Asparagus or Asparagus Salad
Strawberries Merriann*

With this menu we enjoy:

California Johannisberg Riesling

Seedless grapes add an interesting note of flavor to the sauce here.

Sole Veronica

1½ cups water
  1 cup California White Table Wine
  1 tablespoon instant minced onion
  1 bay leaf
  3 or 4 whole peppercorns
    Salt to taste
  2 pounds fillets of sole
  4 tablespoons each: butter and flour
  1 cup light cream or rich milk
  1 tablespoon California Dry
    or Medium Sherry
  1 teaspoon lemon juice
½ teaspoon Worcestershire sauce
    Pepper to taste
  1 cup fresh or well-drained canned
    seedless grapes
  1 (6-oz.) can sliced broiled mushrooms, drained
    Paprika

Combine water, white wine, onion, bay leaf, peppercorns, and salt in a large, heavy skillet; heat to simmering. Lay fillets of sole in this liquid; cover and simmer for 4 to 5 minutes, or just until fish is tender. Drain fillets, reserving liquid, and place in a greased shallow baking dish or on an oven-proof platter. Strain reserved liquid; boil rapidly until reduced to ¾ cup. Melt butter and stir in flour; add cream and the ¾ cup fish liquid; cook, stirring constantly, until mixture boils and thickens. Add Sherry, lemon juice, Worcestershire sauce, salt, and pepper. Stir in grapes and drained mushrooms. Pour hot sauce over fish; sprinkle with paprika. Place under preheated broiler for 1 minute, or until sauce is bubbly and delicately browned. Serves 5 or 6.

Stuffed Potatoes au Gratin

Bake 1 good-sized potato for each person to be served. When done, remove from oven and cut a slice from the flat side. Scoop out the inside with a teaspoon and mash well with a fork. For each potato add ½ tablespoon butter, 1 tablespoon milk, 1 tablespoon grated Parmesan cheese, and salt and pepper to taste. Beat until fluffy; pile mixture lightly into shells. Sprinkle with a little more Parmesan cheese; dust with paprika. Bake in a hot oven (450°F.) for 10 minutes, or until hot and delicately browned.

Strawberries Merriann

  1 cup sugar
½ cup water
½ cup California Port or Sweet Sherry
  1 quart strawberries, washed and hulled (whole, halved, or sliced, depending on size)
  6 bakery shortcake cups (sometimes called "Mary Annes"), or
  6 slices sponge cake
    Whipped cream and 6 whole, unhulled strawberries for garnishing

Combine sugar and water in a saucepan; bring to a boil, stirring until sugar is dissolved, then simmer 5 minutes. Remove from heat. Add wine. Place strawberries in a bowl; pour warm syrup over them; chill for several hours. At serving time, heap strawberries in shortcake cups or on top of cake slices; pour syrup over berries. Top each serving with a generous puff of whipped cream and a whole, unhulled strawberry. Serve at once. Serves 6.

DINNER

Fish Fillets Marguerite*
Parmesan Potato Sticks*
Zucchini & Corn Sauté*
Grapefruit au Cointreau*
Macaroons

With this menu we enjoy:

California Chablis

Fish Fillets Marguerite

1 cup water
1 cup California White Table Wine or
  Dry Vermouth
1 tablespoon instant minced onion
  Pinch of thyme
3 or 4 whole peppercorns
  Salt to taste
1½ pounds fish fillets (sole, halibut, or salmon)
4 tablespoons each: butter and flour
1 cup rich milk
½ cup light cream
1 teaspoon California tarragon wine vinegar
½ teaspoon each: prepared mustard and
  Worcestershire sauce
  Pepper to taste
12 small oysters
¾ cup cooked or canned shrimp
  Paprika

Combine first 7 ingredients in a large pan; heat to simmering. Lay fish fillets in this liquid; cover and simmer 4 to 5 minutes, or just until fish is tender. Drain fillets, reserving liquid, and place in a greased shallow baking dish. Strain reserved liquid; boil rapidly until reduced to ½ cup. Melt butter and stir in flour; add milk, cream, and fish liquid; cook, stirring, until mixture is thickened and smooth. Add vinegar, mustard, Worcestershire sauce, salt, and pepper. Arrange oysters and shrimp over fillets; cover with the hot sauce; dust with paprika. Place under preheated broiler for 1 minute or until sauce is bubbly and delicately browned. Serves 4.

Parmesan Potato Sticks

Heat frozen French-fried potatoes in the oven as directed on the carton. Remove from oven and sprinkle generously with grated Parmesan cheese, shaking pan so potatoes are evenly coated. Add salt to taste. Serve at once.

Zucchini and Corn Sauté

1 pound small zucchini
2 tablespoons butter or salad oil
2 tablespoons water
1 (12-oz.) can vacuum-pack Mexican-style
  whole-kernel corn, drained
  Onion salt, salt, and pepper to taste

Wash zucchini and trim off ends (do not peel); slice crosswise paper-thin. Heat butter in a saucepan or skillet; add zucchini and sauté gently, stirring frequently, until zucchini is lightly browned. Add water. Cover and cook gently for 5 to 10 minutes, or until zucchini is tender, stirring frequently. Add corn; season to taste. Heat piping hot before serving. Serves 4.

Grapefruit au Cointreau

There are two ways to serve this refreshing combination of fruit and liqueur. 1) For each person to be served, section a grapefruit half, drizzle a little Cointreau over it, and chill thoroughly. 2) Sprinkle Cointreau over drained fresh or canned grapefruit sections. Chill thoroughly. Good flavor in either case! California Sweet Sherry is also excellent here in place of the Cointreau.

Crab Rio

Sauté ¼ cup chopped green pepper in 3 tablespoons butter 5 minutes. Stir in 3 tablespoons flour; add 1¼ cups milk, ⅓ cup chili sauce, ¼ cup California Sherry or Dry Vermouth; cook till smooth. Add 2 cups crab or shrimp, salt to taste. Serve in patty shells. Serves 4 or 5. Wine choice: California Dry Semillon.

DINNER
Poached Salmon or Halibut*
with Sour Cream Hollandaise* or Mayonnaise-Caper Sauce*
Crumb Crust Potatoes*
Buttered Chopped Broccoli & Spinach
(use the frozen combination)
Cherry Tomatoes   Cucumber Sticks
Special Apple Crisp*

With this menu we enjoy:
California Pinot Chardonnay

Poached Salmon or Halibut

    4 serving-sized salmon or halibut fillets or steaks
    1 tablespoon *each:* instant minced onion and
      parsley flakes
    ½ bay leaf
    4 peppercorns
    1 teaspoon seasoned salt
      Dash of thyme
    1 cup California Dry Vermouth or
      White Table Wine

Place fish in a single layer in a large skillet. Sprinkle onion, parsley, bay leaf, peppercorns, seasoned salt, and thyme over fish; add wine. Place over low heat and pour in just enough boiling water so that fish is *barely* covered. Let liquid bubble up a minute, then turn off heat, cover skillet, and let stand on burner 10 minutes. Remove fish to heated dinner plates and serve at once with *Sour Cream Hollandaise* or *Mayonnaise-Caper Sauce* (below). Serves 4.

Sour Cream Hollandaise: In a small saucepan combine 1 (6-oz.) can hollandaise sauce, ½ cup dairy sour cream, 2 tablespoons California Dry Vermouth, 1 teaspoon lemon juice, 1 teaspoon dry shredded green onions, and salt to taste. Mix well and heat gently. Serve warm.

Mayonnaise-Caper Sauce: Mix ½ cup mayonnaise, ½ cup dairy sour cream, 1 teaspoon lemon juice, ½ teaspoon prepared horseradish, and ½ teaspoon prepared mustard. Stir in 1 to 2 tablespoons drained capers, 1 teaspoon dry shredded green onions, and seasoned salt to taste. Serve at room temperature.

P. S. Cold poached salmon or halibut is equally delicious, served with *Mayonnaise-Caper Sauce.* Poach the fish for 10 minutes as directed, then remove it from the liquid and place it in a single layer in a shallow dish to cool. Strain the liquid and let cool, also, then pour it over the fish. Cover dish with foil and chill thoroughly before serving. A great warm-weather main dish, served with sliced tomatoes and cucumbers marinated in French dressing.

Crumb Crust Potatoes

Drain canned small whole potatoes. Roll them in melted butter, then in a mixture of equal parts of cornflake crumbs and grated Parmesan cheese. Place on a foil-lined baking sheet. Bake in a moderately hot oven (375°F.) for 20 minutes. Remove from oven and sprinkle lightly with seasoned salt and paprika. Serve at once.

Special Apple Crisp

    1 (1-lb. 4-oz.) can pie-sliced apples
    1½ teaspoons cornstarch
    ⅓ cup sugar
    ¼ teaspoon cinnamon
    ⅛ teaspoon nutmeg
      Dash of salt
    ¼ cup California Sweet Sherry or Muscatel
    ½ teaspoon grated lemon peel
    1 tablespoon butter

Place apples in a colander and drain thoroughly. Mix cornstarch, sugar, spices, and salt in a small saucepan; gradually stir in wine, mixing until smooth; cook over medium heat until mixture is thickened and clear. Add lemon peel and butter. Combine this mixture with the apples, mixing gently but thoroughly. Turn into a greased 9-inch pie plate. With pastry blender or fingers, mix until crumbly for the topping:

    ¼ cup softened butter
    ½ cup sugar
    6 tablespoons flour
      Dash of salt

Sprinkle topping over apples, then pat it down evenly. Bake in a moderate oven (350°F.) for 45 minutes. Serve warm with plain cream, or topped with whipped cream or vanilla ice cream. Serves 4 to 6.

DINNER
Crabmeat or Shrimp Curry*
with Hawaiian Rice Molds*
Curry Condiments
Pattypan Squash with Peas*
Nectar-Glazed Strawberry Tarts*

With this menu we enjoy the indicated
California Wines

Crabmeat or Shrimp Curry

6 tablespoons butter
1 small onion, chopped
½ cup flour
1 tablespoon curry powder (or to taste)
1 teaspoon powdered ginger
2 cups light cream
1 cup chicken stock
½ cup California White Table Wine
2 tablespoons California Dry or Medium Sherry
½ teaspoon each: sugar and Worcestershire sauce
 Salt and garlic salt to taste
3 cups cooked or canned crabmeat or shrimp
2 hard-cooked eggs, coarsely chopped
2 tablespoons parsley flakes

Melt butter in top of a double boiler over direct heat; add onion and sauté gently 5 minutes. Blend in flour, curry powder, and ginger; gradually add cream, chicken stock, and white wine; cook slowly, stirring constantly, until mixture is thickened and smooth. Add Sherry and seasonings; stir in remaining ingredients. Cover; place over simmering water; cook 15 to 20 minutes before serving. (If you want to prepare the dish ahead of time, postpone this cooking over simmering water until just before serving.) Serve with *Hawaiian Rice Molds* (below). Serves 6. Wine choice: California Sauterne.

Hawaiian Rice Molds: Boil or steam 1½ cups long-grain white rice until tender; drain, if necessary. Drain 1 (8½-oz.) can crushed pineapple. Add pineapple to rice along with ¾ cup flaked coconut, 3 tablespoons melted butter, and salt to taste; mix gently with a fork. Heat thoroughly over boiling water before serving. To shape molds, press mixture lightly but firmly into a greased custard cup and unmold on a platter or dinner plates. Serves 6.

Suggested condiments: Chutney (essential), diced banana, chopped salted peanuts, chopped green onions, chopped green pepper, and chopped crisp bacon.

Pattypan Squash with Peas

Scrub 1 pound small pattypan squash; trim stem and blossom ends; slice crosswise in thin slices. Cook, covered, in a small amount of boiling salted water 10 to 15 minutes, or just until tender; drain. Cook 1 (10-oz.) package frozen peas with celery according to package directions; drain. Combine the vegetables; add 2 tablespoons butter, 1 teaspoon dry shredded green onions, and seasoned salt and pepper to taste. Heat gently before serving. Serves 6.

Nectar-Glazed Strawberry Tarts

1½ tablespoons cornstarch
⅓ cup sugar
 Dash of salt
¼ cup California Sweet Sherry or Muscatel
¾ cup canned peach or apricot nectar
1 tablespoon lemon juice
 Red food coloring
3 to 4 cups hulled, washed strawberries (whole, halved, or sliced, depending on size)
8 (4-inch) baked tart shells
 Whipped cream

Mix cornstarch, sugar, and salt in a small saucepan; gradually stir in wine, nectar, and lemon juice, blending until mixture is perfectly smooth. Stir over medium heat until mixture is thickened and clear. Add enough red coloring to give a nice rosy hue. Cool slightly. Fill tart shells with strawberries; spoon glaze over berries. Chill until time to serve. Before serving, top with whipped cream. Makes 8 tarts. Wine choice: California Muscatel.

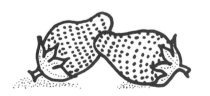

DINNER or LUNCHEON

Crabmeat or Shrimp Jacques*

in Baked Eggplant Ring*
Green Beans Piquant*
Toasted English Muffins
Frozen Lemon Cream*   Ladyfingers

With this menu we enjoy:
California Grey Riesling

Crabmeat or Shrimp Jacques

1 (6-oz.) can sliced broiled mushrooms, drained
2 tablespoons chopped onion
1 tablespoon grated green pepper
4 tablespoons butter
5 tablespoons flour
1 cup light cream
¾ cup bottled clam juice
3 tablespoons California Dry or Medium Sherry
2 tablespoons grated Parmesan cheese
1 tablespoon parsley flakes
1 tablespoon chopped pimiento
  Dash of thyme
  Salt and pepper to taste
2 cups cooked or canned crabmeat or shrimp

In a saucepan sauté mushrooms, onion, and green pepper gently in butter for 5 minutes. Stir in flour; gradually add cream and clam juice; cook slowly, stirring constantly, until mixture is thickened and smooth. Add Sherry, cheese, parsley, pimiento, thyme, salt, and pepper. Last, stir in crabmeat or shrimp. Heat gently and serve piping hot in the center of *Baked Eggplant Ring* (below). Serves 5 or 6.

P. S. For another excellent dish, substitute canned chicken broth for the clam juice in this recipe, and 2 cups diced, cooked chicken for the crabmeat or shrimp.

Baked Eggplant Ring

2 medium-sized eggplants (1¾ to 2 pounds)
1 (10½-oz.) can condensed cream of
  mushroom soup
½ cup shredded Cheddar cheese
¾ cup fine, dry bread crumbs
3 eggs, well beaten
1 tablespoon each: instant minced onion and
  parsley flakes
1 teaspoon Worcestershire sauce
  Salt, garlic salt, and pepper to taste

Pare eggplant and cut in 1-inch cubes; cook, covered, in boiling salted water about 10 minutes, or just until tender. Drain well and mash. Stir soup and cheese together over low heat until cheese melts; combine this sauce with the eggplant; add remaining ingredients. Spoon mixture into a well-oiled 8½-inch (1¼-quart) ring mold; set mold in a shallow pan of hot water; bake in a moderate oven (350°F.) about 50 minutes, or until firm. Remove mold from water; run a small spatula or knife around edges of ring to loosen it from mold; let stand 5 to 10 minutes before unmolding on a heated platter. Serves 5 or 6.

Green Beans Piquant

Drain and rinse 2 (1-lb.) cans vertical-pack green beans. In a skillet heat together 4 tablespoons butter, 2 tablespoons California Dry Vermouth, 2 teaspoons lemon juice, and 1 teaspoon dry shredded green onions. Add beans; heat thoroughly, spooning sauce over them; season to taste with seasoned salt and pepper. To serve, arrange beans neatly in a heated serving dish; pour butter sauce over them; sprinkle with grated Parmesan cheese and paprika. Serves 6.

Frozen Lemon Cream

Mix 1 pint light cream with 1 cup sugar; stir to dissolve sugar. Add the juice and grated peel of 2 lemons. Pour into refrigerator freezing tray; freeze 1 hour. Whip ½ cup heavy cream. Beat 2 egg whites stiff. Remove lemon mixture to a chilled bowl; beat until smooth; fold in cream and egg whites. Return mixture to tray; freeze until firm. Serves 6.

LIGHT DINNER
or LUNCHEON

Celery-Egg Timbales with Lobster Sauce*

or Lobster Tarts Diablo*

Chinese Pea Pods   Canned Shoestring Potatoes

Fruited Lemon Dessert Ring*

With this menu we enjoy:

California Chablis

Celery-Egg Timbales with Lobster Sauce

　2 (10½-oz.) cans condensed cream of celery soup
　½ cup cream or rich milk
　6 large eggs, well beaten
　2 teaspoons parsley flakes
　　Pepper to taste
　¼ cup California Dry Vermouth or
　　White Table Wine
　1 cup shredded Cheddar cheese
　1 tablespoon finely chopped pimiento
　1 teaspoon dry shredded green onions
1½ cups diced, cooked or canned lobster
　　(or crabmeat, shrimp, or tuna)
　1 (3-oz.) can sliced broiled mushrooms, drained

Combine 1 can of the celery soup with the cream, eggs, parsley, and pepper; blend well. Pour into 6 well-greased custard cups. Set cups in a shallow pan containing 1 inch of hot water and bake in a moderate oven (350°F.) for 45 to 50 minutes, or until a knife inserted in the center of a timbale comes out clean. Remove from water and let stand 5 minutes or so before unmolding. While timbales are baking, combine remaining can of soup, wine, and cheese in a saucepan; stir over low heat (or in a double boiler) until cheese melts and ingredients are well blended. Add pimiento, onions, lobster, and mushrooms; heat very gently (do not boil). Serve at once over the timbales, or keep warm over hot water till serving time. Serves 6.

Lobster Tarts Diablo

　4 tablespoons butter
　4 tablespoons flour
1¾ cups rich milk
　¼ cup California Dry or Medium Sherry (or
　　2 tablespoons *each* California Sherry
　　and Brandy)
　1 tablespoon lemon juice

　1 teaspoon Worcestershire sauce
　½ teaspoon prepared mustard
　　Seasoned salt and pepper to taste
　2 cups diced, cooked or canned lobster
　1 (4-oz.) can sliced mushrooms, drained
　1 teaspoon dry shredded green onions
　6 (4-inch) baked tart shells (or patty shells),
　　warmed briefly in the oven
　　Grated Parmesan cheese and paprika

Melt butter and stir in flour; add milk; cook, stirring constantly, until mixture is thickened and smooth; continue cooking and stirring for another minute or two. Add Sherry, lemon juice, and seasonings; stir in lobster and mushrooms; heat gently just until piping hot. Spoon mixture into warm tart shells; sprinkle with Parmesan cheese and paprika. Serve at once. Serves 6.

Fruited Lemon Dessert Ring

　2 envelopes (2 tablespoons) unflavored gelatin
　½ cup cold water
1¼ cups boiling water
　1 cup California Rosé
　1 (6-oz.) can frozen lemonade concentrate
　2 tablespoons sugar
　　Dash of salt
　1 cup diced canned pineapple
　1 cup seedless or halved seeded grapes
　½ cup thinly sliced maraschino cherries

Soften gelatin in the cold water 5 minutes. Add boiling water; stir until gelatin is dissolved. Add wine, frozen lemonade concentrate, sugar and salt. Chill until mixture begins to thicken, then fold in fruits. Turn into a 9½-inch (1½-quart) ring mold that has been rinsed with cold water. Chill until firm. Unmold on a serving platter. Serve with whipped or plain cream. Serves 8.

P. S. If you like, you can fill the center of this ring with washed, hulled, and sweetened strawberries.

DINNER or LUNCHEON

Shrimp and Crabmeat Mold Supreme*

or **Deviled Egg Ring with Shellfish***

Louis Dressing*   **Stuffed Tomato Salad**

(stuff with chopped ripe olives and celery mixed with mayonnaise)

Corn Bread or Muffins

Cranberry Peach Melba*   **Cookies**

With this menu we enjoy:

California Dry Sauterne

Shrimp and Crabmeat Mold Supreme

2 envelopes (2 tablespoons) unflavored gelatin
½ cup California White Table Wine
½ cup boiling water
1 (10½-oz.) can condensed consommé
2 tablespoons lemon juice
1 teaspoon onion juice
1 teaspoon Worcestershire sauce
    Salt and pepper to taste
2 cups cleaned cooked or canned large shrimp
½ pound flaked cooked or canned crabmeat
2 tablespoons chopped parsley

Soften gelatin in the wine for 5 minutes; dissolve in the boiling water. Add consommé, lemon juice, onion juice, Worcestershire sauce, salt, and pepper. Arrange shrimp in the bottom of an oiled 8½-inch (1¼-quart) ring mold, placing them in any attractive geometric pattern. A row of the shrimp may be stood up along the edge of the mold, if desired. Pour 1 cup of the gelatin mixture into the mold; chill until this layer is firm. Meantime, chill remaining gelatin mixture until syrupy; fold in crabmeat and parsley. Spoon crabmeat mixture over firm shrimp layer in mold; chill until crabmeat layer is firm. Unmold on a lettuce-lined platter and garnish as desired with slices of hard-cooked egg, radishes, olives, etc. Serve with *Louis Dressing* or mayonnaise. Serves 6. A really super dish!

Deviled Egg Ring with Shellfish

1 envelope unflavored gelatin
½ cup canned condensed chicken broth
½ cup California White Table Wine
1 cup mayonnaise
1 teaspoon grated onion
½ teaspoon prepared mustard
½ teaspoon Worcestershire sauce

6 hard-cooked eggs, coarsely grated
½ cup finely chopped pimiento-stuffed olives
¼ cup minced parsley
    Salt and pepper to taste
2 cups cooked or canned crabmeat, shrimp,
    or lobster
    French Dressing

Soften gelatin in the chicken broth for 5 minutes; stir over low heat until dissolved. Mix dissolved gelatin and wine; blend in mayonnaise; add onion, mustard and Worcestershire sauce; chill. When mixture begins to thicken, fold in eggs, olives, and parsley; season with salt and pepper. Pour into a well-oiled 8½-inch (1¼-quart) ring mold; chill until firm. Unmold on crisp salad greens and fill center with shellfish that has been mixed with just enough French dressing to moisten it. Serve with *Louis Dressing*. Serves 5 or 6.

Louis Dressing

Mix 1 cup mayonnaise, ¼ cup chili sauce, ¼ cup California Dry Vermouth or Dry or Medium Sherry, 1 tablespoon parsley flakes, 1 teaspoon dry shredded green onions, ½ teaspoon Worcestershire sauce, and seasoned salt to taste. Chill an hour or more to blend flavors. Makes about 1½ cups.

Cranberry Peach Melba

For each serving, fill the hollow of a fresh or canned peach half with a scoop of vanilla ice cream. Spoon *Cranberry Sundae Sauce* over all: In a saucepan combine 1 (1-lb.) can whole cranberry sauce, ⅓ cup California Port, and ¼ cup sugar. Add 1 teaspoon *each* grated orange peel and lemon peel, and a dash *each* of cinnamon, nutmeg, and salt. Bring to a boil, then simmer gently, uncovered, for 10 minutes. Cool thoroughly. Makes almost 2 cups. This is a fine sauce for vanilla, strawberry, or lemon ice cream.

DINNER or LUNCHEON

Emily's Tuna Mousse*
Vermicelli Salad*   Mixed Green Salad
Chilled Vegetable Platter
*(sliced tomatoes, asparagus tips,
and green beans with French dressing)*
Patio Cheddar Bread*
Your Favorite Cake

With this menu we enjoy:

California Dry Sauterne

This Tuna Mousse is smooth and delicious without being too rich. The Vermicelli Salad is light in texture and piquant in flavor.

Emily's Tuna Mousse

1 cup cold water
½ cup California White Table Wine
2 envelopes (2 tablespoons) plus
    1 teaspoon unflavored gelatin
1 tablespoon each: parsley flakes and
    dry shredded green onions
1 (10½-oz.) can cream of celery soup
½ cup salad dressing**
½ cup mayonnaise
3 (6½-oz.) cans chunk-style tuna, rinsed
    and drained
¼ cup lemon juice
1 teaspoon each: grated lemon peel, prepared
    horseradish, and Worcestershire sauce
1 tablespoon chopped pimiento
    Salt to taste

Combine water and wine in a small saucepan; soften gelatin in this mixture for 5 minutes; stir over low heat until gelatin is dissolved. Remove from heat; add parsley and onions. Combine soup, salad dressing and mayonnaise in a blender; gradually add tuna, blending until smooth after each addition. Turn mixture into a large mixing bowl. Add remaining ingredients and dissolved gelatin; mix well. Spoon mixture into a mold that has been brushed with salad oil; chill until firm. (A 5½-cup fish-shaped mold is perfect.) To serve, unmold on a platter; garnish with sprigs of watercress or parsley. Serve with mayonnaise thinned with a little cream or evaporated milk and perked up with a little lemon juice and a few capers. Serves 8.

**I use Miracle Whip for it gives just the flavor this dish requires.

Vermicelli Salad

1 (14-oz.) package coil vermicelli
2 tablespoons olive oil
1 cup bottled Italian dressing
2 tablespoons each: parsley flakes and
    dry shredded green onions
¼ teaspoon each: dried basil and oregano
1¼ cups mayonnaise
2 tablespoons California tarragon red wine vinegar
    Salt to taste (I use seasoned salt and garlic salt)
    Coarse black pepper to taste (I use lemon pepper)

Cook vermicelli in a large kettle of boiling salted water to which you have added the olive oil. Add vermicelli gradually so the water doesn't stop boiling. Stir *constantly* with a two-tined fork until strands of vermicelli are all separated from each other, then continue stirring almost constantly until vermicelli is *just* tender, 10 to 12 minutes cooking. Drain cooked vermicelli immediately; rinse well with cold water; drain again thoroughly. Turn vermicelli into your largest mixing bowl. Add Italian dressing; toss *gently* to coat vermicelli. Add herbs, mayonnaise, and vinegar; toss again. Season to taste. Chill salad thoroughly. Serves 8 to 10.

Patio Cheddar Bread

Have 1 (5-oz.) jar process Cheddar cheese spread at room temperature; blend with ½ cup (¼ pound) soft butter. Gradually beat in 2 tablespoons California Dry or Medium Sherry or Dry Vermouth. Add ½ teaspoon Worcestershire sauce, 1 tablespoon parsley flakes, 1 teaspoon dry shredded green onions, and chopped or pressed garlic to taste. Slash a long loaf of French bread crosswise in thick slices, cutting down to the bottom crust but not through it. Spread slices with cheese mixture. Place loaf on a baking sheet; cover loosely with aluminum foil. Bake at 350°F. about 20 minutes. Serve hot.

V. Pies Mother Never Used to Make

Mouth-watering main-dish pies and tarts

I'm very partial to main-dish pies. I'm not referring to the familiar chicken and beef pies, baked in a casserole with a biscuit or pastry lid, though these are very good. Rather I mean a "real" pie, baked in a pie plate, with a savory filling featuring meat, chicken, seafood, or cheese. Here's an attractive-looking, light main dish that's easy to serve, often an excellent choice for brunch or lunch as well as dinner.

A dinner menu featuring one of these pies usually calls for a hot vegetable and a salad. At brunch, a spiced peach or a skewer threaded with fruit would be the only accompaniment needed, and at lunchtime a fruit or vegetable salad is the perfect plate-mate.

Unless you just *love* to make pastry, take advantage of the excellent frozen pie shells that are readily available. They save precious minutes and are tender as a maiden's heart!

DINNER

Beefburger Pie*
Buttered Lima Beans
(sprinkle with chopped crisp bacon & parsley)
Beet Salad Ring*
Maple-Peanut Sundae*
Cookies

With this menu we enjoy:

California Zinfandel

Beefburger Pie

1 pound lean ground beef
2 tablespoons butter
2 tablespoons flour
3 eggs
1 (10½-oz.) can condensed cream of
    mushroom soup
2 tablespoons California Dry or Medium Sherry
    or Dry Vermouth
2 tablespoons instant minced onion
1 tablespoon parsley flakes
1 teaspoon Worcestershire sauce
    Seasoned salt and pepper to taste
1 (9-inch) baked pastry shell (with a high,
    fluted rim), or 1 Cracker Pie Shell (below)
    Sour cream (if you like)

Sauté beef in butter until it is no longer red, stirring with a fork to separate it into bits. Sprinkle flour over meat; stir well. Remove from heat. Beat eggs slightly; blend in soup and wine; add to meat and mix well. Add onion, parsley, and seasonings. Spoon mixture into pie shell. Bake in a moderate oven (350°F.) for 35 to 40 minutes, or until a knife inserted near the center comes out clean. Remove from oven; let stand a few minutes before cutting. This pie is rich-flavored and delectable as is, or you can gild the lily and pass a bowl of sour cream to be spooned atop each serving. Serves 4 to 6.

Cracker Pie Shell: With a rolling pin or in a blender crush enough plain or cheese-flavored salt crackers to make 2 cups crumbs. (Allow 50 to 60 crackers.) Blend crumbs with 4 tablespoons soft butter and 2 tablespoons water, using a fork and/or fingers. Press mixture evenly over bottom and sides of a 9-inch pie plate. (Wet your fingers so mixture won't stick to them.) Fill shell and bake pie as directed above.

Beet Salad Ring

1 (1-lb.) can diced beets
1 (3-oz.) package orange-flavored gelatin
½ cup California Red Table Wine
1 tablespoon California red wine vinegar
1 tablespoon grated onion
2 teaspoons prepared horseradish
½ teaspoon salt
¾ cup finely cut celery

Drain beets, reserving liquid; chop beets coarsely. Measure beet liquid; add water as needed to make 1¼ cups; heat to simmering; remove from heat. Add gelatin to this hot liquid and stir until dissolved. Add wine, vinegar, onion, horseradish, and salt. Chill. When mixture begins to thicken, fold in beets and celery. Pour into a well-oiled ring mold or individual molds and chill until firm. Unmold on crisp salad greens. Serve with a dressing of equal parts of mayonnaise and sour cream, plus salt to taste, or with plain mayonnaise. Serves 6.

Maple-Peanut Sundae

Spoon vanilla ice cream into sherbet glasses or dessert dishes. Drizzle a little maple syrup over each serving, then sprinkle generously with crushed peanut brittle. Or, serve the ice cream plain, pass the maple syrup and the peanut brittle, and let each person make his own sundae.

Another delectable sundae: Crush 1 or more English toffee bars into coarse crumbs. Drizzle chocolate-flavored wine or crème de cacao over servings of vanilla ice cream, then sprinkle with the crushed candy.

DINNER

Devonshire Beef Pie* or Hash Pasties*
Carrots Julienne
(cook julienne-cut carrots or heat canned ones)
Chilled Broccoli with Mustard Mayonnaise*
Fresh Strawberries   Ladyfingers

With this menu we enjoy the indicated

California Wines

Devonshire Beef Pie

1½ pounds lean ground beef
1 medium-sized onion, chopped
2 tablespoons chopped green pepper (if you like)
2 tablespoons butter
3 tablespoons flour
½ cup California Red Table Wine
2 teaspoons Worcestershire sauce
  Salt and pepper to taste
2 medium-sized potatoes
⅓ cup finely chopped parsley
  Pastry for 2-crust (9-inch) pie, or
  2 (9-inch) frozen pie shells

Sauté beef, onion, and green pepper in butter just until meat is no longer red, stirring with a fork so that meat is separated into bits. Blend in flour; add wine and cook, stirring, until mixture boils and thickens. Season with Worcestershire sauce, salt, and pepper. Remove from heat. Peel and grate potatoes; add to meat mixture; add parsley. Turn mixture into a pastry-lined 9-inch pie plate. Put top crust in place; make several gashes in center to permit escape of steam. Bake in a hot oven (450°F.) for 15 minutes; reduce heat to moderate (350°F.) and continue baking for 1 hour. Remove pie from oven and let stand 20 minutes or so before serving. Serves 5-6. Wine choice: California Claret.

Here's another delicious relative of the Cornish pasty, featuring canned roast beef hash and sautéed ground beef.

Hash Pasties

3 tablespoons bacon drippings or butter
1 large onion, chopped
2 tablespoons chopped green pepper (if you like)
½ pound lean ground beef
1 (1-lb.) can roast beef hash
2 tablespoons parsley flakes
1 teaspoon Worcestershire sauce
  Salt and pepper to taste
3 unbaked (9-inch) pastry shells (homemade, frozen, or bakery-made)
1 tablespoon butter

Heat bacon drippings in a large, heavy skillet. Add onion and green pepper; sauté slowly for 5 minutes. Add ground beef; cook until meat is no longer red, stirring with a fork to separate it into bits. Add hash, parsley, Worcestershire sauce, salt, and pepper; mix well. Spoon some of this filling into the center of each pastry shell; dot with butter. Moisten edges of pastry; fold over to make a semi-circle. Turn rounded edges of pastry inward to make a neat border; crimp with fork or fingers to seal securely; cut several gashes in tops to permit escape of steam. Place pasties on a baking sheet. Bake in a hot oven (450°F.) for 15 minutes; reduce heat to moderate (350°F.) and continue baking for 20 minutes. Serve hot. Makes 3 man-sized pasties, which will serve 6 unless appetites are very hearty. Wine choice: California Gamay.

P. S. Have the pastry shell in its pie pan when you fill it and shape the pasty. This makes it easier to achieve a neat and handsome finished product.

Chilled Broccoli with Mustard Mayonnaise

Arrange stalks of chilled, cooked broccoli on lettuce-lined salad plates. For 6 servings of broccoli, mix 1 cup mayonnaise, 1 tablespoon prepared mustard (the yellow variety), and 1 tablespoon lemon juice. Spoon dressing over broccoli; dust with paprika.

DINNER

Veal and Ham Pie*
Scalloped or au Gratin Potatoes
Peas with Mushrooms
(the frozen combination)
Cranberry-Orange Salad Molds*
Easy Rum Cake*

With this menu we enjoy:

California Rosé

Veal and Ham Pie

1 pound boneless veal round steak, cut ½ inch thick
½ pound cooked ham, cut ½ inch thick
2 hard-cooked eggs, coarsely grated or chopped
2 tablespoons parsley flakes
2 teaspoons dry shredded green onions
2 tablespoons flour
1 teaspoon Worcestershire sauce
   Dash each of thyme and marjoram
   Seasoned salt and pepper to taste
   Pastry for a 2-crust (9-inch) pie, or
   2 (9-inch) frozen pie shells
3 tablespoons canned consommé
1 tablespoon California Dry or Medium Sherry
   or Dry Vermouth

Remove skin from veal. With a sharp knife, cut veal across grain in thin slivers about 1½ inches long. Cut ham in similar slivers. Mix meats, eggs, parsley and onions; sprinkle with flour and seasonings; mix again. Turn mixture into a pastry-lined 9-inch pie plate; sprinkle with consommé and wine. Put top crust in place; make several gashes in center to permit escape of steam. Bake in hot oven (450°F.) for 15 minutes; reduce heat to moderate (350°F.) and bake 1 hour longer. Remove from oven and let stand 10 minutes or so before serving. Serves 4 to 6.

Cranberry-Orange Salad Molds

Dissolve 1 (3-oz.) package lemon-flavored gelatin in 1 cup hot water; add ¼ cup California Red Table Wine. Wash and quarter 1 unpeeled orange; remove seeds; put orange through food chopper. Add orange to gelatin; cool. Crush 1 (1-lb.) can strained cranberry sauce with a fork; blend in gelatin mixture; add a dash of salt. Pour into 5 or 6 oiled individual molds. Chill until firm. Unmold on crisp salad greens and serve with mayonnaise. Serves 5 or 6.

Easy Rum Cake

¼ cup light rum
¼ cup orange juice
1 tablespoon lemon juice
½ cup sugar
½ teaspoon each: orange peel and lemon peel
½ teaspoon rum extract
1 small (6 or 7-inch) unfrosted orange chiffon
   cake (from the bakery)

Combine rum, orange juice, lemon juice, sugar, and grated peels in a small saucepan. Bring to a boil, stirring until sugar is dissolved; simmer 10 minutes. Cool. Add extract. Place cake on a serving platter; prick top all over with a 2-tined kitchen fork; spoon cooled rum syrup evenly over top of cake. Refrigerate for several hours or overnight before serving. Serves 6.

. . . .

Bacon and Egg Pie

Cut 12 slices thick-sliced bacon crosswise in halves; place in a single layer on a rack in a shallow baking pan; bake in a hot oven (400°F.) for 15 to 20 minutes, or until almost done, not brittle. Arrange half of bacon over bottom of a pastry-lined 9-inch pie plate. Carefully break 6 eggs over bacon. Sprinkle eggs with dry shredded green onions, a bit of seasoned salt, coarse black pepper to taste. Arrange rest of bacon over eggs; put top crust in place; cut several gashes to permit escape of steam. Bake in a hot oven (450°F.) for 20 minutes; reduce heat to moderate (350°F.) and continue baking 10 minutes. Serve hot. Serves 4 to 6. Wine choice: California Chablis.

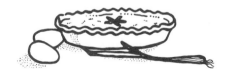

DINNER

Viennese Chicken Pie*
or
Chicken à la King Pie*
Spinach with Onion Crunch*
Tangy Tomato-Avocado Aspic*
Cream Puffs or Eclairs

With this menu we enjoy the indicated

California Wines

Viennese Chicken Pie

3 tablespoons butter
1 cup coarsely chopped onion
2 tablespoons flour
3 eggs
1 cup dairy sour cream
2 tablespoons California Dry or Medium Sherry or Dry Vermouth
1 teaspoon Worcestershire sauce
¼ teaspoon paprika
Salt and pepper to taste
1 cup diced, cooked chicken (or turkey)
1 cup shredded Cheddar cheese
1 tablespoon parsley flakes
1 (9-inch) baked pastry shell (with a high, fluted rim)

Melt butter in a saucepan or skillet; add onion and sauté gently until onion is tender but not brown. Remove from heat; stir in flour. Beat eggs slightly; add sour cream and wine; beat until blended. Add the onion mixture and stir well. Season with Worcestershire sauce, paprika, salt, and pepper. Lightly mix chicken, cheese, and parsley; spread evenly over bottom of pastry shell. Spoon egg mixture over contents of pastry shell. Bake in a moderate oven (350°F.) about 45 minutes, or until a knife inserted near the center comes out clean. Remove from oven and let stand 10 to 15 minutes before cutting. Serves 4 to 6. Wine choice: California Grey Riesling.

P. S. One cup of crabmeat or shrimp, or 1 (6½-oz.) can chunk-style tuna (drained and flaked), may be substituted for the chicken in this pie with excellent results.

Chicken à la King Pie

3 eggs
2 tablespoons flour
1 (10½-oz.) can chicken à la king
2 tablespoons California Dry or Medium Sherry or Dry Vermouth
1 cup shredded Cheddar cheese
1 tablespoon each: instant minced onion and parsley flakes
½ teaspoon Worcestershire sauce
¼ teaspoon nutmeg
Salt and pepper to taste
1 (9-inch) baked pastry shell, or 1 Cracker Pie Shell (page 66)

Beat eggs well with a rotary beater; beat in flour. Add chicken à la king and wine; blend well. Stir in cheese, onion, parsley, and seasonings. Spoon mixture into pastry shell. Bake in a moderate oven (350°F.) about 45 minutes, or until a knife inserted near the center comes out clean. Remove from oven and let stand 10 to 15 minutes before cutting. Serves 4 or more. Wine choice: California Dry Sauterne.

Spinach with Onion Crunch

Nothing to this...just crumble heated canned French-fried onion rings and sprinkle them over hot, cooked spinach a minute before serving. Good flavor and texture.

Tangy Tomato-Avocado Aspic

Heat 1 (8-oz.) can tomato sauce to simmering; add 1 (3-oz.) package lemon-flavored gelatin; stir until dissolved. Remove from heat. Add 1 (10-oz.) can seasoned tomato cocktail, 1 tablespoon lemon juice, and a dash of salt. Chill until mixture begins to thicken, then fold in 1 (2-oz.) bottle pimiento-stuffed olives, chopped, and 1 medium-sized avocado, finely diced. Spoon into 6 well-oiled individual molds; chill until firm. Unmold on crisp lettuce, sprinkle with French dressing; add a dot of mayonnaise. Serves 6.

DINNER

Neapolitan Tuna-Tomato Pie*
Corn on the Cob or Whole-Kernel Corn
Mixed Green Salad
(include some tender spinach leaves)
with
Bohemian French Dressing*
Fruit Cocktail Pudding-Cake*

With this menu we enjoy:

California Rosé

Neapolitan Tuna-Tomato Pie

  2 tablespoons butter
½ cup chopped onion
¼ cup California Dry Vermouth
  2 tablespoons flour
  2 eggs
½ cup cream
¼ teaspoon oregano
    Seasoned salt and pepper to taste
  1 (6½-oz.) can chunk-style tuna, rinsed and drained
¾ cup shredded Swiss or Cheddar Cheese
  1 (9-inch) baked pastry shell
  1 large tomato, peeled and cut crosswise in 12 slices
  5 or 6 anchovy fillets, cut in small bits
  1 to 2 teaspoons drained capers
  3 tablespoons grated Parmesan cheese
    Paprika

Melt butter in a saucepan or skillet; add onion and wine; cook gently 10 to 15 minutes, or until onion is tender but not brown. Remove from heat; stir in flour. Beat eggs slightly; add cream and beat until blended; add the onion mixture and stir well. Season with oregano, seasoned salt, and pepper. Lightly mix tuna and cheese; spread evenly over bottom of pastry shell. Arrange tomato slices overlapping on top of tuna-cheese mixture; dot with the anchovy bits and capers. Carefully spoon egg mixture over tomatoes; sprinkle with Parmesan cheese and paprika. Bake in a moderate oven (350°F.) about 45 minutes, or until a knife inserted near the center comes out clean. Remove from oven and let stand 20 minutes or so before cutting. Serve warm. Serves 4 to 6.

Bohemian French Dressing

  2 hard-cooked eggs, yolks and whites separated
¼ cup grated Parmesan cheese
  3 tablespoons chopped parsley
1½ cups bottled Italian dressing

Grate egg whites or chop very fine. Mash yolks with a fork; add cheese and parsley; mix well. Gradually blend in the dressing. Add egg whites. Pour into a 1-pint jar and shake well. Chill several hours. Shake again before using. Makes about 2 cups. Good with all mixed green and vegetable salads.

The first time I tasted this dessert at a luncheon party, I couldn't guess the ingredients. It was a delicious mystery!

Fruit Cocktail Pudding-Cake

  1 cup all-purpose flour
  1 cup granulated sugar
  1 teaspoon baking soda
¼ teaspoon salt
  1 egg, unbeaten
  1 (1-lb.) can fruit cocktail
  1 cup (firmly packed) brown sugar
½ cup chopped walnuts or pecans
    Whipped cream or vanilla ice cream

Sift flour, granulated sugar, soda, and salt together into a mixing bowl. Make a slight hole in the center of these dry ingredients; add egg and the fruit cocktail (undrained); beat until thoroughly mixed. Pour into a greased 9 by 9 by 2-inch baking pan. Mix brown sugar and nuts; sprinkle over batter. Bake in a moderate oven (350°F.) for 45 minutes. Serve warm or cold, topped with whipped cream or vanilla ice cream. Serves 6 to 8.

DINNER

Bacon-Mushroom Pie*
or Ham-Mushroom Pie*
or Bacon-Onion Pie*
Shoestring Potatoes
(the canned ones)

Hot Asparagus   Olives & Celery Hearts
Raspberry Sherbet   Frosted Date Brownies*

With this menu we enjoy the indicated

California Wines

Bacon-Mushroom Pie

    8 slices thick-sliced bacon
    1 (9-inch) baked pastry shell (with a high,
        fluted rim)
    ½ pound fresh mushrooms
    2 tablespoons chopped onion
    2 tablespoons flour
    1 cup (¼ pound) shredded Swiss or
        Cheddar cheese
    4 eggs
    1⅔ cups light cream (or 1 cup heavy cream and
        ⅔ cup milk)
    2 tablespoons California Dry or Medium Sherry
        or Dry Vermouth
    1 teaspoon dry shredded green onions
    ½ teaspoon Worcestershire sauce
    ¼ teaspoon nutmeg
        Salt and pepper to taste

Cook bacon until crisp. (I arrange the slices on a rack in a shallow baking pan and bake at 400°F. for 20 to 25 minutes. No turning necessary.) Crumble the cooked bacon and spread evenly over bottom of the pastry shell. Scrub mushrooms gently; remove stems; chop mushrooms coarsely. Heat 3 tablespoons of the bacon drippings in a large skillet; add mushrooms and chopped onion; sauté slowly for 5 minutes, stirring often. Sprinkle flour over mushrooms and blend well; remove from heat; stir in cheese. Spread mushroom mixture evenly over bacon in pie shell. Beat eggs slightly; beat in cream; add wine, green onions, and seasonings. Pour egg mixture carefully over contents of pie shell. Bake in a moderate oven (350°F.) for 50 to 60 minutes, or until a knife inserted near the center comes out clean. Remove from oven and let stand 10 to 15 minutes before cutting. Serves 4 to 6. Wine choice: California Dry Sauterne.

Ham-Mushroom Pie

Follow the recipe for *Bacon-Mushroom Pie,* but substitute ¾ cup slivered boiled or baked ham for the crumbled bacon, and sauté the mushrooms and onion in 3 tablespoons butter instead of bacon drippings. Wine choice: California Rosé.

Bacon-Onion Pie

Follow the recipe for *Bacon-Mushroom Pie,* but omit the mushrooms and increase the chopped onion to 1½ cups. Sauté the onion for 10 minutes; do not let it brown. This pie is good warm or cold (not chilled). Wine choice: California Rosé.

Frosted Date Brownies

    2 eggs
    ¾ cup (firmly packed) brown sugar
    ½ cup all-purpose flour
    1⅔ cups packaged graham cracker crumbs
    ½ teaspoon vanilla
    1 (8-oz.) package chopped dates
    ½ cup chopped walnuts or pecans

Beat eggs until light. Mix brown sugar, flour, and graham cracker crumbs; add to eggs, blending well. Stir in vanilla, dates, and nuts. Spread mixture evenly in a greased and floured 8-inch square pan. Bake in a moderate oven (350°F.) for 25 to 30 minutes. While still warm, frost with *Orange Icing* (below), then cut into 20 bars.

Orange Icing: Blend together 1 cup confectioners' sugar, 1 tablespoon melted butter, 1 tablespoon orange juice, and 1 teaspoon grated orange peel. Spread as directed above.

DINNER

Ham and Cheese Tarts* or Pie*
Green Beans with Almonds
(the frozen combination)
Celery Heart & Tomato Salad*
Orange Dessert Ring with Fruit*
Macaroons

With this menu we enjoy the indicated
California Wines

Ham and Cheese Tarts

4 eggs
1 (10½-oz.) can condensed cream of chicken soup
⅔ cup evaporated milk
2 tablespoons California Dry or Medium Sherry
½ teaspoon Worcestershire sauce
1 teaspoon dry shredded green onions
　Salt to taste
½ pound (2 cups) shredded Cheddar cheese
¾ cup slivered cooked ham, or 1 (3-oz.) package
　sliced smoked ham, cut fine
12 (4-inch) baked tart shells (homemade or
　bakery-made)
　Paprika

Beat eggs well; add soup and beat until blended. Stir in evaporated milk, Sherry, Worcestershire sauce, onions, and salt. With fingers, lightly mix cheese and ham; put ¼ cup of mixture in each tart shell. Carefully pour a scant ¼ cup of the egg mixture into each shell. Place filled shells on baking sheets. Bake in a moderate oven (350°F.) for 30 minutes. Remove from oven and sprinkle with paprika. Cool 5 to 10 minutes before serving. Makes 12 tarts. One apiece will suffice at a "ladies' luncheon"; men usually enjoy two. Wine choice: California Dry Chenin Blanc.

Ham and Cheese Pie

Follow the recipe above for *Ham and Cheese Tarts,* but substitute 2 (9-inch) baked pastry shells for the tart shells. Bake in a moderate oven (350°F.) for about 45 minutes, or until a knife inserted near the center comes out clean. Wine choice: California Rosé.

Celery Heart and Tomato Salad

Drain canned celery hearts thoroughly; marinate in homemade or bottled well-seasoned oil-vinegar French dressing in the refrigerator for several hours. Peel and chill tomatoes, or chill canned tomato aspic. To assemble salad: Cut tomatoes or aspic in thin slices; lay a slice in the center of a lettuce-lined individual salad plate; top tomato with 1 or more celery hearts (depending on size). Drizzle a little French dressing over the salad; top with a bit of mayonnaise. Garnish with a sprinkling of hard-cooked egg and a dash of paprika.

Orange Dessert Ring with Fruit

2 (3-oz.) packages orange-flavored gelatin
2 cups hot water
1¼ cups orange juice
½ cup California Sweet Sherry or Muscatel
2 tablespoons lemon juice
¼ cup sugar
　Dash of salt

Dissolve gelatin in the hot water. Add remaining ingredients; stir well. Pour into an 8-inch ring mold that has been rinsed with cold water. Chill until firm. Unmold on a platter and fill center with *Fruit Medley* (below). Serve plain or accompanied by a bowl of sour cream. Serves 8. Wine choice: California Muscatel.

Fruit Medley: Drain 1 (11-oz.) can mandarin orange sections; mix with 1 cup fresh or canned seedless (or halved, seeded) grapes. Add sugar to taste and sprinkle with a little California Sweet Sherry or Muscatel. Cover and chill thoroughly. Just before serving, peel and dice a good-sized banana; add to fruit mixture. Spoon into center of ring. (Other fruits may be substituted.)

VI. A Casserole's Full of a Number of Things

Versatile one-dish meals with real character

A casserole dish can be an anonymous concoction, undistinguished in flavor and texture, or it can be a happy mingling of ingredients with real character. I hope you'll agree with me that the casserole dishes in this chapter fall into the latter category. Serve one of these when you want a not-too-hearty main dish for dinner, and keep them in mind for luncheons and supper, too.

Many of these casseroles are do-ahead dishes. They can be prepared early in the day, covered and refrigerated, and then baked before serving. Allow time for the refrigerated mixture to come to room temperature before putting it in the oven.

When you want to reheat a leftover casserole dish in the oven, cover it (with foil if the dish has no lid) and set it in a shallow pan of hot water. This will prevent the mixture from drying out and ensure its tasting as good as it did the first time around.

DINNER

Pastetseo*
Vegetable Bouquet Salad*
Lemony Angel Pie*

With this menu we enjoy:

California Zinfandel

Pastetseo

2 large onions, diced
6 tablespoons butter
2 pounds *lean* ground beef
1 (1-lb.) can stewed tomatoes (dice large pieces with scissors)
½ cup California Red Table Wine
1 teaspoon cinnamon
½ teaspoon nutmeg
   Salt and pepper to taste
6 ounces elbow macaroni
6 eggs
1⅓ cups grated Parmesan cheese
2 tablespoons parsley flakes
3 tablespoons flour
2 cups milk
   Paprika

In a large, heavy skillet sauté onions gently in 3 tablespoons butter for 10 minutes. (Do not let them brown.) Add beef and sauté until no longer red, stirring with a fork to break it into bits. Add tomatoes, wine, spices, salt, and pepper; simmer, uncovered, for 15 to 20 minutes, or until mixture is no longer juicy. Meantime, cook and drain macaroni. When meat mixture is quite dry, add macaroni, 3 well-beaten eggs, 1 cup cheese, and the parsley. Taste and add salt, if needed. Turn into a greased baking dish. Melt remaining 3 tablespoons butter and stir in flour; add milk and cook, stirring, until mixture boils and thickens. Beat remaining 3 eggs well; stir in a little of the cream sauce; add to remaining cream sauce, blending well. Season with salt and pepper. Spoon mixture evenly over contents of casserole; sprinkle with remaining ⅓ cup cheese. Bake at 350° F. for 1 hour. Remove from oven; sprinkle with paprika. Let stand 5 minutes or so before serving. Serves 6 to 8.

Vegetable Bouquet Salad

Line a large round platter with crisp lettuce leaves. In the center place a chilled head of cooked cauliflower. Around the cauliflower arrange some of the following vegetables (well chilled): bundles of asparagus, broccoli spears, cooked carrot or zucchini strips, mounds of cooked or canned green beans, lima beans, artichoke hearts. Add beets (pickled or plain) or sliced tomatoes. Before serving, sprinkle French dressing over salad; dust with paprika and/or chopped parsley. Serve mayonnaise on the side. This can be as pretty as a prize-winning flower arrangement!

Lemony Angel Pie

Meringue Shell: Beat 3 egg whites until foamy; sprinkle with ¼ teaspoon cream of tartar; continue beating until stiff but not dry. Gradually add ¾ cup sugar, beating until meringue is smooth and glossy. Spread over bottom and sides (not rim) of a well-greased 9-inch pie plate, making a depression in center. Bake in a slow oven (275° F.) about 1 hour, or until delicately browned. Cool.

Filling: Make up 1 (3¼-oz.) package lemon pudding and pie filling according to directions on carton for pie filling, but substitute ¼ cup California Sweet Sherry for ¼ cup of the required water, and add 1 teaspoon grated lemon peel. Pour into a bowl; cool thoroughly at room temperature, stirring occasionally.

Spoon filling into meringue shell; chill several hours or overnight. Before serving, whip 1 cup heavy cream and spread over pie; garnish with a bit of grated lemon peel. Serves 6 generously, 8 modestly.

DINNER or LUNCHEON

Cannelloni à la Emily*
Bowl of Mixed Lettuces with French Dressing
Vegetable Kabobs*
Basket of Fresh Fruits
(apples, pears, grapes)
Cheese Tray   Crackers

With this menu we enjoy:

California Dry Semillon

These beef-filled pancakes, covered with a creamy sauce and garnished with tomato sauce, are a delightful main dish for buffet suppers and luncheons. Much of the preparation can be done ahead of time.

Cannelloni à la Emily

Pancakes:
1½ cups sifted all-purpose flour
1½ teaspoons salt
3 large eggs, well beaten
1⅔ cups milk
1 tablespoon salad oil

Mix flour and salt in a bowl. Combine beaten eggs and milk; add gradually to flour, stirring until smooth. Add oil. Cook pancakes one at a time in a well-greased skillet (6½ inches across bottom), turning once. Use a *scant* ¼ cup batter per pancake; tilt skillet as you pour in batter so it covers bottom evenly. Stack cooked pancakes on a plate until needed. Makes 16. (These can be made a day ahead.)

Filling:
1 pound lean ground beef
 Chopped or pressed garlic to taste
1 tablespoon butter
1 (10-oz.) package frozen chopped spinach, cooked and *thoroughly* drained
1 (3-oz.) can liver pâté
¼ cup grated Parmesan cheese
2 eggs, slightly beaten
 Pinch each of nutmeg and oregano
 Seasoned salt and pepper to taste

Sauté beef and garlic in butter until meat is no longer red, stirring with a fork to separate it into bits. Add remaining ingredients; mix well. (Filling can be made a day ahead.)

Cream Sauce:
¾ cup each: butter and flour
4 cups chicken stock
1 cup milk
⅓ cup California Dry or Medium Sherry or White Table Wine
1 cup (4 ounces) shredded or finely diced process Swiss cheese
 Nutmeg, salt, and pepper to taste

Melt butter and stir in flour; gradually add stock and milk; cook, stirring, until mixture is thickened and smooth. Add wine and cheese; stir over low heat until cheese melts. Add seasonings.

To assemble the dish: Spread a scant ¼ cup filling down center of each pancake. Roll up; place side by side in two greased 12 by 8 by 2-inch baking dishes. Pour hot cream sauce over pancakes; spoon half of an 8-oz. can of tomato sauce over each casserole; sprinkle ¼ cup grated Parmesan cheese over each one. Bake in a moderately hot oven (375°F.) for 20 to 25 minutes, or just until bubbly. Pass extra Parmesan cheese. Makes 16 cannelloni, serving 8 or more. P.S. You can put the filled cannelloni in the baking dishes ahead of time, but don't sauce them until just before baking.

Vegetable Kabobs

You might call these "finger salads." For each kabob allow a canned artichoke heart, a large pitted ripe olive (or a canned broiled mushroom crown), a canned baby carrot, and a canned baby beet. Marinate vegetables in French dressing in the refrigerator for several hours, keeping beets separate from the others. Shortly before serving, drain vegetables and string them on wooden or metal skewers, or on long cocktail picks. Arrange on a lettuce-lined platter. Allow one or more kabobs per person.

DINNER

Italian Noodle Casserole*
or Sunday Night Casserole*
Bowl of Mixed Greens with French Dressing
Relish-Salad Platter*
Fruit Turnovers
(frozen or from the bakery)

With this menu we enjoy the indicated

California Wines

Italian Noodle Casserole

1 pound lean ground beef
1 tablespoon olive oil
1 (1-lb.) can stewed tomatoes
1 (6-oz.) can tomato paste
½ cup California Red Table Wine
2 tablespoons instant minced onion
1 clove garlic, chopped or pressed
1 teaspoon mixed Italian seasoning
    Salt and pepper to taste
1 (12-oz.) package wide noodles
2 (1-pt.) cartons large-curd cottage cheese
    (chive or plain)
½ cup grated Parmesan cheese
1 (10-oz.) package frozen chopped spinach,
    cooked and drained
2 eggs, well beaten
1 pound Cheddar cheese, thinly sliced (or two
    8-oz. packages sliced process Cheddar)

Sauté beef in olive oil until it is no longer red, stirring with a fork to separate it into bits. Add tomatoes, tomato paste, wine, onion, garlic, and seasonings. Bring to a boil; cover and simmer gently for 1 hour, stirring occasionally. Meantime, cook noodles in boiling salted water just until tender; drain. Mix cottage cheese, Parmesan cheese, spinach, and eggs; season with salt and pepper. In a 13 by 9 by 2-inch baking dish spread half the noodles, then half the cottage cheese mixture, then half the Cheddar cheese; cover with half the sauce. Repeat layers. Bake in a moderate oven (350°F.) about 50 minutes, or until bubbly all the way through. Serves 8. Wine choice: California Claret.

Sunday Night Casserole

1 pound lean ground beef
1 tablespoon butter
1 medium-sized onion, chopped
½ green pepper, chopped
2 tender stalks celery, chopped
2 (8-oz.) cans tomato sauce
½ cup California Red Table Wine
1 (4-oz.) can sliced mushrooms, drained
½ teaspoon oregano
    Salt and pepper to taste
8 ounces wide noodles
½ pint (1 cup) large-curd cottage cheese
½ pint (1 cup) dairy sour cream
1 teaspoon poppy seeds
⅓ cup grated Parmesan cheese
1 cup shredded Mozzarella or Cheddar cheese

In a large, heavy skillet sauté beef in butter until it's no longer red, stirring to separate it into bits. Add onion, green pepper, and celery; sauté 5 minutes longer. Add tomato sauce, wine, mushrooms, oregano, salt, and pepper; cover and simmer 10 minutes, stirring often. Cook noodles in boiling water *just* until tender; drain. Mix noodles, cottage cheese, sour cream, and poppy seeds. In a greased 3-quart casserole spread half the noodle mixture, then half the meat sauce; sprinkle with half the cheeses. Repeat layers. Bake at 350°F. for 45 to 50 minutes, or until hot and bubbly. Pass extra Parmesan cheese. Serves 5 or 6. Wine choice: California Gamay.

Relish-Salad Platter

Line a platter with crisp salad greens. On it, in groups, arrange any or all of the following: garbanzos (ceci beans), ripe and green olives, crisp celery hearts, raw carrot sticks, pepperoncini (little hot peppers), artichoke hearts, and radishes. (Marinate the garbanzos and artichoke hearts in bottled Italian-style French dressing first.) Sometimes I add thinly sliced salami to the platter, too.

DINNER

Mushroom Ham Loaf*
with
Hunter's Sauce*
Scalloped or au Gratin Potatoes
Buttered Broccoli Spears
Fruit or Sherbet   Cherry Wine Bars*

With this menu we enjoy:

California Rosé

Mushroom Ham Loaf

1½ pounds ground smoked ham
1½ pounds ground lean pork
    2 cups (firmly packed) soft bread crumbs
    1 (10½-oz.) can condensed cream of
        mushroom soup
¼ cup water
    2 eggs, slightly beaten
¼ cup grated green pepper
    2 tablespoons parsley flakes
    1 tablespoon instant minced onion
½ teaspoon salt
¼ teaspoon pepper

Have meat dealer grind ham and pork together.
Mix all ingredients lightly but thoroughly. Pack
mixture into a 10 by 5 by 3-inch loaf pan. Bake in
moderate oven (350°F.) 1½ hours. Pour off juices,
then let stand 5 minutes or so before unmolding.
Serve with *Hunter's Sauce* (below). Serves 6 to 8.

Hunter's Sauce

In a small saucepan combine ¾ cup red currant
jelly, 6 tablespoons *each:* California Port and catsup, ¾ teaspoon Worcestershire sauce, and 3 tablespoons butter. Stir over low heat until jelly and
butter are melted and ingredients are well blended.
Serve warm. Makes about 1½ cups. Leftover sauce
can be stored in the refrigerator and reheated
gently.

Cherry Wine Bars

Cherry Filling:
    1 cup drained canned sour red pitted cherries,
        chopped and drained again
¼ cup California Port
    1 teaspoon grated lemon peel
    1 tablespoon cornstarch

½ cup sugar
    Dash of salt
¼ cup finely chopped walnuts

Combine cherries, wine, and lemon peel in a saucepan; heat to simmering. Mix cornstarch, sugar, and
salt; add to cherry-wine mixture and cook, stirring
constantly, until mixture is thickened and clear.
Remove from heat. Stir in nuts. Let mixture cool
while you prepare the crust.

Crust:
    1 cup sifted all-purpose flour
    1 cup quick-cooking rolled oats
⅔ cup (firmly packed) brown sugar
½ teaspoon baking soda
¼ teaspoon salt
½ cup melted butter

Mix dry ingredients in a bowl. Add melted butter
and work with the fingers until mixture is crumbly.
Pat half of crumbly mixture firmly over bottom of
an 8-inch square pan. Spread filling evenly over this
layer. Pat rest of crumbly mixture gently but firmly
over filling. Bake in a moderate oven (350°F.) for
35 minutes. Let cool in the pan, then cut in squares
or bars. Makes 16 or more. Truly *delectable!*

•••••••••••••••••••••••

*A baked ham would fit nicely into this menu in
place of the ham loaf.*

Marmalade-Glazed Ham

Place a 5-lb. piece of fully cooked boneless ham in
a shallow baking pan. Spread thinly with prepared
mustard. Mix ½ cup orange marmalade, ½ cup California Sweet Sherry (or Sweet Vermouth), 1 tablespoon California wine vinegar, and generous dash
of powdered cloves; pour over ham. Bake in a slow
oven (325°F.) about 1 hour, basting frequently.
Serves 8 to 12. Wine choice: California Champagne.

DINNER

Delphine's Chili-Cheese Custard*
Chili Beans Diego*
Corn Chips
Mixed Green Salad
(with thinly sliced avocado & radishes)
Orange-Pineapple Cup*   Cookies

With this menu we enjoy:

California Zinfandel or Chablis

Delphine's Chili-Cheese Custard

2 (4-oz.) cans peeled green chili peppers
½ pound (2 cups) shredded Cheddar cheese
½ pound (2 cups) shredded firm Monterey Jack
  cheese (or an additional ½ pound Cheddar
  cheese, if you can't get the Monterey Jack)
5 eggs
  Salt to taste
  Paprika

Split the chili peppers; wash out seeds under running water; drain peppers on paper towels. Arrange half of peppers over bottom of a greased 8 by 8 by 2-inch baking dish. Mix cheeses lightly with fingers; sprinkle half over peppers in baking dish. Repeat layers with remaining peppers and cheese. Beat eggs well; beat in salt; spoon mixture carefully over contents of baking dish. Dust with paprika. Bake in a moderate oven (350° F.) about 45 minutes, or until firm in the center. Serves 6.

Chili Beans Diego

Wash and pick over 1 pound pink or red beans; soak overnight in cold water to cover. Drain. Place beans in a Dutch oven or other heavy kettle; add 2 cups boiling water, 1 (1-lb.) can chili con carne (without beans), 1 (1-lb.) can stewed tomatoes, 1 cup California Red Table Wine, 2 tablespoons instant minced onion, bit of chopped or pressed garlic, and 1 teaspoon cumin seed. Bring to a boil, then cover and simmer gently for 2½ to 3 hours, or until beans are tender and sauce is a nice, rich consistency. Stir gently with a fork from time to time and add a little more boiling water, if necessary. Add salt to taste during the last hour of cooking. Serves 6.

Orange-Pineapple Cup

Drain canned mandarin oranges and canned pineapple chunks or tidbits. Combine in a bowl in any proportion you wish. Sprinkle with confectioners' sugar and then with California Sweet Sherry or Muscatel. (Don't drown the fruit!) Mix well; chill. At serving time, heap in dessert dishes and (if you like) sprinkle with flaked coconut.

••••••••••••••••••••••••

Cheese-Stuffed Peppers Marinara

6 medium-sized green peppers
½ pound (2 cups) shredded Cheddar cheese
½ pound (2 cups) shredded firm Monterey Jack
  cheese (or another ½ pound shredded Cheddar)
4 eggs, slightly beaten
1 (15½-oz.) can marinara sauce (or two
  7¾-oz. cans)
2 tablespoons California Dry or Medium Sherry
  or Dry Vermouth
  Pinch of oregano
  Salt to taste

Cut a thin slice from stem end of each pepper; remove seeds and fibrous white portion. Drop peppers into boiling salted water; parboil 5 minutes; drain thoroughly. Mix cheese and eggs; stuff peppers with mixture; arrange in greased baking dish. Mix remaining ingredients; heat to simmering; pour around (not over) peppers. Bake, uncovered, in a moderately hot oven (375° F.) for 35 to 40 minutes, or until cheese filling is firm and delicately browned. Serve peppers with sauce over them. Serves 6. Wine choice: California Burgundy. Good with Vienna sausages or crisp bacon, corn, and a tossed salad.

DINNER

Sausage and Zucchini Torta*
or
Stuffed Zucchini with Tomato Sauce*
Corn on the Cob or Whole-Kernel Corn
French Bread Venetia*
Olives and Radishes
Your Favorite Chocolate Cake

With this menu we enjoy the indicated
California Wines

Sausage and Zucchini Torta

2 pounds small zucchini
1 pound bulk pork sausage meat
1 (10-oz.) package frozen chopped spinach,
    cooked and drained
½ cup packaged corn flake crumbs
½ cup plus 2 tablespoons grated Parmesan cheese
4 eggs, slightly beaten
1 tablespoon instant minced onion
1 tablespoon parsley flakes
    Bit of chopped or pressed garlic (if you like)
    Pinch each of thyme and rosemary
    Seasoned salt and pepper to taste

Wash zucchini and trim off ends. Cook whole in boiling salted water for about 15 minutes, or *just* until tender. Drain thoroughly; chop coarsely; drain again. Cook sausage meat until it is no longer pink, stirring with a fork to separate it into bits. Remove from heat. To the sausage add the zucchini, spinach, corn flake crumbs, ½ cup grated Parmesan cheese, eggs, onion, parsley, garlic, and seasonings. Turn mixture into an oiled 8 by 8 by 2-inch baking dish; smooth top; sprinkle with remaining Parmesan cheese. Bake in a moderate oven (350°F.) about 45 minutes, or until firm. Remove from oven and let stand a few minutes before serving. Serves 5 or 6. Wine choice: California Rosé.

P. S. If you'd like to doll up the torta a bit, serve *Mushroom Sauce* (page 83) with it.

Stuffed Zucchini with Tomato Sauce

8 or 9 medium-sized zucchini (about 2 pounds)
1 pound ground beef
1 medium-sized onion, chopped
1 clove garlic, chopped or pressed
2 tablespoons chopped green pepper
1 tablespoon olive oil
½ cup grated Parmesan cheese
⅔ cup fine cracker crumbs
1 egg, well beaten
    Pinch each of rosemary, thyme, and marjoram
    Salt and pepper to taste
1 (8 oz.) can tomato sauce
½ cup California Red Table Wine
½ cup canned consommé

Wash zucchini; trim off ends. Parboil whole in salted water for 10 minutes; drain. When cool enough to handle, cut lengthwise in halves; scoop out insides. Drain scooped-out portion; mash well. Sauté beef, onion, garlic, and green pepper gently in oil for 5 minutes, stirring with a fork to separate meat into bits. Add mashed zucchini, all but 2 tablespoons each of the cheese and crumbs, the egg, and seasonings. Heap mixture into zucchini shells. Place in a greased shallow baking dish. Heat tomato sauce, wine, and consommé together; pour over zucchini. Sprinkle with reserved cheese and crumbs. Bake in a moderate oven (350°F.) for 45 minutes; baste once or twice. Pass extra Parmesan cheese. Serves 6. Wine choice: California Claret.

French Bread Venetia

Slash a long loaf of sourdough French bread crosswise in thick slices, cutting down to the crust but not through it. Blend together ½ cup soft butter, ½ cup grated Parmesan cheese, 2 tablespoons olive oil, bit of chopped or pressed garlic, 2 teaspoons dry shredded green onions, and ½ teaspoon mixed Italian seasoning. Spread mixture between slices of bread. Wrap loaf in foil. Bake in hot oven (400°F.) for 15 to 20 minutes, or until piping hot.

DINNER

Yorkshire Sausage Pudding*
Sautéed Pineapple Rings
(brown canned pineapple lightly in butter)
Green Bean Salad*
with Sour Cream Dressing*
Graham Cracker Ice Cream*

With this menu we enjoy:

California Gamay

Yorkshire pudding being one of my favorite foods, I was delighted to find a way to serve it other than as an accompaniment to roast beef.

Yorkshire Sausage Pudding

1 pound pork sausage links
1 cup sifted all-purpose flour
½ teaspoon salt
2 eggs, well beaten
1 cup milk

Arrange sausages in a shallow baking dish (8 by 8 by 2 inches); bake in a hot oven (450°F.) for 10 to 15 minutes, or until sausages begin to brown and have exuded a goodly amount of their fat. Meantime, mix flour and salt; stir in combined eggs and milk; beat with a rotary or electric beater until smooth. (Or, put all ingredients in a blender and whirl until smooth.) Now remove the baking dish from the oven, pour off all but about ¼ cup of the fat, and pour the batter over the sausages. Immediately return the dish to the oven and bake for 25 to 30 minutes, or until pudding is puffy and nicely browned. Serve at once. This will take care of 3 very hearty appetites or 4 moderate ones.

P. S. This is also a wonderful Sunday breakfast dish, accompanied by scrambled eggs and sautéed pineapple rings or warm applesauce.

Green Bean Salad

Drain canned French-cut green beans. Moisten sparingly with well-seasoned oil-vinegar French dressing, using 1 to 2 tablespoons dressing per 1-lb. can of beans. Cover; chill 1 hour or more. Just before serving, drain beans thoroughly; mix with just enough *Sour Cream Dressing* (below) to make them moist. Heap in a lettuce-lined bowl or on lettuce-lined salad plates; sprinkle with paprika. Garnish the salad with sliced pickled beets or tomato.

Sour Cream Dressing

Mix 1 cup dairy sour cream, ½ cup mayonnaise, 2 tablespoons California Dry Vermouth, 1 tablespoon prepared horseradish, 2 teaspoons dry shredded green onions, 1 teaspoon lemon juice, and salt and coarse black pepper to taste. Chill. Makes 1½ cups. Serve this same dressing with a tomato aspic or molded beet salad, and mix it with shredded cabbage and a sprinkling of celery to make cole slaw.

Graham Cracker Ice Cream

1 cup milk
1 cup heavy cream
½ cup sugar
1 cup (heaping) packaged graham cracker crumbs
1 teaspoon vanilla

Mix all ingredients well; pour into refrigerator freezing tray. Freeze until mixture is frozen about 1 inch around the edge. Turn into a bowl; beat until smooth. Return to freezing tray; freeze until firm. Serves 6. This is good by itself, or you can top it with maple syrup or chocolate sauce.

DINNER or LUNCHEON

Baked Deviled Eggs with Shrimp Sauce*
Rice
Watermelon Pickles
Zucchini with Peas*
(or a salad)
Orange Sherbet
(top with mandarin oranges and Cointreau)
Cookies

With this menu we enjoy:

California Grey Riesling

Baked Deviled Eggs with Shrimp Sauce

6 shelled, hard-cooked eggs
3 tablespoons mayonnaise
1 teaspoon prepared mustard
  Salt and pepper to taste
1 (4-oz.) can sliced mushrooms
4 tablespoons each: butter and flour
1 cup milk
1 chicken bouillon cube (or 2 teaspoons
  chicken stock base)
1 cup shredded Cheddar cheese
⅓ cup California White Table Wine
1 cup cooked or canned shrimp (or crabmeat, or
  a 6½-oz. can tuna, drained and flaked)
  Paprika

Cut eggs in halves lengthwise; remove yolks. Mash yolks; blend in mayonnaise, mustard, salt, and pepper; fill whites with mixture. Arrange, filled side up, in a greased shallow baking dish. Drain mushrooms, reserving liquid. Melt butter and stir in flour; add milk, mushroom liquid, and bouillon cube; cook, stirring, until mixture boils and thickens and bouillon cube dissolves. Add cheese and wine; stir over low heat until cheese melts. Add shrimp and mushrooms. Pour sauce over eggs; sprinkle with paprika. Bake in a moderate oven (350°F.) for 20 to 25 minutes. Serves 4 to 6.

Zucchini with Peas

To serve 6, wash 1 pound small zucchini; trim off ends. Slice crosswise paper thin. Heat 2 tablespoons salad oil in a skillet; add zucchini and sauté gently, stirring frequently, until zucchini begins to brown. Add 2 tablespoons water, a sprinkling of thyme, and salt and pepper to taste. Cover and cook gently for 5 to 10 minutes, or just until zucchini is tender, stirring occasionally. Cook 1 (10-oz.) package frozen peas with celery according to carton directions; drain, if necessary. Combine vegetables. Serve piping hot.

....

Mushroom-Stuffed Eggs Parisienne

1 (8-oz.) can mushroom stems and pieces
6 shelled, hard-cooked eggs
¼ cup mayonnaise
1 teaspoon dry shredded green onions
½ teaspoon Worcestershire sauce
  Salt and pepper to taste
2 (10-oz.) packages frozen chopped broccoli,
  cooked and thoroughly drained
6 tablespoons each: butter and flour
1 cup each: chicken stock and rich milk
1 cup shredded Cheddar cheese
⅓ cup California White Table Wine
  Paprika

Drain mushrooms, reserving liquid; chop fine. Cut eggs lengthwise in halves; remove yolks. Mash yolks; blend in mayonnaise; add mushrooms, onions, Worcestershire sauce, salt, and pepper. Fill whites heaping full with mixture. Arrange broccoli in a greased shallow baking dish; place egg halves, filled side up, on top. Melt butter and stir in flour; add reserved mushroom liquid, stock, and milk; cook, stirring, until mixture boils and thickens. Add cheese; stir over low heat until melted. Add wine salt, and pepper. Pour sauce over eggs and broccoli, dust with paprika. Bake in moderate oven (350°F.) 20 to 25 minutes. Serves 6. Wine choice: California Dry Sauterne.

LIGHT DINNER
or LUNCHEON

Baked Eggs Florentine*
Waffle Potato Chips
Vegetable Consommé Molds*
Sour Cream Mincemeat Pie*

With this menu we enjoy:

California Chablis

Baked Eggs Florentine

3 tablespoons each: butter and flour
1 cup milk
¼ cup California White Table Wine or
   Dry Vermouth
1 cup shredded Cheddar cheese
½ teaspoon Worcestershire sauce
¼ teaspoon prepared mustard
   Salt and pepper to taste
2 (10-oz.) packages frozen chopped spinach,
   cooked and *thoroughly* drained
¼ cup mayonnaise
6 eggs
   Paprika

Melt butter and stir in flour; add milk and cook, stirring constantly, until mixture boils and thickens. Add wine and cheese; stir over low heat until cheese is melted. Add Worcestershire sauce, mustard, salt, and pepper. Mix spinach and mayonnaise; spoon into 6 greased individual casseroles, making a depression in the center to form a "nest." Break an egg into each casserole; spoon some of the cheese sauce over the egg; dust with paprika. Bake in a moderately hot oven (375°F.) about 15 minutes, or until egg is set. Serves 6. To make this a really man-sized dish, serving 3, divide the ingredients among three oval individual baking dishes.

Vegetable Consommé Molds

1 envelope (1 tablespoon) unflavored gelatin
1 (10½-oz.) can condensed consommé
   (or chicken broth)
⅓ cup California Dry Vermouth or Dry or
   Medium Sherry
1 teaspoon lemon juice
   Seasoned salt to taste
1 cup each finely diced cooked carrots, celery,
   and zucchini
1 teaspoon each grated onion, dried green onion
   Crisp salad greens
   French dressing, mayonnaise and paprika

Soften gelatin in ½ cup of the consommé for 5 minutes; stir over medium heat until gelatin is dissolved. Add remaining consommé, wine, lemon juice, and salt. Toss diced vegetables, grated onion, and green onions together lightly with a fork; divide among 6 oiled individual molds or custard cups; press vegetables down gently into cups. Pour gelatin mixture over vegetables; chill until firm. Unmold on lettuce-lined salad plates; sprinkle with French dressing. Top each mold with a bit of mayonnaise and a dusting of paprika. Tomato wedges or pickled beets may be added as a garnish, if you like. Serves 6.

Sour Cream Mincemeat Pie

2 eggs, slightly beaten
¾ cup sugar
¾ cup dairy sour cream
¼ cup California Medium or Sweet Sherry
1 tablespoon flour
¼ teaspoon salt
1 teaspoon grated lemon peel
2 cups prepared mincemeat
1 (9-inch) unbaked pastry shell

Mix eggs and sugar; gradually stir in sour cream and Sherry. Mix flour and salt; add lemon peel and mincemeat; stir into egg-sour cream mixture. Pour into pastry shell. Bake in a hot oven (450°F.) for 10 minutes; reduce heat to moderate (350°F.) and continue baking about 40 minutes, or until a knife inserted in the center comes out clean. Serve warm or cold, plain or topped with whipped cream.

DINNER or LUNCHEON

Chicken Rice Torta* with Mushroom Sauce*
Spinach Soufflé
(use the frozen)
Grapefruit Avocado Salad*
with Lorraine Dressing*
Meringue Shells
(from the bakery)
with Vanilla Ice Cream & Butterscotch Topping

With this menu we enjoy:

California Chablis

Chicken Rice Torta

 1 cup uncooked white rice
 2 cups diced, cooked chicken (or turkey)
 1 cup shredded Cheddar cheese
 ¼ cup grated Parmesan cheese
 2 tablespoons parsley flakes
 1 tablespoon instant minced onion
1¼ cups milk
 ¼ cup California Dry or Medium Sherry or
    White Table Wine
 3 eggs, slightly beaten
 3 tablespoons melted butter or salad oil
 ½ teaspoon Worcestershire sauce
    Dash of mace or nutmeg
    Salt, celery salt, and pepper to taste

Boil or steam rice until tender; drain, if necessary. Mix rice with all remaining ingredients. Turn into a well-greased baking dish (8 by 8 by 2 inches); smooth top. Bake in a moderate oven (350° F.) about 45 minutes, or until firm and lightly browned. Cut in squares and serve with *Mushroom Sauce.* Serves 6.

P. S. An excellent way to prepare the chicken for this or any dish that calls for cooked chicken is to buy chicken breasts and bake them. Arrange breasts, skin side up, in a shallow pan; dot each with ½ teaspoon butter; pour in just enough white table wine or water to cover bottom of pan; cover loosely with aluminum foil. Bake at 325°F. for 1 hour, basting occasionally. Cool chicken; remove bones and skin; dice meat with scissors. Three pounds of chicken breasts will yield a generous quart of diced meat; 1½ pounds will yield approximately 1 pint (2 cups).

Mushroom Sauce

 ¼ cup each: butter and flour
 1 cup chicken stock
 ½ cup cream
 1 (4-oz.) can sliced mushrooms
 ¼ cup California Dry or Medium Sherry
    or White Table Wine
 ½ cup shredded Cheddar cheese
 ½ teaspoon Worcestershire sauce
    Salt, pepper, and paprika to taste

Melt butter and stir in flour; add stock, cream, and liquid from mushrooms; cook, stirring, until mixture boils and thickens. Add mushrooms, wine, and cheese; stir over low heat until cheese melts. Add seasonings. Serve hot with *Chicken Rice Torta.*

Grapefruit Avocado Salad

Line individual salad plates with crisp salad greens. On the greens arrange fresh or canned grapefruit sections alternately with slices of avocado. Serve with *Lorraine Dressing* (below).

Lorraine Dressing

 1 cup salad oil
 ½ cup *each* California red wine vinegar and
    dark corn syrup
 3 tablespoons catsup
 1 clove garlic, chopped or put through garlic press
 2 tablespoons sugar
 1 teaspoon Worcestershire sauce
 ½ teaspoon dry mustard
1½ teaspoons salt

Combine all ingredients in a jar or bowl; shake or beat until thoroughly blended. Cover and chill several hours to blend flavors. Makes about 2 cups.

LIGHT DINNER
or LUNCHEON

Creamed Artichokes with Chicken au Gratin*
Zucchini and Tomato Salad*
with Mushroom French Dressing*
Mocha Chiffon Pie*

With this menu we enjoy:

California Grey Riesling

Creamed Artichokes with Chicken au Gratin

  6 *large*, fresh artichokes
  4 tablespoons butter
  3 tablespoons flour
  ¾ cup cream or rich milk
  ½ cup chicken stock
  ¼ cup California White Table Wine
  2 tablespoons California Dry or Medium Sherry
  1 tablespoon parsley flakes
  ½ teaspoon grated lemon peel
  ½ teaspoon Worcestershire sauce
    Salt and pepper to taste
  2 to 2½ cups diced cooked or canned chicken
    (crabmeat, shrimp, or tuna may be substituted)
  ½ cup shredded Cheddar cheese
    Paprika

Wash artichokes and cut off stems. Cook, covered, in a large amount of boiling salted water for 45 minutes to 1 hour, or until bottoms are tender when pierced with a fork. (I add a clove of garlic, half a lemon, and a spoonful of olive oil to the water for extra flavor.) Drain cooked artichokes upside down. When cool enough to handle, separate leaves from bottoms and remove fuzzy chokes. Place bottoms, cup side up, in a single layer in a greased shallow baking dish. With a spoon, scrape edible portion from each leaf. Melt butter and stir in flour; add cream, stock, and white wine; cook, stirring, until mixture boils and thickens. Remove from heat. Add scraped artichoke pulp, Sherry, parsley, lemon peel, Worcestershire sauce, salt, and pepper. Heap chicken in the artichoke bottoms. Spoon sauce over all; sprinkle with grated cheese and paprika. Bake in a moderately hot oven (375°F.) about 20 minutes, or until bubbly and delicately browned. Serves 6.

Zucchini and Tomato Salad

Line individual salad plates with crisp lettuce. In the center of each, place a thick slice of peeled tomato or tomato aspic. Top tomato with several strip s of chilled, cooked zucchini. Spoon *Mushroom French Dressing* (below) over the salad.

Mushroom French Dressing: Drain 1 (4-oz.) can mushroom stems and pieces; chop mushrooms very fine. Pour 1⅓ cups Italian oil-vinegar dressing into a 1-pint jar; add mushrooms and 2 teaspoons dry shredded green onions; shake well before using. Makes about 1¾ cups.

Mocha Chiffon Pie

  1 envelope (1 tablespoon) unflavored gelatin
  ¼ cup cold water
  ½ cup California Sweet Sherry
  2 (1-oz.) squares unsweetened chocolate
  1 cup sugar
  1 tablespoon instant coffee powder
  ¼ teaspoon cinnamon
    Dash of salt
  3 eggs, separated
  1 (9-inch) baked pastry shell
    Whipped cream and a few shavings of
    unsweetened chocolate for garnish

Soften gelatin in the cold water. Combine wine, chocolate, ½ cup sugar, coffee, cinnamon, and salt in top of double boiler; heat, stirring occasionally, until chocolate melts and ingredients are blended. Beat egg yolks slightly; add chocolate mixture; return to double boiler and cook, stirring, for a minute or two. Remove from heat. Add gelatin and stir to dissolve. Cool thoroughly at room temperature. Beat egg whites until stiff; gradually beat in remaining ½ cup sugar; fold in chocolate mixture. Pour into pie shell. Chill until firm. Serve topped with whipped cream and chocolate shavings.

DINNER or LUNCHEON

Tuna Noodle Special*
or Seafood and Rice Casserole Delecta*
Chinese Pea Pods *(the frozen ones)*
Pineapple Cucumber Salad Molds*
Coffee or Peppermint Ice Cream
(top it with chocolate-flavored wine or crème de cacao)
Cookies

With this menu we enjoy the indicated

California Wines

Tuna Noodle Special

8 ounces fine noodles
2 tablespoons each: chopped onion and
    green pepper
¼ cup each: butter and flour
2 cups milk
2 (3-oz.) packages cream cheese (plain or pimiento)
⅓ cup California Dry or Medium Sherry or
    White Table Wine
1 teaspoon Worcestershire sauce
    Salt and pepper to taste
2 (6½ or 7-oz.) cans tuna, drained and flaked
    (or a 1-lb. can salmon)
1 (4-oz.) can mushroom stems and pieces, drained
½ to 1 cup shredded Cheddar cheese
    Paprika

Cook noodles in boiling salted water *just* until tender; drain. Sauté onion and green pepper gently in butter for 5 minutes. Blend in flour; add milk and cook, stirring, until mixture boils and thickens. Add cream cheese; stir over low heat until melted and blended with the sauce. Add wine, Worcestershire sauce, salt, and pepper. Stir in tuna, noodles, and mushrooms. Turn into a greased casserole; sprinkle with Cheddar cheese; dust with paprika. Bake in moderately hot oven (375°F.) about 25 minutes, or until bubbly and delicately browned on top. Serves 6. Wine choice: California Dry Sauterne.

Seafood and Rice Casserole Delecta

2 cups well seasoned chicken stock
1 cup uncooked long-grain white rice
⅓ cup each: butter and flour
2 cups milk
⅓ cup California Dry or Medium Sherry or
    White Table Wine
1 (4-oz.) can mushroom stems and pieces
    (undrained)
1 pimiento, chopped

2 tablespoons parsley flakes
    Dash of thyme
    Salt and pepper to taste
1 cup each: cooked or canned crabmeat and shrimp
    (or 2 cups of either one)
½ cup shaved unblanched almonds
½ cup shredded Cheddar cheese
    Paprika

Heat chicken stock to boiling in a saucepan; slowly sprinkle in rice; stir well, then cover and simmer very gently for 25 minutes, or until rice is tender and stock is absorbed. Melt butter and stir in flour; add milk and cook, stirring, until mixture boils and thickens. Add wine, mushrooms with their liquid, pimiento, parsley, thyme, salt, and pepper. Combine this sauce with the crabmeat, shrimp, and rice. Turn into a greased casserole. Sprinkle almonds and cheese over the top; dust with paprika. Bake in a moderately hot oven (375°F.) for 25 to 30 minutes, or until bubbly and delicately browned on top. Serves 6. Wine choice: California Chablis.

Pineapple Cucumber Salad Molds

Drain 1 (1-lb., 4-oz.) can crushed pineapple, reserving syrup. Add California White Table Wine to syrup to make 1½ cups liquid. Heat liquid to simmering; add 1 (3-oz.) package lemon-flavored gelatin, ¼ cup sugar, and a generous dash of salt; stir until dissolved. Remove from heat; add 3 tablespoons vinegar. Cool, then chill. When mixture begins to thicken, fold in pineapple, 1 cup grated, seeded cucumber (1 large cucumber), ¼ cup chopped pimiento-stuffed olives, and 1 teaspoon grated onion. Pour into 6 well-oiled individual molds; chill until firm. Unmold on crisp salad greens; serve with mayonnaise. Serves 6.

DINNER or LUNCHEON

Cheese Pudding*
with Chicken Livers in Wine Sauce*
Bacon Curlicues*
Green Beans
Brandied Fruit & Sherbet Cup*
Ladyfingers

With this menu we enjoy:
California Claret or Chablis

Cheese Pudding

8 slices white bread, buttered and cubed
½ pound (2 cups) shredded Cheddar cheese
1 tablespoon parsley flakes
4 eggs
1 (10½-oz.) can condensed cream of chicken soup
1¼ cups milk
2 tablespoons California Dry or Medium Sherry
1 teaspoon Worcestershire sauce
Salt and pepper to taste

Toss bread cubes, cheese, and parsley together lightly with a fork; turn into a greased 8 by 8 by 2-inch baking dish. Beat eggs well; blend in soup, milk, Sherry, and seasonings; pour over bread and cheese. Let stand an hour or more. Bake in a slow oven (325°F.) for 1 hour. Serves 4.

Chicken Livers in Wine Sauce

Cut one pound chicken livers in bite-sized pieces. Melt 4 tablespoons butter in a skillet; add 1 tablespoon chopped onion; sauté gently for 2 to 3 minutes. Add chicken livers; sauté about 5 minutes, turning frequently. Remove livers from pan. Add 3 tablespoons flour to pan drippings and blend well; add 1 cup canned condensed consommé and ⅓ cup California Dry or Medium Sherry; cook, stirring, until mixture is thickened and smooth. Add ½ teaspoon Worcestershire sauce and salt and pepper to taste. Add chicken livers, 1 (3-oz.) can sliced broiled mushrooms (drained), and 1 tablespoon parsley flakes; heat gently. Serve at once. Serves 4.

P. S. Creamed chicken or creamed mushrooms are good with *Cheese Pudding* in place of the chicken livers. For *Cheese Pudding Mexicano,* remove seeds from all or part of 1 (4-oz.) can peeled green chili peppers; cut peppers fairly fine and toss with the bread-cheese mixture. Also add ½ teaspoon oregano. With the pudding serve canned chili con carne (without beans).

Bacon Curlicues

Roll strips of bacon loosely; fasten with toothpicks. Place on a rack in a shallow baking pan. Bake in a hot oven (400°F.) for 15 to 20 minutes, or until crisp. Remove toothpicks before serving. Allow 2 or 3 curlicues per person.

Brandied Fruit and Sherbet Cup

Choose any fruits you like for the fruit cup portion of this dessert. Seedless grapes, canned mandarin orange sections, and diced pineapple are one good combination. Grapefruit sections, strawberries, and pineapple chunks are another. Place the fruit in a bowl and sweeten with sugar, if need be. Then sprinkle just enough California Brandy over it to moisten and flavor it. Cover and chill thoroughly. At serving time, place the fruit in sherbet glasses or dessert dishes, top each serving with a small scoop of your favorite sherbet, and spoon a little of the Brandy marinade over all.

....

Cheese Timbales with Chili

Scald 1½ cups milk; add ¾ cup shredded process Cheddar cheese; stir over low heat until melted. Gradually stir hot mixture into 4 slightly beaten eggs; season with ½ teaspoon Worcestershire sauce and seasoned salt to taste. Pour into 4 well-greased custard cups; set in a shallow pan of hot water; bake at 350°F. about 45 minutes, or until firm in center. Heat 1 (15-oz.) can chili con carne (without beans) to simmering; stir in ⅓ cup California Red Table Wine. Unmold timbales; pour some chili over each. Serves 4. Wine choice; California Rosé. Creamed chicken, shrimp, or crabmeat can replace the chili.

DINNER or LUNCHEON

Crabmeat Sandwich Puff*
Hot Asparagus
Mandarin Orange Molds with Pineapple*
Wonderful Chocolate Pie*

With this menu we enjoy:

California Dry Sauterne

Crabmeat Sandwich Puff

  1 cup cooked or canned crabmeat (or shrimp,
     or a 6½-oz. can tuna, drained and flaked
½ teaspoon dry shredded green onions
¼ cup mayonnaise
  8 slices white bread, buttered
  4 sandwich-sized slices process Cheddar cheese
  3 eggs, slightly beaten
1¾ cups milk
¼ cup California Dry or Medium Sherry or
     White Table Wine
½ teaspoon Worcestershire sauce
     Seasoned salt and pepper to taste

Mix crabmeat, onions, and mayonnaise; spread over 4 slices of bread. Top with cheese slices, then with remaining 4 slices of bread. Cut sandwiches diagonally in halves; arrange in a greased baking dish (8 by 8 by 2 inches). Mix remaining ingredients; pour over sandwiches. Let stand for an hour or more. Bake in a slow oven (325°F.) for 1 hour. To serve, separate sandwiches with a sharp knife and lift onto plates with a broad spatula. Serves 4.

Mandarin Orange Molds with Pineapple

Dissolve 1 (3-oz.) package orange-flavored gelatin in 1 cup hot water. Remove from heat. Stir in ½ cup orange juice, 1 tablespoon vinegar, dash of salt. Cool, then chill. When mixture begins to thicken, fold in 1 (11-oz.) can mandarin orange sections (drained), 2 tablespoons grated green pepper, 1 teaspoon grated onion. Pour into 4 oiled individual molds; chill until firm. At serving time, line 4 salad plates with lettuce; top lettuce with a ring of canned pineapple; top pineapple with an orange mold. Sprinkle with French dressing; serve with mayonnaise. Serves 4.

Wonderful Chocolate Pie

¼ pound butter (at room temperature)
¾ cup sugar
  2 eggs
  1 (1-oz.) square unsweetened chocolate, melted
  1 (8-inch) graham cracker pie shell or baked
     pie shell
  1 cup heavy cream, whipped
     Additional unsweetened chocolate, grated,
     for garnish

Cream butter and sugar together thoroughly; add eggs, one at a time, beating *hard* after each one is added. Blend in melted chocolate. Turn into pie shell; chill several hours. Before serving, cover pie with whipped cream; garnish with grated chocolate.

• •

This dish, serving 12, was originally designed as an entrée for a "ladies' luncheon," but it's easily cut.

Baked Stuffed Mushrooms Lundi

Select 36 large mushrooms about 2¼ to 2½ inches in diameter (approximately 2 pounds). Scrub mushrooms gently; remove stems. Put stems through food grinder with a bit of onion; sauté for 5 minutes in ¼ cup butter. Prepare 1 (8-oz.) package bread stuffing according to directions on bag; add sautéed mixture and about 1½ cups *finely* diced, cooked chicken. Fill mushroom caps; place, filled side up, in 2 (13 by 9 by 2-inch) baking dishes. Mix and heat 1 cup chicken stock, ¼ cup butter, and ¼ cup California Dry or Medium Sherry or Dry Vermouth; pour around mushrooms. Cover dish with aluminum foil; bake at 350°F. for 25 minutes. Uncover; continue baking 20 minutes, basting several times. Serve with a sauce made by heating 1 (10¾-oz.) can chicken gravy with enough of the pan juices to give it a medium-thin consistency. Serves 12. Wine choice: California Chablis.

VII. It Pays to Be Sneaky

Quick-to-fix dinners that taste like hours of work

There are times when even the most dedicated, I-love-every-minute-in-the-kitchen cook wants to produce a good meal with a minimum of fuss and bother. This is the moment to reach for some of the many excellent convenience foods on your grocer's shelves, enhance them with a few personal, home-cooked touches, and serve them proudly forth.

The important thing to remember: Just don't tell anybody you didn't slave over the hot stove all day. True, this is the sneaky approach, but prestige in the kitchen seems to involve doing things the hard way. The cook who confesses to culinary sleight of hand is sure to lose status!

The menus in this chapter feature some of my sneaky favorites.

DINNER

Mexican Meat Balls* & Chili-Cheese Rice*
or
Meat Balls Marinara* & Farina Mia*
Mixed Green Salad   Two-Bean Salad*
Pineapple Sherbet
(top with canned crushed pineapple)
Cookies

With this menu we enjoy the indicated
California Wines

Mexican Meat Balls

1 (11-oz.) can chili beef soup
½ cup California Red Table Wine
   Bit of chopped or pressed garlic
1 tablespoon instant minced onion
½ teaspoon oregano ¼ teaspoon cumin seed
3 (15-oz.) cans meat balls in gravy

In a large, heavy skillet combine all ingredients except meat balls; heat to simmering. Add meat balls with their gravy; mix gently, being careful not to break the tender balls. Simmer very slowly for 5 minutes or so. Set aside; let stand 1 hour or more to blend flavors. Reheat gently before serving. Serves 6. Wine choice: California Zinfandel.

Chili-Cheese Rice

Heat 3 cups canned beef or chicken stock to boiling; add 3 cups 5-minute rice, 2 tablespoons instant minced onion, 2 tablespoons butter, and salt to taste. Cover; remove from heat; let stand 5 minutes. With a fork, gently stir in ¾ cup shredded process Cheddar cheese and 3 canned peeled green chili peppers, seeded and finely chopped. Cover; let stand another 5 minutes over hot water. Serve with *Mexican Meat Balls*. Serves 6.

Meat Balls Marinara

1 (15-oz.) can marinara sauce
3 tablespoons California Dry or Medium Sherry
   or Dry Vermouth
1 tablespoon instant minced onion
   Dash (just a dash!) of cinnamon
   Garlic salt and salt to taste
3 (15-oz.) cans meat balls in gravy

In a large, heavy skillet combine all ingredients except meat balls; heat to simmering. Add meat balls with their gravy; mix gently. Simmer very slowly for 5 minutes or so. Set aside; let stand 1 hour or more to blend flavors. Reheat before serving. Serves 6. Wine choice: California Barbera.

Farina Mia

Heat 2¼ cups milk, 1½ cups water, and ¼ cup butter to boiling. *Slowly* sprinkle in ¾ cup quick-cooking farina,** stirring constantly while mixture thickens. Then turn heat low, cover, and continue cooking, stirring occasionally, for 5 minutes. Add ⅓ cup grated Parmesan cheese and seasoned salt to taste. Serve at once, or keep warm over hot water. Serve with *Meat Balls Marinara*. Pass extra grated Parmesan cheese. Serves 6.

**I use Cream of Wheat for it gives just the flavor this dish requires.

Two-Bean Salad

Drain and rinse 1 (1-lb.) can of garbanzos (ceci beans) and 1 (1-lb.) can red kidney beans. Combine in a bowl with 1 teaspoon dry shredded green onions and chopped or pressed garlic to taste. Add enough bottled Italian-style French dressing to moisten the beans nicely but not to make them juicy. Season with coarsely ground black pepper and, if needed, with a little salt. Cover and chill at least 1 hour. Serve as a side dish with a green salad.

DINNER

Super Roast Beef Hash*
with Mustard Sauce* or Brown Gravy
Frozen Broccoli or Spinach
Baked Peaches*   "My" French Bread*
Marmalade Sundae*

With this menu we enjoy:
California Gamay

Super Roast Beef Hash

1 tablespoon butter
1 pound lean ground beef
2 (1-lb.) cans roast beef hash
¼ cup California Red Table Wine
1 teaspoon Worcestershire sauce
  Onion salt and pepper to taste

Melt butter in a large skillet; add ground beef and sauté until no longer red, stirring with a fork to separate meat into bits. Pour off any drippings. Add hash, wine and seasonings; mix well; turn into a greased casserole. Bake in a moderate oven (350°F.) for 30 minutes. If you like a brown crust on your hash, turn on the broiler for a minute before serving. Serves 5 or 6. Good with *Mustard Sauce* (below) or, if you prefer gravy with it, heat a can of brown gravy and season to taste with a bit of onion salt and pepper.

Mustard Sauce: Mix ½ cup each mayonnaise and evaporated milk; stir in 2 tablespoons prepared mustard. Makes about 1 cup. (Store leftover sauce in a covered jar in the refrigerator.) This is also an excellent sauce for baked ham and ham loaf.

Baked Peaches

Drain canned peach halves; place cut side up in a shallow baking dish. Fill hollows with catsup; dot with butter; sprinkle lightly with brown sugar. Bake at 350°F. for 20 minutes or so. Allow 1 or 2 peach halves per person, depending on size.

"My" French Bread

1 cup mayonnaise
2 tablespoons cream or evaporated milk
⅔ cup grated Parmesan cheese
2 tablespoons dry shredded green onions
1 teaspoon Worcestershire sauce
1 long loaf sourdough French bread
  Paprika

Blend mayonnaise and cream; add cheese, onions, and Worcestershire sauce; mix well. Cut loaf of bread lengthwise in halves; slice halves crosswise, cutting down to bottom crust but not through it. Spread cut surface of each half with mayonnaise mixture; dust with paprika. Bake in a hot oven (450°F.) about 10 minutes, or until topping is delicately browned. Before serving, finish cutting through slices with kitchen scissors.

P. S. For an elegant hot sandwich (we like it for Sunday brunch), toast slices of French bread on one side, cover untoasted side with thin slices of tomato, and spread the above mayonnaise mixture generously over the tomato. Dust with paprika and bake at 450°F. until nicely browned. Top each sandwich with a strip or two of crisp bacon and serve at once. Glorious!

Marmalade Sundae

Thin orange marmalade with just enough orange-flavored liqueur or California Muscatel or Sweet Sherry to give it a nice sauce-like consistency. Spoon over servings of vanilla ice cream.

....

Hash with Eggs Hollandaise

Chill 1 (1-lb.) can of roast beef hash or a can of corned beef hash; cut into 4 slices. Melt 2 tablespoons butter in a skillet; put hash slices in skillet and make "nests" by pressing each slice with the back of a spoon. Put an egg in each one; sprinkle with seasoned salt and coarse black pepper. Cover and cook slowly until eggs are done. Serve with this sauce: Mix and heat gently 1 (6-oz.) can hollandaise sauce, 2 tablespoons California Dry Vermouth, 1 tablespoon butter, ½ teaspoon lemon juice, ½ teaspoon dry shredded green onions, and salt to taste. Serves 2 to 4, depending on the occasion. Wine choice: California Rosé.

DINNER

Baked Spanish Rice with Chili Con Carne*
Buttered Whole-Kernel Corn
(use canned Mexican-style corn)
Green Salad with Artichoke Hearts & Mushrooms*
Cheesecake Pie*

With this menu we enjoy:

California Zinfandel

Baked Spanish Rice with Chili Con Carne

3 (1-lb.) cans Spanish rice
4 eggs, slightly beaten
½ cup shredded Cheddar cheese
   Salt and pepper to taste
2 (1-lb.) cans chili con carne without beans
½ cup California Red Table Wine
   Grated Parmesan cheese

Mix rice, eggs, Cheddar cheese, salt, and pepper. Turn into a well-oiled 8 by 8 by 2-inch baking dish. Bake in a moderate oven (350°F.) about 1¼ hours, or until a knife inserted in the center comes out clean. Remove from oven; let stand 10 to 15 minutes before serving. Add wine to chili con carne; heat and serve over rice. Pass grated Parmesan cheese. Serves 6.

Variation: Substitute *Mexican Meat Balls* (page 89) for the two cans of chili con carne, and you'll have another very good combination. This rice is also good with creamed chicken or seafood.

Green Salad with Artichoke Hearts & Mushrooms

Tear chilled, crisp salad greens into a salad bowl. Halve well-drained canned artichoke hearts, or use cooked frozen ones; in either case they should be chilled. Scrub and slice fresh mushrooms, or drain canned sliced ones. Add artichoke hearts and mushrooms to the greens (amounts up to you), along with a grated hard-cooked egg, if you like. Add French dressing (bottled Italian-style French dressing is good here), toss gently, and serve at once.

This easy-as-pie dessert has a delightful cheesecake flavor.

Cheesecake Pie

1 (15-oz.) can sweetened condensed milk
1 cup dairy sour cream
⅓ cup fresh lemon juice
½ teaspoon grated lemon peel
1 teaspoon vanilla
1 (8-inch) packaged graham cracker pie shell

Blend sweetened condensed milk and sour cream; gradually stir in lemon juice; add lemon peel and vanilla. Pour into pie shell. Chill at least 3 hours. Serves 6.

• • • • • • • • • • • • • • • • • • • •

Serve this flavorful dish with a tomato-avocado salad (thick slices of tomato topped with frozen guacamole), ripe olives and celery, and corn chips.

Two-Minute Enchilada Casserole

4 (15-oz.) cans beef enchiladas
4 (8-oz.) cans tomato sauce
1½ cups canned consommé or chicken broth
½ cup California Red Table Wine
2 to 3 teaspoons chili powder
1 teaspoon oregano
½ teaspoon cumin seed
   Salt to taste
3 (4-oz.) packages shredded Cheddar Cheese
   (3 cups)

Arrange enchiladas in 2 greased 12 by 8 by 2-inch baking dishes. Mix all remaining ingredients except cheese; heat to simmering; spoon over enchiladas. Sprinkle with the cheese. Bake in a moderately hot oven (375°F.) for 20 to 25 minutes, or until bubbly and piping hot. Serves 8. Wine choice: California Gamay.

DINNER

Mario's Baked Spaghetti*
or
Macaroni Marinara*
Tomato Aspic & Green Bean Salad*
Sesame Bread Sticks*
Raspberry Parfait Pudding*

With this menu we enjoy the indicated

California Wines

Mario's Baked Spaghetti

1 pound lean ground beef
2 tablespoons butter
1 (4-oz.) can mushroom stems and pieces, drained
½ cup shredded Cheddar cheese
2 (1-lb.) cans Italian-style spaghetti in tomato sauce
¼ cup California Red Table Wine
½ teaspoon Worcestershire sauce
    Onion salt, garlic salt, and pepper to taste
    Pinch of oregano
¼ cup grated Parmesan cheese

Sauté beef in butter until no longer red, stirring with a fork to separate it into bits. Drain off fat. Add all ingredients except Parmesan cheese. Turn into a casserole; sprinkle with Parmesan cheese. Bake in a hot oven (400°F.) for 20 minutes. Remove from oven and let settle a few minutes before serving. Serves 5 or 6. Wine choice: California Claret.

Macaroni Marinara

Prepare 2 (7¼-oz.) packages macaroni and cheese dinner according to directions on carton; add 2 teaspoons dry shredded green onions to macaroni along with the other ingredients. Prepare sauce:

1 pound lean ground beef
2 tablespoons butter
2 (15-oz.) cans marinara sauce
¼ cup California Dry or Medium Sherry or
    Dry Vermouth
2 tablespoons each: instant minced onion and
    parsley flakes
    Bit of chopped or pressed garlic
    Dash of cinnamon
    Salt and pepper to taste

Sauté beef in butter until no longer red, stirring with a fork to separate it into bits. Drain off excess fat. Add remaining ingredients. Cover; simmer gently 30 minutes, stirring often. To serve, spoon hot macaroni onto heated dinner plates; pour sauce over macaroni. Pass grated Parmesan cheese. Serves 6. Wine choice: California Zinfandel.

Tomato Aspic and Green Bean Salad

Drain 2 (1-lb.) cans French-style green beans. Combine in a bowl with 1 cup finely cut celery, 1 teaspoon dry shredded green onions, and chopped or pressed garlic to taste. Add enough bottled Italian-style French dressing to moisten vegetables nicely without making them juicy. Season with salt to taste and coarsely ground black pepper. Cover; chill at least 1 hour. Cut 1 can tomato aspic in 6 to 8 slices; sprinkle with French dressing; chill. At serving time, line chilled salad plates with crisp lettuce; top lettuce with a slice of aspic; top aspic with marinated beans. Top each serving with a bit of mayonnaise. Serves 6 to 8.

Sesame Bread Sticks

Cut 6 hot-dog buns lengthwise in quarters; brush with ½ cup melted butter. Mix 6 tablespoons grated Parmesan cheese and 3 tablespoons sesame (or poppy) seeds; roll bread sticks in mixture. Place on baking sheet; bake at 350°F. about 12 minutes, or until crisp. Serve hot. Makes 24 bread sticks.

Raspberry Parfait Pudding

Dissolve 1 (3-oz.) package raspberry-flavored gelatin in 1¼ cups hot water. Add 3 tablespoons orange-flavored liqueur and ½ teaspoon grated orange peel. Gradually stir in 1 pint vanilla ice cream, blending until it melts. Chill until mixture begins to thicken, then stir well and spoon into 6 stemmed glasses or dessert dishes; chill until firm. Serve topped with whipped cream and a trickle of the liqueur used in the pudding. Serves 6.

DINNER or LUNCHEON

Chicken or Tuna à la King*
or Special Creamed Chicken or Seafood*
Macaroni and Cheese Torta*
Green Beans with Almonds   Beet Aspic Salad
(the frozen combination)   *(the canned aspic)*
Heaven Cake*

With this menu we enjoy the indicated
California Wines

Chicken or Tuna à la King

2 (10½-oz.) cans chicken à la king
1 to 2 tablespoons California Dry or Medium Sherry
2 cups diced, cooked or canned chicken, or
  2 (7-oz.) cans tuna, drained and flaked
1 (4-oz.) can sliced mushrooms, drained
½ teaspoon dry shredded green onions
  Salt and pepper to taste

Combine all ingredients in a saucepan; heat, uncovered, *very* gently *just* until piping hot. Serve over squares of *Macaroni and Cheese Torta,* with rice, or in patty shells. (Frozen patty shells are excellent.) Serves 4. Wine choice: California Dry Sauterne.

Special Creamed Chicken or Seafood

1 (10½-oz.) can white sauce
½ cup shredded Cheddar cheese
2 tablespoons mayonnaise
2 teaspoons parsley flakes
½ teaspoon Worcestershire sauce
  Salt and pepper to taste
2 cups diced cooked or canned chicken, or
  2 (7-oz.) cans tuna, drained and flaked, or 2 cups
  shrimp, crabmeat, or lobster
1 to 2 tablespoons California Dry or Medium Sherry

In a saucepan mix white sauce, cheese, mayonnaise, parsley, and seasonings; stir over *very* low heat until cheese melts and blends with the sauce. Add chicken or seafood and Sherry; heat, uncovered, *very* gently, *just* until piping hot. Serve over squares of *Macaroni and Cheese Torta,* with rice, or in patty shells. Serves 4. Wine choice: California Chablis.

Macaroni and Cheese Torta

Beat 2 eggs well; blend in ½ cup evaporated milk and ½ teaspoon *each* Worcestershire sauce and prepared mustard. Stir in 1 cup soft bread crumbs, ⅔ cup shredded Cheddar cheese, and 2 teaspoons dry shredded green onions. Gently combine this mixture with 2 (15-oz.) cans macaroni with cheese sauce; season with seasoned salt and pepper. Turn mixture into a greased 10 by 6 by 2-inch baking dish; dust with paprika. Bake in a moderate oven (350°F.) for 1 hour, or until firm in center. Remove from oven; let settle 10 minutes or so before cutting. Serves 6.

Heaven Cake

Buy a pound cake (frozen or otherwise) or a loaf-shaped angel food cake. With a very sharp knife, slice cake into 3 or 4 layers. Whip 1½ cups heavy cream; gently fold in ⅓ cup *instant* cocoa and 2 tablespoons coffee or chocolate-flavored wine or liqueur. Put cake layers together with the cream filling between them, and frost cake all over. Sprinkle top with finely chopped toasted almonds or shaved unsweetened chocolate. Refrigerate several hours or overnight.

• •

Ham and Celery Rolls au Gratin

Drain 1 (1-lb.) can celery hearts; cut lengthwise as necessary to make 6 equal portions. Wrap each portion in a thin, sandwich-sized slice of boiled ham. Place rolls, "seam" down, in a greased 10 by 6 by 2-inch baking dish. In a saucepan mix 1 (10¾-oz.) can condensed Cheddar cheese soup, ¼ cup evaporated milk, 1 tablespoon California Dry or Medium Sherry, and ½ teaspoon dry shredded green onions; stir over low heat until smooth and warm. Pour sauce over ham rolls; dust with paprika. Bake in a moderately hot oven (375°F.) for 20 to 25 minutes. Serves 3. Wine choice: California Rosé.

DINNER or LUNCHEON

Scalloped Chicken and Noodles*
or Chicken and Stuffing Casserole*
Cranberry Jelly
Celery or Asparagus Vinaigrette*
Brownies à la Mode
(brownies, vanilla ice cream, & chocolate sauce)

With this menu we enjoy the indicated

California Wines

Scalloped Chicken and Noodles

3 (14-oz.) jars noodle chicken dinner or 3 (15-oz.) cans noodle turkey dinner
1 (approximately 3-lb.) canned whole chicken
⅓ cup butter
½ cup flour
¾ cup cream or evaporated milk
¼ cup California Dry or Medium Sherry or White Table Wine
½ cup grated Parmesan cheese
1 (4-oz.) can sliced mushrooms (undrained)
2 tablespoons chopped pimiento
1 tablespoon parsley flakes
1 teaspoon dry shredded green onions
½ teaspoon Worcestershire sauce
Nutmeg, seasoned salt, and pepper to taste
Paprika

Drain and reserve broth from noodle chicken dinners and the whole chicken. Remove whole chicken from bones; cut meat in good-sized pieces. Melt butter and stir in flour; gradually add 2 cups of the reserved chicken broth and the cream; cook, stirring, until mixture boils and thickens. Add wine, ¼ cup of the cheese, and all remaining ingredients, except paprika. Spread noodle chicken dinners in a greased 12 by 8 by 2-inch baking dish; top with cut-up chicken; pour sauce over all. Sprinkle with remaining cheese and paprika. Bake in a moderately hot oven (375°F.) about 25 minutes, or until bubbly and delicately browned. Serves 6 to 8. Wine choice: California Johannisberg Riesling.

Chicken and Stuffing Casserole

1 (approximately 3-lb.) canned whole chicken
1 (8-oz.) package bread stuffing
¾ cup butter
1 (4-oz.) can mushroom stems and pieces, drained
1 tablespoon parsley flakes
¼ cup flour

¾ cup cream or evaporated milk
1 egg, slightly beaten
3 tablespoons California Dry or Medium Sherry
Seasoned salt and pepper to taste
Paprika

Drain chicken, reserving broth. Remove chicken from bones; discard skin and cut meat in good-sized pieces. Prepare stuffing according to package directions, using 1 cup reserved chicken broth as the liquid and ½ cup butter. Measure ¾ cup prepared stuffing; set aside. Add mushrooms and parsley to remaining stuffing. Melt remaining ¼ cup butter; stir in flour; gradually add 1 cup reserved chicken broth and the cream; cook, stirring, until mixture boils and thickens. Remove from heat. Stir a little sauce into beaten egg; stir mixture back into remaining sauce. Add Sherry, seasoned salt, and pepper. To assemble dish: Spread all but reserved ¾ cup stuffing over bottom of a greased 10 by 6 by 2-inch baking dish; top with chicken; spoon sauce over chicken. Sprinkle with reserved stuffing; dust with paprika. Bake in a moderately hot oven (375°F.) for 30 minutes. Serves 5 or 6. Wine choice: California Dry Sauterne.

Celery or Asparagus Vinaigrette

Arrange chilled, drained canned celery hearts or asparagus tips on lettuce-lined salad plates; spoon *Vinaigrette Dressing* (below), over them. Garnish with tomatoes or pickled beets, if you like.

Vinaigrette Dressing: To ¾ cup bottled Italian-style French dressing add 2 tablespoons drained sweet pickle relish, 1 teaspoon dry shredded green onions, and 1 grated, hard-cooked egg. Mix well. Cover and chill at least 1 hour; mix again before serving. Makes enough dressing for 6 servings. This dressing is also excellent on broccoli spears, canned vertical-pack green beans, strips of cooked zucchini, and sliced tomatoes.

DINNER or LUNCHEON

Chicken Pancakes au Gratin*
Peas with Celery *(use the frozen)*
Pear and Orange Salad*
with Rosy Honey Dressing*
Fudge Pound Cake*

With this menu we enjoy:
California Chablis

Chicken Pancakes au Gratin

1 (approximately 3-lb.) canned whole chicken
½ cup California White Table Wine
   Milk (the richer the better)
½ cup butter
⅔ cup flour
¾ cup grated Parmesan cheese
2 tablespoons California Dry or Medium Sherry
2 tablespoons parsley flakes
1 teaspoon Worcestershire sauce
   Generous dash of nutmeg
   Seasoned salt and pepper to taste
1 (10-oz.) package frozen chopped spinach,
   cooked and *thoroughly* drained
1 (8-oz.) can mushroom stems and pieces, drained
   and chopped
1 package flour tortillas (12 tortillas)
   Paprika

Drain chicken. Measure broth; add wine and enough milk to make 6 cups. Melt butter and stir in flour; gradually add the 6 cups liquid and cook, stirring constantly, until mixture is thickened and smooth. Remove from heat. Add ¼ cup Parmesan cheese, Sherry, parsley, Worcestershire sauce, nutmeg, seasoned salt, and pepper. Remove skin from chicken and cut meat fairly fine; add spinach, mushrooms, ½ cup of the sauce, and salt to taste. Spread some of this mixture down the center of each tortilla; fold over top and bottom (to keep filling from escaping) and roll up tortillas loosely. Place side by side in two greased 12 by 8 by 2-inch baking dishes. Spoon simmering sauce over tortillas; sprinkle ¼ cup Parmesan cheese over each dish; dust with paprika. Bake in a moderately hot oven (375°F.) for 20 to 25 minutes, or until bubbly. Serves 6 or more. Lock the kitchen door while you're preparing this dish and nobody will guess that you didn't make the "pancakes" and cook the chicken. It looks and tastes like a real production!

P. S. The tortillas can be filled, rolled, and placed in the casseroles well ahead of baking time. The sauce can also be prepared in advance. Just before the casseroles go into the oven, reheat the sauce to simmering and pour it over the tortillas.

Pear and Orange Salad

Line a platter or individual salad plates with crisp lettuce cups. In the lettuce cups arrange chilled, drained canned pear halves, cut side up. Top pear halves with chilled, drained canned mandarin orange sections. (Seedless grapes are a good addition here when available.) Sprinkle a little bottled Italian-style French dressing over the salad and serve with *Rosy Honey Dressing* (below).

Rosy Honey Dressing: Mix ¾ cup honey, ½ cup mayonnaise, and ½ teaspoon paprika. Stir until thoroughly blended. Makes 1¼ cups dressing. Good with any fruit salad. Store in refrigerator but bring to room temperature before using.

Fudge Pound Cake

With a sharp knife (and a steady hand!) slice a bakery-made or frozen pound cake into 4 or 5 layers. Mix canned milk chocolate fudge topping with just enough California Sweet Sherry to give a good consistency for spreading. Put cake layers back together with this as the filling. Wrap in waxed paper, then in aluminum foil. Chill overnight. Slice just before serving.

Another good pound cake dessert: Slice a pound cake as directed above. Sprinkle slices sparingly with rum. Put cake back together again with a filling of apricot-pineapple or peach preserves between the layers. Wrap as directed; chill overnight.

DINNER or LUNCHEON

Jeanne's Chicken Mousse*
Garnished with
Vegetables, Hard-Cooked Eggs, & Olives
Sour Cream Dressing*   Poppy Cheese Buns*
Brandied Peach Pudding*

With this menu we enjoy:

California Rosé

Chicken à la king is rather a novel ingredient for a salad, I'll admit, but once you taste this mousse I think you'll see why it's one of my easy-does-it pets.

Jeanne's Chicken Mousse

½ cup canned chicken broth
½ cup California White Table Wine
2 envelopes (2 tablespoons) unflavored gelatin
1 tablespoon parsley flakes
2 teaspoons dry shredded green onions
2 (10½-oz.) cans chicken à la king
½ cup salad dressing**
½ cup mayonnaise
4 hard-cooked eggs, chopped or shredded
1 (4-oz.) jar sliced pimientos, drained and cut fine
1 tablespoon lemon juice
½ teaspoon Worcestershire sauce
   Seasoned salt and pepper to taste

Combine chicken broth and wine in a small saucepan; soften gelatin in this mixture for 5 minutes; stir over low heat until gelatin is dissolved. Remove from heat; add parsley and onions. In a large bowl combine chicken à la king with all remaining ingredients; stir in gelatin mixture, blending thoroughly. Set bowl in the refrigerator just until mixture begins to thicken; stir frequently and watch carefully lest mixture get too firm. Spoon slightly thickened mixture into a 5-cup mold that has been brushed with mayonnaise or salad oil; chill until firm. To serve, unmold on a lettuce-lined platter. Garnish with quartered or sliced tomatoes, asparagus tips, quartered or sliced hard-cooked eggs, and ripe olives. Sprinkle tomatoes and asparagus tips with French dressing, and serve *Sour Cream Dressing* (below) with the salad. Serves 6.

Sour Cream Dressing: Mix equal parts of mayonnaise and dairy sour cream. Season with a touch of prepared mustard and salt to taste. If you like capers, add some, drained. Chill before serving.

**I use Miracle Whip for it gives just the flavor this dish requires.

Poppy Cheese Buns

½ cup softened butter
¼ cup prepared mustard (the yellow variety)
1 tablespoon instant minced onion, soaked 15 minutes in warm water and drained
1 tablespoon poppy seeds
6 sandwich-sized slices process Swiss cheese
1 (2¼-oz.) can deviled ham
6 hamburger buns, sliced in halves

Blend butter and mustard together; stir in onion and poppy seeds. Spread each cheese slice evenly with some of the deviled ham. Spread cut sides of hamburger buns with some of the butter mixture; put halves back together with a slice of cheese between; spread remaining butter mixture over tops. Place buns on a baking sheet. Bake in a moderate oven (350°F.) for 15 minutes. Before serving, cut buns in halves. Makes 6 buns. Wonderful flavor!

Brandied Peach Pudding

Drain 1 (1-lb.) can sliced freestone peaches, reserving syrup. Divide peaches among 6 stemmed glasses or dessert dishes; sprinkle 1 teaspoon or so of California Brandy per glass over peaches. Combine ½ cup reserved peach syrup and 1½ cups cream in a mixing bowl; add 1 (3¾-oz.) package instant vanilla pudding mix; beat slowly with rotary or electric beater 1 minute. Pour pudding over peaches; sprinkle with nutmeg. Chill at least 1 hour. (Pudding will remain soft and creamy.) Serves 6.

LIGHT DINNER or LUNCHEON

A Creamy, Flavorful Soup*
(see recipes below)

Toasted English Muffins   Mixed Green Salad
Celery Hearts & Cherry Tomatoes
Layer Cake or Pie
(from your favorite bakery)

With this menu we enjoy:
California Chenin Blanc or Chablis

Shrimp Supper Soup

1 (10-oz.) can frozen condensed cream of
    shrimp soup
1 cup rich milk (or ½ cup milk and ½ cup cream)
1 cup cooked or canned shrimp (whole if small,
    cut up if large)
¼ cup California Dry or Medium Sherry or
    Dry Vermouth
½ teaspoon grated lemon peel
    Salt and paprika to taste
    Dash of cayenne

Heat soup and milk to simmering; add remaining ingredients. Pour into heated soup bowls. Serves 2 or 3.

Willipa Oyster Stew

1 (10-oz.) can oysters
    Evaporated milk
1 (10¼-oz.) can condensed (not frozen) oyster stew
½ teaspoon dry shredded green onions
½ teaspoon Worcestershire sauce
    Salt and pepper to taste
    Generous lump of butter
    Paprika

Drain oysters, reserving liquid. If oysters are large, cut in halves or thirds. Measure oyster liquid; add evaporated milk to make 1¼ cups. In a saucepan combine this 1¼ cups liquid with the oysters, oyster stew, onions, seasonings, and butter; heat gently, stirring occasionally, until piping hot. Pour into heated bowls. Dust with paprika. Serves 3.

Happy Clam Chowder

1 (10¼-oz.) can frozen condensed clam chowder
1 (10¼-oz.) can frozen condensed potato soup
1¼ cups cream
1 (7-oz.) can minced clams

¼ cup California White Table Wine
1 tablespoon parsley flakes
    Salt, onion salt, and pepper to taste
    Paprika

Heat soups, cream, and clam liquid to simmering. Add clams, wine, parsley, salt, onion salt, and pepper. Pour piping hot into heated soup bowls. Dust with paprika. Serves 4 generously.

••••••••••••••••••••••

With rice and a salad this casserole makes fine eating.

Crabmeat and Artichoke Casserole

1 (10½-oz.) can condensed cream of celery soup
1 (4-oz.) package shredded Cheddar cheese (1 cup)
2 tablespoons each; evaporated milk and California
    Dry Sherry or Vermouth
1 teaspoon dry shredded green onions
½ teaspoon Worcestershire sauce
    Pepper to taste (no salt)
2 (6½-oz.) cans crabmeat, drained (or shrimp
    or tuna)
1 (14-oz.) can artichoke hearts, drained and
    halved or quartered
1 (4-oz.) can sliced mushrooms, drained
¼ cup grated Parmesan cheese
    Paprika

In a saucepan combine soup, Cheddar cheese, milk, Sherry, onions, and seasonings; stir over *very* low heat until cheese melts and blends with the sauce. Arrange crabmeat, artichoke hearts, and mushrooms in a greased shallow casserole; spoon sauce over them; sprinkle with Parmesan cheese and paprika. Bake in a moderately hot oven (375° F.) for 20 minutes. Remove from oven and let stand 5 minutes before serving. Serves 6. Wine choice: California Dry Sauterne.

LIGHT DINNER

Ann's Cheddar Fondue with Dunkers*
Hasty Tasty Tomato Molds*
Asparagus Tips
Pudding Shortcakes*

With this menu we enjoy:

California Grey Riesling

Ann's Cheddar Fondue

1 (11-oz.) can Cheddar cheese soup
¼ cup California Dry Vermouth or White
    Table Wine
1¼ cups shredded Cheddar cheese (I use the
    packaged shredded cheese)
    Bit of chopped or pressed garlic
1 teaspoon Worcestershire sauce
¼ teaspoon dry mustard

Combine all ingredients in a fondue pot or small double boiler; stir over gentle heat until cheese is melted and ingredients are well blended. Serve with any of the following Dunkers:

Cubes of crusty French bread or French rolls
Cooked large shrimp
Tiny meat balls, or cubes of meat loaf or ham
Vienna sausages, cocktail frankfurters, or chunks
    of regular-sized frankfurters
Drained canned whole mushrooms

Serves 2 or 3 as a main dish, more as an appetizer.

P. S. For another delightful luncheon or supper dish, serve the fondue over slices of hot toast, with strips of crisp bacon on the side. For extra heartiness, top toast with a poached egg or two. Another good idea: Cover slices of toast with slices of meat loaf, then top with the fondue. Try it, too, as a sauce for hamburgers or frankfurters.

Hasty Tasty Tomato Molds

1 (1-lb.) can stewed tomatoes
    Small piece of onion
1 (3-oz.) package lemon or strawberry-flavored
    gelatin
1 tablespoon California wine vinegar
    Seasoned salt to taste

Put tomatoes and onion in a blender; run blender until vegetables are liquefied. Pour into a saucepan; bring to a boil. Add gelatin, vinegar, and salt; stir

until gelatin is dissolved. Pour into 4 (½-cup) molds that have been rinsed with cold water (or into a 1-pint mold). Chill until firm. Unmold on crisp salad greens; arrange canned asparagus tips around molds. Sprinkle with a little bottled Italian-style French dressing. Pass mayonnaise. Serves 4.

Pudding Shortcakes

For each serving, sprinkle a bakery shortcake cup (or a slice of frozen or bakery pound cake) sparingly with California Medium or Sweet Sherry. Spoon thawed frozen chocolate or butterscotch pudding into cup. Top with whipped cream (from a pressurized can) or with prepared cream-like dessert topping. If desired, sprinkle a little crushed English toffee over the cream. Serve at once. A no-effort dessert with a lot of flavor and glamour!

....

Sunday Chipped Beef

1 tablespoon butter
1 (3-oz.) package smoked sliced beef, cut up
    with scissors
2 tablespoons California Dry or Medium Sherry
1 (10½-oz.) can white sauce
¼ cup shredded Cheddar cheese
½ teaspoon Worcestershire sauce
¼ teaspoon prepared mustard
    Dash of pepper
½ teaspoon dry shredded green onions

Melt butter in a skillet or saucepan; add beef and Sherry; stir over medium heat until mixture is heated through. Add white sauce and cheese; stir over low heat until cheese melts and ingredients are well blended. Stir in remaining ingredients. Serve over hot, crisp toast. Serves 2 generously, 3 modestly. This is also good as a supper dish with baked potatoes. Sliced, hard-cooked eggs may be added.

VIII. Something A Little Special

Menus and recipes to enhance any cook's reputation

Breathes there a hostess-cook who hasn't sat down at her own dinner party too weary to enjoy it? I doubt it, because a groaning board and hospitality have been synonymous since time immemorial, and the temptation to show off our culinary talents when company's coming is too strong for most of us to resist.

Doing most of the preparation well ahead of time and thereby avoiding a lot of frantic last-minute kitchen activity is the best way to ensure a good time with one's guests. So in this chapter I'm giving you some of my favorite company menus built around do-ahead dishes. I hope that by following each menu with its "Timing Tips," I've pointed the way to some entertaining-without-tears!

DINNER

Canapé Pierre*
Veal Capri*
Zucchini & Rice Torta*
Peas with Celery
(the frozen combination)
Ripe & Green Olives
Glazed Cherry Port Tarts*

With this menu we enjoy the indicated

California Wines

Canapé Pierre

      8 (3-inch) rounds of white bread
        Butter
        Anchovy paste
      8 thin slices peeled tomato (or canned
        tomato aspic)
      1 good-sized avocado (or 2 smaller ones), peeled
        and thinly sliced
    1½ cups cooked or canned crabmeat
        (or small shrimp)
        Canapé Dressing (below)
      2 hard-cooked eggs, sieved or shredded
        Paprika
        Sprigs of watercress or parsley for garnishing

Spread both sides of bread rounds rather generously
with butter. Place on a baking sheet and bake in a
slow oven (300°F.) until crisp and light golden
brown. (Watch them lest they get *too* brown.) Cool.
To assemble canapés: Spread toast rounds thinly
with anchovy paste; place each on a salad or dessert
plate. Top toast with a tomato slice; cover tomato
with slices of avocado; top avocado with a mound
of crabmeat. Just before serving, spoon *Canapé
Dressing* (below) over all; sprinkle with hard-cooked
egg and dust with paprika. Garnish each canapé
with watercress or parsley. Serves 8.

Canapé Dressing: Blend together ¾ cup mayonnaise, ⅓ cup chili sauce, 1 tablespoon California Dry
or Medium Sherry or Dry Vermouth, 1 tablespoon
lemon juice, 1 teaspoon dry shredded green onions,
and salt to taste. Chill.

Veal Capri

      3 pounds veal round steak, cut about ½ inch thick
    ¾ cup grated Parmesan cheese
      3 tablespoons each: butter and salad oil
      4 tablespoons flour
      2 cups canned consommé or chicken broth
    ½ cup California White Table Wine
      1 (8-oz.) can mushroom stems and pieces
        (undrained)
      2 tablespoons drained capers
      2 tablespoons instant minced onion
      1 clove garlic, pressed or chopped
      2 tablespoons parsley flakes
    1½ teaspoons Worcestershire sauce
        Pinch each of thyme and marjoram
        Salt and pepper to taste
      2 tablespoons California Dry
        or Medium Sherry

Remove bone and skin from veal. Sprinkle veal with
some of the cheese; pound cheese into meat with a
wooden mallet or the edge of a heavy plate. Turn
slices over; sprinkle with cheese; pound. Repeat
until all cheese is used. Cut veal in 1 by 2-inch
pieces. Heat butter and oil in a large, heavy skillet
or a Dutch oven; brown veal nicely on all sides, a
few pieces at a time. Remove browned veal from
pan and set aside. Blend flour with drippings in
pan; add consommé, white wine, and mushrooms
with their liquid; cook, stirring, until mixture boils
and thickens. Add capers, onion, garlic, parsley,
Worcestershire sauce, thyme, marjoram, salt, and
pepper. Return veal to pan. Cover and simmer
gently, stirring frequently, for about 45 minutes, or
until veal is meltingly tender. Before serving, add
Sherry; taste and add more salt and pepper, if
needed. Serves 8. Wine choice: California Sauvignon
Blanc.

In addition to being a good meat accompaniment, this torta also makes a good base for creamed chicken, crabmeat, shrimp or tuna in a luncheon menu. As a luncheon dish it should serve 10 or even 12. If you want to halve the recipe, bake it in a 9-inch pie plate.

Zucchini and Rice Torta

1 cup uncooked long-grain white rice
2 pounds small zucchini
4 eggs, slightly beaten
⅓ cup melted butter or salad oil
1 cup shredded Cheddar cheese
⅓ cup grated Parmesan cheese
2 tablespoons instant minced onion
  Bit of chopped or pressed garlic
2 tablespoons parsley flakes
1 teaspoon Worcestershire sauce
  Pinch each of thyme and rosemary
  Salt and pepper to taste

Boil or steam rice until tender; drain, if necessary. Scrub zucchini and trim off ends; cook whole in boiling water about 10 minutes, or *just* until tender. Drain cooked zucchini; chop coarsely; drain again. Combine rice and zucchini with all remaining ingredients; mix well. Turn into a well-oiled baking dish (12 by 8 by 2 inches). Bake in a moderate oven (350°F.) for 45 to 50 minutes, or until firm in the center. Serves 8.

Glazed Cherry Port Tarts

1½ tablespoons cornstarch
3 tablespoons sugar
  Dash of cinnamon
  Dash of salt
½ cup syrup from canned sour red pitted cherries
½ cup California Port
1 (3-oz.) package cream cheese
1 tablespoon milk
8 (4-inch) baked tart shells
3 cups drained canned sour red pitted cherries

Mix cornstarch, sugar, cinnamon, and salt in a saucepan; gradually add cherry syrup and wine, stirring until mixture is smooth. Stir over medium heat until sauce is thickened and clear. Remove from heat. Mash cream cheese with a fork; blend in milk; spread mixture evenly over bottom of tart shells. Place cherries in tart shells; pour sauce over cherries. Chill thoroughly before serving. Serve topped with whipped cream. Makes 8 tarts. Wine choice: California Port.

Timing Tips for the Hostess-Cook

Canapé Pierre: The morning of the party, prepare the toast rounds. Peel the tomatoes and chill, or remove the aspic from the can and chill. Make *Canapé Dressing* and chill. Hard-cook the eggs; chill. Wash and chill the watercress or parsley. If refrigerator space permits, assemble the canapés on individual plates shortly before the guests arrive, chill them, and then spoon the dressing over them and garnish just before serving. Otherwise, before the guests arrive, slice the tomatoes or aspic; peel and slice the avocado and sprinkle with lemon juice to prevent darkening; chill tomatoes and avocado. Spread toast rounds with anchovy paste; sieve or shred the eggs. Assemble, dress, and garnish canapés just before serving.

Veal Capri: Prepare early in the day, or even the day before. Reheat gently before serving; add a little more consommé or chicken broth if sauce seems on the thick side after standing.

Zucchini and Rice Torta: Prepare mixture early in the day. Stir well, turn into baking dish, and bake just before serving.

Peas with Celery: For the best flavor and texture, wait until the last possible moment to cook this frozen vegetable. Or, if the last-minute aspect "nervouses" you, cook the vegetable before the guests arrive; drain, reserving liquid, and let cool. Reheat with a very little bit of the liquid and a pat of butter *just* before serving.

Glazed Cherry Port Tarts: If you make your own tart shells, you can have them ready well in advance of party day. If you buy them, they're no problem. Prepare filling and fill shells the morning of the dinner; chill. Top with whipped cream just before serving.

DINNER

Celery Victor*
Parmesan Sticks*
Baked Stuffed Lamb Chops*
with Sauce Bergère*
Peasant Pilaf*   Mushroom Puff*
Crème d'Orange*

With this menu we enjoy:

California Cabernet Sauvignon

Celery Victor

Drain 2 (1-lb.) cans celery hearts *thoroughly*. Arrange in a single layer in a shallow dish. Over the hearts spoon well-seasoned oil-vinegar French dressing (you'll need about ¾ cup). Cover (with aluminum foil, if dish has no lid) and chill thoroughly. Before serving, arrange hearts on 6 lettuce-lined salad plates. (You'll have some celery left for your lunch the next day.) Spoon any dressing remaining in the dish over the hearts; sprinkle with 2 grated hard-cooked eggs and paprika; top each serving with 2 or 3 anchovy fillets (flat or rolled with capers). Pass mayonnaise, if desired. Serves 6.

P.S. A few crab flakes or small shrimp can replace the anchovies here. When assembling the salad, top the celery hearts with the crab or shrimp before spooning on the French dressing. For *Hearts of Palm Victor* (elegant indeed!), halve or quarter canned hearts of palm lengthwise; substitute for the celery hearts. You can "underline" the celery or hearts of palm with slices of tomato or canned tomato aspic, if you like. Not strictly "Victor," but good.

Parmesan Sticks

Trim crusts from slices of white bread; cut each slice in 4 strips. Dip strips in melted butter, then roll in grated Parmesan cheese. (Be generous with butter and cheese.) Place on foil-lined baking sheet. Bake in a moderate oven (350°F.) about 15 minutes, or until a very pale golden brown. Serve warm or cold.

Baked Stuffed Lamb Chops

12 double rib lamb chops
 1 (2¼-oz.) can deviled ham
¼ cup canned chopped ripe olives
 2 teaspoons dry shredded green onions
   Dash of thyme
   Seasoned salt and pepper

With a sharp paring knife, split chops from fat side to bone to form a pocket. Mix deviled ham, olives, onions, and thyme; spread mixture in pocket of each chop. Sprinkle chops with salt and pepper; place on a rack in a shallow pan. Bake in a moderate oven (350°F.) for 50 minutes. Spoon a little *Sauce Bergère* (below) over each chop; pass remainder at the table. Serves 6.

Sauce Bergère: In a saucepan mix 2 (10¾-oz.) cans beef gravy, ½ cup California Red Table Wine, 1 teaspoon dry shredded green onions, bit of chopped or pressed garlic, 1 teaspoon Worcestershire sauce, and salt and pepper to taste. Cover; simmer 5 minutes, stirring occasionally. Just before serving, stir in 2 tablespoons butter and 2 tablespoons California Dry or Medium Sherry. Excellent with plain broiled lamb chops and roast leg of lamb, too.

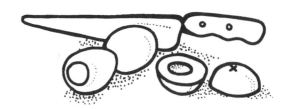

Peasant Pilaf

6 tablespoons butter
1½ cups long-grain white rice
1 cup each: coarsely shredded raw carrots and
  finely cut celery
2 tablespoons each: instant minced onion and
  parsley flakes
3 cups chicken broth
  Seasoned salt and pepper to taste

Melt 4 tablespoons butter in a large skillet; add rice; sauté gently, stirring frequently, for 5 minutes. Stir in carrots, celery, onion, and parsley; add broth and seasonings. Bring to a boil, then cover, turn heat as low as possible, and cook for 25 minutes, or until rice is tender and all liquid has been absorbed. Uncover; add remaining 2 tablespoons butter and stir gently into mixture with a fork. Serves 6 or more. Leftover pilaf can be reheated in a double boiler.

Mushroom Puff

4 tablespoons butter
1 pound fresh mushrooms, scrubbed gently and
  coarsely chopped
4 tablespoons flour
1 (10½-oz.) can condensed cream of
  mushroom soup
2 tablespoons California Dry or Medium Sherry
  or Dry Vermouth
4 eggs, yolks and whites separated
2 tablespoons parsley flakes
1 tablespoon instant minced onion
½ teaspoon Worcestershire sauce
  Nutmeg, salt, and pepper to taste
¼ teaspoon cream of tartar

Melt butter in a skillet; add mushrooms; cover and sauté over medium heat, stirring frequently, for 5 minutes. Uncover; sauté 5 minutes longer, or until mixture is no longer juicy. Reduce heat. Stir in flour; add mushroom soup and wine; cook, stirring, until mixture is thick and well blended. Blend in well-beaten egg yolks; continue stirring over low heat for another minute. Remove from heat. Add parsley, onion, and seasonings; cool. Beat egg whites until foamy; sprinkle with cream of tartar; continue beating until stiff but not dry. Gently fold mushroom mixture into egg whites; blend carefully until no trace of egg white remains. Taste; correct seasoning. Pour mixture into an ungreased 10 by 6 by 2-inch baking dish. Bake in a moderate oven (350°F.) for 1 hour, or until puffed and toasty brown. Serves 6. A lovely vegetable dish!

Crème d'Orange

Mix 2 envelopes (2 tablespoons) unflavored gelatin, ½ cup sugar, and dash of salt in a small saucepan. Add ½ cup water; stir over low heat until gelatin is dissolved. Empty 1 (6-oz.) can frozen orange juice concentrate into a bowl; blend in 1½ cups cold water; add gelatin mixture. Chill until mixture begins to thicken, then whip and fold in 1 cup heavy cream. Pour into a 1½-quart mold; chill until firm. Unmold and serve with this sauce: Mix 1 cup orange marmalade and 2 to 3 tablespoons Cointreau or Triple Sec; cover; let stand at room temperature an hour or longer so flavor can mellow. Serves 6.

Timing Tips for the Hostess-Cook

Celery Victor: Early in the day, put drained celery hearts in the refrigerator to marinate. Wash and chill lettuce. Hard-cook and chill eggs. If there's room in the refrigerator, assemble salads on the individual plates shortly before the guests arrive and leave them to chill. Otherwise, assemble them on chilled plates just before serving.

Parmesan Sticks: Prepare early in the day; bake just before serving; serve warm. Or, prepare and bake them ahead; cool; store tightly covered; serve cold.

Baked Stuffed Lamb Chops: Stuff and season lamb chops early in the day. Make sauce early in the day; cover; reheat gently before serving.

Peasant Pilaf: Sauté rice early in the day; remove from heat; add carrots, celery, onion, and parsley. Set aside. About 30 minutes before dinnertime, add broth and seasonings; cook pilaf as directed; let stand in a warm place until time to serve. Or, prepare pilaf early in the day; cool; turn into a covered casserole. To reheat before serving, set casserole in a shallow pan of hot water; bake at 350°F. about 30 minutes.

Mushroom Puff: Prepare mixture early in the day, up to the point where egg whites are added. Finish just before baking.

Crème d'Orange: Prepare early in the day or the day before. If you make the sauce well ahead, refrigerate it, then let stand at room temperature for an hour or so before serving.

DINNER

Oysters Henriette*
Roast Rack of Lamb*
with
Currant Sauce Piquant*
Baked Barley with Mushrooms*
Artichoke Bottoms with Creamed Spinach*
Masquerade Pie*

With this menu we enjoy the indicated

California Wines

Oysters Henriette

       6 (3-inch) rounds of white bread
          Butter
1½ teaspoons flour
1¼ cups catsup
¼ cup California Dry Vermouth or Dry or
   Medium Sherry
½ teaspoon Worcestershire sauce
1 pint drained oysters (the smaller the better)
   Sprigs of watercress or parsley for garnishing

Spread both sides of bread rounds rather generously with butter. Place on a baking sheet; bake in a slow oven (300°F.) until crisp and light golden brown. (Watch carefully lest they get *too* brown.) Melt 6 tablespoons butter and blend in flour; add catsup, wine, and Worcestershire sauce; cook, stirring constantly, until mixture boils. Just before serving, add oysters; heat gently just to boiling point. Do not allow sauce to continue to boil. Place toast rounds on warm plates (salad or dessert size); arrange oysters on toast; spoon sauce over them. Garnish with watercress or parsley and serve at once. Serves 6. P. S. This also makes a very good supper main dish for four people. Serve it on toast or toasted English muffins. Crisp bacon is a good companion on the plate.

Roast Rack of Lamb

To serve 6, you will need 2 racks of lamb (each 7 or 8 ribs, weighing about 2 pounds). Ask your meat dealer to trim them so that ends of rib bones are exposed. Have meat at room temperature when you're ready to put it in the oven. Score fat surface lightly with the tip of a sharp knife; rub with a cut clove of garlic, if you like. Place meat, fat side up, on a rack in a shallow baking pan. If you're using a meat thermometer, insert it in the fleshiest part, making sure tip does not touch bone. Roast in a very hot oven (450°F.) for 15 minutes. Reduce heat to 350°F. and continue roasting for 40 to 50 minutes (160° to 165°F. on a meat thermometer) if you like your lamb slightly rare; allow a few minutes longer (170° to 175°F.) if you prefer it better done. Remove from oven and let stand 5 minutes or so before serving. Serve on a heated platter, with bunches of watercress or parsley for garnish. (You can doll up the rib bones with those little paper chop frills, if you like.) Pass *Currant Sauce Piquant* (below). Wine choice: California Cabernet Sauvignon.

Currant Sauce Piquant

1 (10¾-oz.) can beef gravy
½ cup red currant jelly
1½ tablespoons butter
⅓ cup California Red Table Wine
¼ cup catsup
   Bit of chopped or pressed garlic, if you like
1 teaspoon Worcestershire sauce
1 teaspoon *each:* parsley flakes and dry shredded
   green onions
   Seasoned salt to taste

Combine all ingredients in a saucepan. Place over medium heat and stir frequently until jelly and butter melt and ingredients are well blended. Serve piping hot. Makes about 2 cups.

Baked Barley with Mushrooms

6 tablespoons butter
1⅓ cups pearl barley
1 (4-oz.) can mushroom stems and pieces
1 (10½-oz.) can condensed onion soup
½ cup California White Table Wine or
 Dry Vermouth
 Seasoned salt and pepper to taste
2 cups finely diced celery
2 tablespoons parsley flakes

Melt 4 tablespoons of the butter in a 10-inch skillet; add barley and sauté until it's a nice golden brown, stirring frequently. Drain mushrooms, reserving liquid. Mix mushroom liquid, onion soup, and wine; add boiling water to make 4 cups; season to taste. Add this liquid to barley; stir well; bring to a boil. Pour into a 2-quart casserole; cover tightly. Bake in a moderate oven (350°F.) for 1 hour. Meantime, sauté celery in remaining 2 tablespoons butter for 5 minutes. Add to barley at end of 1 hour baking period, along with mushrooms and parsley, mixing lightly with a fork. Cover; continue baking another 10 to 15 minutes, or until barley is tender and all liquid is absorbed. Taste; add more salt and pepper, if needed. Serves 6.

Artichoke Bottoms Filled with Creamed Spinach

12 canned artichoke bottoms (about 2 inches in
  diameter) rinsed and drained
1 (10-oz.) package frozen chopped spinach
1 (3-oz.) package cream cheese
1 teaspoon dry shredded green onions
 Dash of nutmeg, salt and pepper to taste
 Parmesan cheese and paprika

Arrange artichoke bottoms, cup-side up, in a greased shallow baking dish. Cook spinach and drain *thoroughly*. Mix spinach, cream cheese, onions, nutmeg, seasoned salt, and pepper. Spoon mixture into artichokes; sprinkle with Parmesan cheese and paprika. Bake in a moderate oven (350°F.) about 15 minutes, or until thoroughly heated. Serves 6.

Masquerade Pie

1 envelope unflavored gelatin
¼ cup cold water
1 cup sugar
4 teaspoons cornstarch
¼ teaspoon salt
4 eggs, separated
1½ cups milk, scalded
½ cup California Sweet Sherry

2 (1-oz.) squares unsweetened chocolate,
  melted over hot water
1 (9-inch) baked pastry shell (with *high* fluted rim)
⅛ teaspoon cream of tartar
¼ teaspoon almond extract
¾ cup heavy cream, whipped
 Shaved unsweetened chocolate for garnish

Soften gelatin in the cold water. Mix ½ cup sugar, cornstarch, and salt. Beat egg yolks well in the top of a double boiler; gradually stir in scalded milk, then the sugar mixture. Cook over hot water, stirring occasionally until mixture coats a metal spoon. Remove pan from water. Add softened gelatin and stir until dissolved. Add wine. Take out half of this custard mixture; add melted chocolate; pour into pie shell. Cool remaining half at room temperature. Beat egg whites until frothy; beat in cream of tartar; gradually add ½ cup sugar, beating until whites stand in soft peaks. Fold into custard; add almond extract; spoon over chocolate layer. Chill until firm. Before serving, spread whipped cream over top of pie and sprinkle with shaved chocolate. Wine choice: California Cream Sherry.

Timing Tips for the Hostess-Cook

Oysters Henriette: Early in the day, prepare toast rounds and sauce. Place toast rounds on a baking sheet; cover loosely with aluminum foil. Shortly before dinner, warm toast rounds *briefly* in the oven; reheat sauce. Heat oysters in sauce just before serving.

Roast Rack of Lamb: Don't forget to remove meat from refrigerator so it will be at room temperature when it goes into the oven.

Currant Sauce Piquant: Prepare early in the day. Reheat gently just before serving.

Baked Barley with Mushrooms: Sauté barley early in the day and set aside; measure the 4 cups liquid; sauté the celery. About an hour before dinnertime, heat liquid to boiling and add to barley; bake dish as directed. Or, finish dish early in the day; to reheat, set the covered casserole in a shallow pan of hot water; bake about 30 minutes at 350°F.

Artichoke Bottoms with Creamed Spinach: Prepare spinach mixture and fill artichoke bottoms early in the day. Cover; refrigerate. Bring to room temperature before baking.

Masquerade Pie: Prepare the day before. Top with whipped cream and shaved chocolate just before serving.

DINNER

Avocado Crabmeat Cocktail Salad*
Cheese Crisps*
Beef Romanoff*
Asparagus or Broccoli with Lemon-Butter Sauce*
Creamy Noodle Casserole*
Chocolate Angel Refrigerator Cake*

With this menu we enjoy the indicated
California Wines

Avocado Crabmeat Cocktail Salad

1¼ cups catsup
¼ cup California Dry or Medium Sherry or
    Dry Vermouth
¼ cup salad oil
1 tablespoon lemon juice
1 teaspoon each: grated onion, Worcestershire
    sauce, and prepared horseradish
3 cups cooked or canned crabmeat
    (or small shrimp)
1 cup finely cut celery
4 small avocados
    Lemon wedges

Mix catsup, wine, oil, lemon juice, onion, Worcestershire sauce, and horseradish. Combine this sauce with the crabmeat and celery. Cover; chill 1 hour or longer. At serving time, cut avocados lengthwise in halves; remove seed and peel. Place halves on lettuce-lined salad plates; fill cavities with crabmeat mixture. Garnish with lemon wedges. Serves 8.

Cheese Crisps

Cream together *well* ½ pound softened butter or margarine and ½ pound (2 cups) shredded sharp Cheddar cheese. Blend in ¾ cup yellow corn meal, 1¼ cups all-purpose flour, ¼ teaspoon seasoned salt, and ½ teaspoon Worcestershire sauce. Chill dough thoroughly. Take up bits of dough (1 level measuring teaspoonful at a time); roll into little balls; place on ungreased baking sheets. Flatten by pressing crisscross with wet fork. Bake in a slow oven (300°F.) about 30 minutes, or just until light golden brown. Remove from baking sheets immediately; sprinkle with Parmesan cheese and paprika. Cool. Store tightly covered. Makes about 100.

Beef Romanoff

3 pounds round steak, cut ½ inch thick
4 tablespoons each: butter and flour
1 (10¾-oz.) can condensed tomato soup
1 (10½-oz.) can condensed consommé
½ cup California Dry or Medium Sherry or
    Dry Vermouth
2 tablespoons instant minced onion
    Bit of chopped or pressed garlic (if you like)
1 (8-oz.) can mushroom stems and pieces, drained
1 teaspoon Worcestershire sauce
    Salt and pepper to taste
1 cup dairy sour cream
2 tablespoons parsley flakes
½ teaspoon paprika

Remove skin and fat from meat; cut meat across grain in strips about ½ inch wide and 2 inches long. Heat butter in a large, heavy skillet or a Dutch oven; add meat and cook, stirring frequently, until nicely browned. Sprinkle flour over meat; stir well. Add tomato soup, consommé, and wine; cook, stirring, until sauce boils and thickens. Add onion, garlic, drained mushrooms, Worcestershire sauce, salt, and pepper. Cover; simmer gently, stirring occasionally, for about 1½ hours, or until meat is fork-tender. If gravy thickens too much, add a little of the mushroom liquid. Before serving, stir in sour cream, parsley, and paprika; taste; add salt, if needed. Serves 8. Wine choice: California Zinfandel.

Asparagus or Broccoli with Lemon-Butter Sauce

Melt ½ cup butter in a skillet; stir in 2 teaspoons lemon juice, 1 tablespoon parsley flakes, 2 teaspoons dry shredded green onions, and a dash of salt. Spoon mixture over hot, cooked asparagus or broccoli just before serving. Plenty for 8 servings.

Creamy Noodle Casserole

8 ounces wide noodles
½ pint (1 cup) large-curd cottage cheese (chive or plain)
½ pint (1 cup) dairy sour cream
1 (10½-oz.) can condensed cream of chicken soup
2 tablespoons California Dry or Medium Sherry
1 tablespoon parsley flakes
2 teaspoons dry shredded green onions
2 teaspoons Worcestershire sauce
Seasoned salt, garlic salt, and pepper to taste
¼ cup grated Parmesan cheese
Paprika

Cook noodles in boiling salted water *just* until tender; drain. Mix all remaining ingredients except Parmesan cheese and paprika; add noodles. Spread mixture in a greased 12 by 8 by 2-inch baking dish; sprinkle with Parmesan cheese and paprika. Cover dish loosely with foil. Bake in a moderate oven (350° F.) for 25 minutes. Uncover; continue baking 15 minutes. Remove from oven and let settle 5 minutes or so before serving. Serves 8.

Chocolate Angel Refrigerator Cake

1 envelope (1 tablespoon) unflavored gelatin
¼ cup Kahlua or Tia Maria, or California Sweet Sherry
6 eggs
1½ cups sugar
¾ cup milk
Dash of salt
2 (1-oz.) squares unsweetened chocolate, melted
1 teaspoon vanilla
1 homemade or bakery angel food cake (baked in a 10 by 4-inch tube pan)
1½ cups heavy cream, whipped
Additional unsweetened chocolate, shaved, for garnish

Soften gelatin in the Kahlua, Tia Maria, or Sherry. Beat egg yolks slightly in the top of a double boiler; stir in ¾ cup of the sugar, the milk, and salt; cook, stirring frequently, over hot (not boiling) water for about 10 minutes, or until mixture thickens. Add softened gelatin; stir until dissolved. Blend in melted chocolate and vanilla. Cool thoroughly. Beat egg whites stiff; gradually beat in remaining sugar; fold gently but thoroughly into egg yolk mixture. Tear cake into good-sized pieces; place in a large bowl. Add chocolate mixture; mix lightly but well. Pack into a 10 by 4-inch tube pan that has been rinsed with cold water. Chill several hours or overnight. Unmold on a large platter; frost with the whipped cream and sprinkle all over with the shaved chocolate. Serves 8 to 10. Wine choice: California Cream Sherry.

Timing Tips for the Hostess-Cook

Avocado Crabmeat Cocktail Salad: Prepare crabmeat mixture early in the day and get the lettuce ready; refrigerate. Shortly before the guests arrive, prepare the avocado half shells; brush with lemon juice to prevent darkening; refrigerate. Put the salad plates in the refrigerator to chill. Assemble salad just before serving.

Cheese Crisps: These can be made several days ahead. Store in a tin or large jar with a tight-fitting lid.

Beef Romanoff: Prepare early in the day, but don't add the sour cream until time to reheat *gently* before serving.

Asparagus or Broccoli with Lemon-Butter Sauce: Prepare sauce early in the day; leave in skillet; reheat before serving. If you're using fresh asparagus or broccoli, wash and trim it early in the day; refrigerate. Cook vegetable (fresh or frozen) just before serving.

Creamy Noodle Casserole: Prepare early in the day; refrigerate. Bring to room temperature and bake before serving.

Chocolate Angel Refrigerator Cake: Prepare cake-chocolate mixture the day before; pack into tube pan; chill. Unmold, frost, and garnish the afternoon of the party; refrigerate until time to serve.

DINNER

Mushroom Consommé Imperial*
Herb Toasties*
Roast Prime Ribs of Beef*
with Brown Gravy*
Yorkshire Pudding* or Green Onion Tart*
Celery Hearts Parmesan*
Cheese Tray
including
Trio Cheese*
Crackers & Melba Toast

With this menu we enjoy the indicated

California Wines

Mushroom Consommé Imperial

1 (6-oz.) can chopped broiled mushrooms
1 (10½-oz.) can condensed consommé
1 (10½-oz.) can condensed bouillon
⅔ cup water
2 slices lemon
6 whole cloves
6 tablespoons California Dry or Medium Sherry
  Salt and pepper to taste
  Sour cream and paprika for garnishing

Drain mushrooms, reserving liquid. In a saucepan, combine mushroom liquid, consommé, bouillon, water, lemon, and cloves; heat to boiling; simmer 5 minutes; strain. Reheat; add mushrooms, Sherry, salt, and pepper. Pour piping hot into bouillon cups; top with a spoonful of sour cream and a dusting of paprika. Serve at once. Serves 6. Wine choice: California Dry Sherry.

Herb Toasties

Spread packaged melba toast rounds evenly with butter; place on baking sheet; sprinkle lightly with mixed Italian seasoning. Bake in a moderate oven (350°F.) for 5 minutes. Serve warm or cold, with soups and salads or as an hors d'oeuvre. For *Herb-Cheese Toasties,* sprinkle with Italian seasoning, then with grated Parmesan cheese.

When I first heard about this unorthodox and relaxed way of cooking roast beef, I was skeptical. However, it produces an ideal "middle of the road" doneness. If you enjoy pink-rare beef, give the recipe a try. If you prefer your meat otherwise, follow the rest of the menu, but do the roast your way.

Roast Prime Ribs of Beef

To serve 6, select a 3-rib roast (*not* boned). Start it cooking in the afternoon, 3 to 5 hours before you plan to serve it. Have the meat at room temperature. Preheat the oven to moderately hot (375°F.). Place the roast, fat side up, in a shallow pan. Put it in the preheated oven and cook it *exactly* 1 hour. At the end of the hour, turn off the oven, leaving the roast inside. *Do not open the oven door at any time!* (I Scotch-tape a note to the oven door to remind myself and everybody else in the house about this vital point.) Let the roast remain in the oven and forget about it (if you can forget anything that sends forth such a delicious aroma) until about 1¼ hours before it is to be carved. At this magic moment, turn the oven to 300°F. and let the roast stay in exactly 45 minutes. *Remember:* Don't open the door! At the end of the 45 minutes, take the roast out and put it on a carving board or platter to rest while you make *Brown Gravy* (below), and bake the *Yorkshire Pudding* or *Onion Tart*.

P.S. I'm told this method will work for any size roast; my own experience has been with 2 and 3-ribbers. The three "musts" are: bone in, meat at room temperature, *and* a mental padlock on the oven door! Wine choice: California Pinot Noir.

Brown Gravy: After you take the roast out of the pan, pour off all the fat. (You'll need some of it if you plan to make *Yorkshire Pudding*.) Pour ¼ cup California Red Table Wine into the pan; set over low heat while you stir and scrape the bottom of the pan to capture any little crusty brown bits. Pour wine into a saucepan; add 2 (10¾-oz.) cans brown gravy, ½ teaspoon Worcestershire sauce, and seasoned salt and pepper to taste; simmer 5 minutes or so. Serve gravy very hot with the roast.

Yorkshire Pudding

Preheat oven to 450°F. Mix 1½ cups sifted all-purpose flour and ¾ teaspoon salt. Combine 3 well-beaten eggs and 1½ cups milk; add gradually to flour, beating just until smooth. Pour 3 tablespoons beef drippings (or a mixture of butter and bacon drippings) into *each* of 2 (9-inch) pie plates; heat sizzling hot in the oven. Pour half of batter into each hot pie plate; put immediately into the 450°F. oven and bake for 25 to 30 minutes, or until puffed and brown. To serve, cut in pie-shaped wedges. Serves 6.

Green Onion Tart

 1 cup prepared biscuit mix
⅓ cup milk
 2 cups thinly sliced green onions, including
    some of the green tops (4 bunches)
 2 tablespoons butter
 2 tablespoons California Dry Vermouth or Dry or
    Medium Sherry
 1 (8-oz.) package cream cheese (at room
    temperature)
½ cup milk
 2 large eggs, slightly beaten
 1 teaspoon Worcestershire sauce
½ teaspoon seasoned salt
    Paprika

Combine biscuit mix and milk according to package directions. Roll or pat out thin on a lightly floured board to fit over bottom and sides of a 9-inch pie plate (not over rim). Melt butter in a skillet or saucepan; add wine and onions; sauté, stirring frequently, until onions are wilted and bright green. With a fork, blend cream cheese, milk, and eggs together, then beat with a rotary beater until mixture is smooth. Stir in Worcestershire sauce and seasoned salt. Spread onions over bottom of biscuit shell; spoon cheese mixture over them. Dust with paprika. Bake in a moderate oven (350°F.) for 35 minutes, or until a knife inserted near the center comes out clean. Remove from oven and let stand 10 minutes or so before cutting. Makes 1 (9-inch) tart. P. S. This tart also makes a good light main dish, with a salad and slices of Canadian bacon or strips of crisp bacon. A baked 9-inch pastry shell can be substituted for the biscuit shell, if you like.

Celery Hearts Parmesan

To serve 6, drain 2 (1-lb.) cans celery hearts. Arrange hearts, cut side up, in a single layer in a greased shallow baking dish. Spread *generously* with softened butter, then sprinkle *generously* with grated Parmesan cheese. Season with salt, pepper, and paprika. Cover dish loosely with aluminum foil. Bake in a very hot oven (450°F.) about 10 minutes (or longer in a slower oven) to heat the hearts thoroughly and melt the cheese.

Trio Cheese

Have at room temperature: ½ pound shredded Cheddar cheese, ¼ pound crumbled blue cheese, and 1 (3-oz.) package cream cheese. Place cheeses in a bowl; blend well with a fork. Gradually beat in ¼ cup California Dry Vermouth or Dry or Medium Sherry. Add ½ teaspoon *each:* Worcestershire sauce and paprika, and salt and cayenne to taste. Beat until smooth and creamy. Makes about 2¼ cups. Wine choice: California Port. This is an excellent keeper. Store it, covered, in the refrigerator, then bring to room temperature before serving.

Timing Tips for the Hostess-Cook

Mushroom Consommé Imperial: Prepare early in the day; reheat just before serving.

Roast Prime Ribs of Beef: Be sure to have the meat at room temperature when it goes into the oven.

Brown Gravy: Early in the day, combine all ingredients except wine in a saucepan. After roast is out of the oven, deglaze the pan with the wine as directed; add wine to contents of saucepan and heat.

Yorkshire Pudding: Shortly before guests arrive, mix pudding batter; cover and refrigerate. Just before baking time, beat briefly again, then pour into the heated pie plates.

Onion Tart: Early in the day, prepare biscuit shell and fit into pie plate; sauté onions and set aside; blend cream cheese with milk, eggs, etc., and refrigerate. Before baking the tart, bring cream cheese mixture to room temperature. At oven time, put onions in biscuit shell; pour cheese mixture over them and dust with paprika.

Celery Hearts Parmesan: Prepare early in the day; cover with foil; refrigerate. Bring to room temperature before baking.

Trio Cheese: Tastes even more delicious if made a day or more ahead. Cover and refrigerate. Bring to room temperature before serving.

DINNER

Tomato Shrimp Appetizer, Green Goddess*
Braised Stuffed Pork Chops*
Butter-Baked Mushrooms*
Gnocchi Parmesan*
Pickled Peaches
Heavenly Torte*

With this menu we enjoy the indicated

California Wines

Tomato Shrimp Appetizer, Green Goddess

1 cup mayonnaise
1 tablespoon anchovy paste
2 tablespoons cream or evaporated milk
2 tablespoons California tarragon wine
   vinegar
1 teaspoon lemon juice
1 tablespoon parsley flakes
1 teaspoon dry shredded green onions
   Chopped or pressed garlic to taste
4 medium-sized tomatoes, peeled and chilled
16 canned artichoke hearts, rinsed, halved,
   and chilled
1 cup small cooked or canned shrimp
   Salad greens, washed and chilled (I use
   butter lettuce)
2 hard-cooked eggs, sieved or shredded
   Paprika

Blend mayonnaise and anchovy paste; add cream, vinegar, lemon juice, parsley, onions, and garlic; mix well; chill thoroughly. To assemble salad: Halve tomatoes crosswise; place a half, cut side up, on a lettuce-lined individual salad plate. Top tomato with 4 artichoke halves; arrange shrimp over artichokes. Just before serving, spoon some of the dressing over each salad; sprinkle with hard-cooked egg and dust with paprika. Serves 8. Crabmeat is also good in this salad in place of the shrimp.

Braised Stuffed Pork Chops

8 pork chops, cut about 1¼ inches thick
3 cups (firmly packed) fine, soft bread crumbs
⅔ cup seedless raisins, rinsed with boiling water
   and drained
1 medium-sized onion, minced
6 tablespoons melted butter
½ teaspoon poultry seasoning
   Salt and pepper to taste
   Flour
1 cup each California White Table Wine and
   chicken or beef stock
1 tablespoon parsley flakes

Have chops slit from fat side to bone to form a pocket. Mix bread crumbs, raisins, onion, butter, poultry seasoning, salt, and pepper; stuff into pockets of pork chops; fasten openings securely with skewers or toothpicks. Dredge chops with flour; brown nicely on both sides in a heavy skillet, using a bit of fat trimmed from the chops. Add wine and stock; cover tightly and simmer gently for about 1 and ¼ hours, or until chops are tender, turning and basting occasionally. Remove chops to a heated platter. Blend ¼ cup flour with 1 cup cold water; stir into drippings in skillet; cook, stirring, until mixture boils and thickens. (Add a little more water if gravy seems too thick.) Taste and correct seasoning; add parsley. Pour gravy over chops or pass separately. Serves 8. Wine choice: California Rosé.

Butter-Baked Mushrooms

Scrub 1½ pounds medium-sized mushrooms gently and remove stems; place, stem side up, in one or more shallow baking dishes. In a saucepan combine ½ cup (¼ pound) butter, 2 chicken bouillon cubes, ½ cup water, ¼ cup California Dry Vermouth, 1 tablespoon parsley flakes, 1 teaspoon dry shredded green onions, and a dash *each* of thyme, marjoram, and pepper. Heat, stirring often, until butter melts and bouillon cubes are completely dissolved; spoon mixture over mushrooms. Cover baking dish (or dishes) loosely with foil. Bake in a moderate oven (350°F.) for 45 minutes, basting occasionally. Serves 8 in this menu, perhaps fewer if the dinner is less hearty. These are wonderful with steak... hamburger or filet!

Gnocchi Parmesan

Mix 1½ cups white corn meal, 2½ teaspoons salt, and 1½ cups cold water. In a saucepan heat 1½ cups water and 3 cups milk to boiling; gradually stir in the moistened corn meal; cook slowly, stirring almost constantly, for 5 minutes. Remove from heat; blend in 3 well-beaten eggs. Spread half of mixture in a well-greased 12 by 8 by 2-inch baking dish; sprinkle with 3 tablespoons melted butter and ⅓ cup grated Parmesan cheese. Repeat with remaining corn meal mixture, another 3 tablespoons melted butter, and another ⅓ cup grated Parmesan cheese. Dust with paprika. Bake in a moderate oven (350°F.) for 45 minutes. Serves 8.

Heavenly Torte

3 eggs
1 cup sugar
   Dash of salt
1 teaspoon vanilla
1 (5¾-oz.) package zwieback, crushed
1 teaspoon baking powder
1 cup finely chopped walnuts or pecans

Beat eggs until thick and lemon-colored; gradually beat in sugar; add salt and vanilla. Mix zwieback crumbs, baking powder, and nuts; add to egg mixture, stirring until well blended. Pour into 2 (9-inch) layer cake tins that have been greased, lined with waxed paper, and greased again. Bake in a moderately hot oven (375°F.) for 25 minutes. Let cool slightly, then turn out on a wire rack and peel off paper. Cool thoroughly. Prepare filling as follows:

1 envelope (1 tablespoon) unflavored gelatin
2 tablespoons cold water
¾ cup hot, strong coffee
¾ cup sugar
   Dash of salt
1 pint heavy cream, whipped

Soften gelatin in cold water; dissolve in hot coffee. (Or, dissolve in ¾ cup hot water and add 1 heaping teaspoon instant coffee.) Add sugar and salt; stir until dissolved. Cool, then chill. When mixture begins to thicken, fold in whipped cream.

To assemble the torte: Spread half of filling between layers and remainder over top. Garnish with a few walnut or pecan halves. Chill several hours or overnight before serving. Serves 8. Wine choice: California Sweet Sauterne.

Timing Tips for the Hostess-Cook

Tomato Shrimp Appetizer, Green Goddess: Prepare the dressing early in the day; chill. Also peel the tomatoes; rinse and halve the artichoke hearts; chill. Chill the shrimp. Wash and chill the salad greens. Hard-cook the eggs; chill. If refrigerator space permits, assemble the salads on individual plates shortly before guests arrive, chill, and then spoon the dressing over them and garnish just before serving. Otherwise, assemble and dress the salads on chilled plates just before serving.

Braised Stuffed Pork Chops: Early in the day, stuff and cook the chops. Remove cooked chops from pan; set aside. Make the gravy. Before serving, reheat chops in the gravy, adding a little water if gravy needs thinning.

Butter-Baked Mushrooms: Wash and de-stem mushrooms early in the day; place in baking dish; cover with foil and refrigerate. Make butter sauce early in the day. At baking time, reheat sauce and pour over mushrooms.

Gnocchi Parmesan: Prepare early in the day; refrigerate. Bring to room temperature before baking.

Heavenly Torte: Prepare the day before the party; refrigerate.

DINNER

Mushroom Canapé Belleview*
Sole with Crabmeat Mephisto*
Spinach Soufflé
(use the frozen)
Shoestring Potatoes
(use the canned)
Crisp Celery Hearts & Cherry Tomatoes
Coconut Bavarian Cream*
with
Almond Butterscotch Sauce*

With this menu we enjoy the indicated

California Wines

Mushroom Canapé Belleview

8 (3-inch) rounds of white bread
    Butter
1 (4¾-oz.) can liver pâté
1 hard-cooked egg
1 pound fresh mushrooms
2 tablespoons flour
1 cup canned chicken broth or consommé
¼ cup California Dry or Medium Sherry or
    White Table Wine
1 tablespoon parsley flakes
1 teaspoon dry shredded green onions
    Dash each of thyme and marjoram
    Salt and pepper to taste
    Paprika
    Sprigs of watercress or parsley for garnishing

Spread both sides of bread rounds rather generously with butter. Place on a baking sheet; bake in a slow oven (300°F.) until crisp and light golden brown. (Watch carefully lest they get *too* brown.) Blend liver pâté with hard-cooked egg yolk; sieve or shred hard-cooked egg white. Scrub mushrooms gently; remove stems; chop mushrooms coarsely. Melt 4 tablespoons butter in a skillet; add mushrooms; cover and sauté over medium heat, stirring frequently, for 5 minutes. Uncover; sauté 5 minutes longer, or until mixture is no longer juicy. Stir in flour; add chicken broth and wine; cook, stirring, until mixture bubbles and thickens; continue cooking and stirring for another minute or two. Add parsley, onions, and seasonings. To assemble canapés: Spread each toast round with some of the pâté mixture; place on warm plates (salad or dessert size). Spoon piping hot mushroom mixture over toast rounds; sprinkle with egg white and paprika. Garnish with watercress or parsley; serve at once. Serves 8. Wine choice: California Dry Sherry. Most of the preparation for this canapé can be done well ahead of time, so it's not the last-minute dish that it may appear to be at first reading. (See "Timing Tips" on page 113.)

Sole with Crabmeat Mephisto

3 to 3¼ pounds fillets of sole
3 tablespoons butter
3 tablespoons flour
¾ cup rich milk
¾ cup mayonnaise
3 tablespoons California Dry or Medium
    Sherry or Dry Vermouth
2 teaspoons dry shredded green onions
1 teaspoon grated lemon peel
1½ teaspoons Worcestershire sauce
½ teaspoon prepared mustard
    Salt and pepper to taste
1½ pounds cooked or canned crabmeat
    Melted butter
    Grated Parmesan cheese and paprika

Divide sole into 16 even portions. Arrange 8 of these in 8 shallow individual baking dishes (or in two 12 by 8 by 2-inch baking dishes). Melt butter and stir in flour; gradually add milk and cook, stirring constantly, until mixture boils and thickens. Remove from heat. Blend in mayonnaise; add wine, onions, lemon peel, Worcestershire sauce, mustard, salt, and pepper; add crabmeat. Spread over sole in dishes; cover with remaining fillets. Brush with melted butter; sprinkle with Parmesan cheese. Bake in a hot oven (400°F.) for 20 minutes. Remove from oven; dust with paprika. Let settle a few minutes before serving. Serves 8. Wine choice: Pinot Chardonnay.

Here's a rich and luscious creation that wasn't designed for weight-watchers. But show me a truly partified dessert that was!

Coconut Bavarian Cream

1½ envelopes (1½ tablespoons) unflavored gelatin
⅓ cup cold water
1¼ cups milk, scalded
¾ cup sugar
  Dash of salt
⅓ cup California Sweet Sherry
2 cups flaked coconut
1 teaspoon lemon juice
1 cup heavy cream, whipped

Soften gelatin in the cold water; dissolve in the hot milk. Add sugar and salt; stir to dissolve. Add wine. Cool, then chill. When mixture begins to thicken, stir in coconut and lemon juice, then fold in whipped cream. Pour into a mold; chill until firm. Unmold and serve with *Almond Butterscotch Sauce* (below). Serves 8. Wine choice: California Sweet Sherry.

Here's a butterscotch sauce that is not only good in this menu but also shines as a sundae topping. It's excellent over vanilla, toasted almond, maple-nut, butter brickle, or coffee ice cream.

Almond Butterscotch Sauce

¾ cup white corn syrup
¾ cup (firmly packed) brown sugar
⅓ cup California Medium Sherry
2 tablespoons cream
2 tablespoons butter
  Dash of salt
½ cup slivered, toasted almonds

Combine all ingredients except nuts in a saucepan; bring to a boil, then simmer, uncovered, for 10 minutes, stirring frequently. Remove from heat. Add nuts. Cool to room temperature (1 hour or longer) before serving. Stir well to distribute nuts evenly before spooning over *Coconut Bavarian Cream* or ice cream. Makes about 1⅔ cups. Leftover sauce may be stored in the refrigerator; set container in a pan of warm water to bring to proper consistency before serving.

P. S. Another topping that makes a good alternate for *Almond Butterscotch Sauce* here is bottled coconut syrup, thinned with a little California Medium Sherry. If you use this, you can pass a bowl of chopped walnuts or pecans to be sprinkled atop the dessert.

Timing Tips for the Hostess-Cook

Mushroom Canapé Belleview: Early in the day, prepare toast rounds, pâté mixture, sieved egg white, and mushroom mixture. Wash and chill watercress or parsley. Before guests arrive, spread toast rounds with pâté mixture; place on baking sheet; cover loosely with aluminum foil. About 5 minutes before dinner, place covered baking sheet in a slow oven to heat toast rounds; heat mushroom mixture to simmering, adding a little chicken broth if it seems to need thinning. Warm the plates and assemble canapés just before serving.

Sole with Crabmeat Mephisto: Prepare early in the day; cover and refrigerate. Bring to room temperature before baking. Don't forget to allow time for that brief "rest" period before serving.

Spinach Soufflé: Nothing to worry the hostess here. Use frozen spinach soufflé and bake as directed. If you have little individual soufflé dishes, you can thaw the frozen soufflé enough so that it can be spooned into them before baking; or, you can bake it in the foil containers in which it comes and then serve it in the little soufflé dishes.

Shoestring Potatoes: Another carefree item on the menu! It's nice (but not essential) to warm these *very* briefly in the oven before serving.

Coconut Bavarian Cream: Prepare early in the day, or the day before.

Almond Butterscotch Sauce: Prepare early in the day, or the day before. Before serving, warm to proper consistency as the recipe directs.

DINNER

Pâté Maison*
with
Sourdough French Bread and Melba Toast
Roast Rock Cornish Game Hens
with
Grape Stuffing*
Mushroom Rice* **Green Beans**
Crème de Menthe Mousse*

With this menu we enjoy the indicated
California Wines

For years I was content to leave baked pâtés to the chefs in good French restaurants, thinking that they were too complex and time-consuming for a place in my culinary repertoire. Then I fell heir to this recipe for a handsome aspic-coated pâté loaf, and found I could achieve a flavorsome "specialty of the house" with no trouble at all. Here it is featured as the first course of our dinner, but it also makes a fine hors d'oeuvre and a good main dish for an al fresco luncheon.

Pâté Maison

1 pound rather lean pork, ground twice
1 pound chicken livers, cut as fine as possible
  with sharp scissors
1 egg, well beaten
¼ cup California Brandy (or Bourbon, if you prefer)
1 teaspoon salt
⅛ teaspoon allspice
3 strips thick bacon
2 envelopes (2 tablespoons) unflavored gelatin
2 (10½-oz.) cans condensed consommé
  Watercress or small lettuce leaves for garnishing

Mix together pork, chicken livers, egg, Brandy, salt, and allspice. Pack mixture into a round 1-quart Pyrex casserole. Cover top completely with bacon, cutting strips as necessary to fit. (You may have part of a strip left over.) Cover casserole; set in a shallow pan of hot water; bake in a moderate oven (350°F.) for 2 hours. Remove casserole from water; let stand 5 to 10 minutes, then carefully pour off any liquid that remains and turn loaf out onto a platter. While pâté is cooling, wash casserole thoroughly and prepare the aspic coating: Soften gelatin in 1 cup of the consommé for 5 minutes; stir over medium heat until gelatin is dissolved. Remove from heat; stir in remaining consommé. Pour ½ cup of this mixture over bottom of casserole; chill until firm. Leave remainder of gelatin mixture at room temperature. When pâté is completely cold, replace it in the casserole on top of the firm layer of gelatin; refrigerate. Now (and no earlier) chill remaining gelatin mixture *just* until it's the consistency of unbeaten egg white; remove casserole from refrigerator and pour enough of the syrupy gelatin mixture over the pâté to fill casserole to the brim; chill until gelatin is very firm. Pour any extra syrupy gelatin into a small, shallow dish; chill until very firm. About half an hour before serving the pâté, unmold it and leave at room temperature to take off the chill. Unmold the little extra round of firm gelatin; chop it finely with a sharp knife; refrigerate. To serve, cut loaf in wedges with a very sharp knife; place wedges on individual salad plates; garnish with watercress or small lettuce leaves and some of the chopped aspic. Pass thinly sliced sourdough French bread and melba toast. Serves 16 or more, so you'll have some left to enjoy later. Refrigerate, covered, in the casserole. Wine choice: California Dry Sherry.

P. S. If you prefer to slice the pâté at the table, unmold it on a platter; garnish with chopped aspic and watercress or lettuce.

Roast Rock Cornish Game Hens with Grape Stuffing

8 (1-lb. 6-oz.) Rock Cornish game hens
½ cup butter
3 cups broth from giblets (or canned chicken broth)
1 (8-oz.) package bread stuffing
1 cup halved seedless grapes
   Salt and pepper
8 slices bacon, halved crosswise
2 cups California White Table Wine

Remove giblets from game hens; cook in seasoned water (with onion, celery, etc.) to make the 3 cups broth for the stuffing and basting, if desired. Prepare stuffing: In a saucepan heat butter and 1 cup broth together until butter melts; add stuffing mix; stir lightly with a fork to moisten crumbs; stir in grapes. Pack stuffing loosely into cavity of each bird; truss birds. Place birds in a shallow baking pan; sprinkle with salt and pepper; lay two bacon halves over each one. Roast in a very hot oven (450°F.) for 25 minutes. Reduce heat to 350°F.; pour wine and remaining 2 cups broth over birds; continue roasting for 45 to 50 minutes, or just until birds are tender, basting often with liquid in pan. When birds are tender, remove from oven, un-truss them, and place on a serving platter or a pan. Cover them loosely with aluminum foil and let them rest for 10 minutes or so before serving. Pour off all liquid from roasting pan into a pitcher or bowl; let stand a few minutes, then skim off as much fat as possible. Make gravy (below) to serve with the hens. Serves 8. Wine choice: California Johannisberg Riesling.

To make the gravy: In a saucepan mix 2 (10¾-oz.) cans chicken gravy and 1 can of beef gravy. Stir in ½ cup of the de-fatted pan drippings, 2 tablespoons California Dry or Medium Sherry, 2 tablespoons parsley flakes, and salt and pepper to taste. Heat piping hot. Spoon a little gravy over each bird when you serve them, and pass remainder separately. Sliced canned mushrooms or sautéed fresh ones can be added to the gravy, if you wish. (No, they won't interfere with the *Mushroom Rice;* they'll just enhance it.)

P. S. If you use smaller (about 14-oz.) birds, you can reduce the 350°F. baking period to 35 or 40 minutes. If you have stuffing left over, wrap it lightly in foil; bake along with the birds during the last 15 to 20 minutes they're in the oven.

Mushroom Rice

2 cups long-grain white rice
1½ pounds fresh mushrooms
4 tablespoons butter
   Salt to taste

Boil or steam rice until tender; drain, if necessary. Scrub mushrooms gently and remove tough portion of stems; put mushrooms through coarse blade of the food grinder. Melt butter in a large skillet; add mushrooms and sauté gently, uncovered for 5 minutes, stirring frequently. With a fork, lightly mix rice and mushrooms; add salt. Serve piping hot. Serves 8.

Crème de Menthe Mousse

¼ pound (16) marshmallows
⅔ cup green crème de menthe
1 pint heavy cream, whipped

Place marshmallows and crème de menthe in top of double boiler. Stir over boiling water until marshmallows are melted. Cool thoroughly, then fold into whipped cream. Pour into refrigerator freezing tray or a pan of similar size. Cover with foil; freeze until firm. Serves 8. This dessert may be served plain or topped with chocolate sauce, crème de cacao, or crème de menthe.

Timing Tips for the Hostess-Cook

Pâté Maison: Can be prepared several days before the party.

Roast Rock Cornish Game Hens with Grape Stuffing: Early in the day, make giblet broth; prepare stuffing; mix all ingredients for gravy except "juice of the bird." Stuff and truss birds shortly before roasting. Finish gravy and heat piping hot before serving.

Mushroom Rice: Prepare early in the day. Before serving, reheat in a double boiler. Or, turn into a covered casserole; set in a shallow pan of hot water; reheat at 350°F. about 30 minutes.

Green Beans: If you want to cook fresh or frozen beans before the guests arrive, drain them, reserving liquid, and let cool. Before serving, reheat with a little of the liquid and a generous pat of butter. Don't overcook!

Crème de Menthe Mousse: Prepare the day before.

DINNER

Caviar Eggs in Aspic*
Breast of Chicken Sans Souci*
Buttered Noodles
Summer Squash Cups with Peas*
Zabaglione Ring with Fruit*

With this menu we enjoy the indicated

California Wines

Caviar Eggs in Aspic

2 envelopes (2 tablespoons) unflavored gelatin
1 cup water
2 (10½-oz.) cans condensed consommé
2 tablespoons California Dry or Medium Sherry
  or Dry Vermouth
1 tablespoon lemon juice
  Salt to taste
4 large eggs, hard-cooked and chilled
1 (2-oz.) jar caviar
1 teaspoon dry shredded green onions
1 tablespoon (approximately) mayonnaise
  Watercress or butter lettuce,
  washed and chilled
  Paprika

Soften gelatin in the water for 5 minutes; stir over medium heat until gelatin is dissolved. Remove from heat; stir in consommé, wine, lemon juice, and salt. Spoon 2 tablespoons of this mixture into each of 8 well-oiled individual molds or custard cups; chill until very firm. Keep remaining gelatin mixture at room temperature. Cut eggs lengthwise in halves; remove yolks. Put some of the caviar in each egg white. Mash 2 of the yolks; blend in onions and just enough mayonnaise to make a spreadable mixture; carefully spread this over cavity of each egg white to seal in the caviar. Place filled egg whites, face down, on top of firm gelatin layer in molds; refrigerate. Now (and no earlier) chill remaining gelatin mixture just until it's the consistency of unbeaten egg white; spoon mixture into molds; chill until very firm. Grate or sieve remaining 2 egg yolks for garnish; cover and refrigerate. To serve, turn molds out on chilled salad plates lined with watercress or small lettuce leaves; spoon *Lemon Cream Mayonnaise* over molds; sprinkle with sieved egg yolk and paprika. Serves 8.

Lemon Cream Mayonnaise: Blend 1 cup mayonnaise with ¼ cup evaporated milk and 2 tablespoons lemon juice; add 1 teaspoon dry shredded green onions and salt to taste. Chill until serving time.

Breast of Chicken Sans Souci

3 tablespoons butter
3 tablespoons salad oil
4 large chicken breasts, boned and halved
5 tablespoons flour
2 cups canned chicken broth
3 (4-oz.) cans sliced mushrooms
⅓ cup California Dry or Medium Sherry or
  White Table Wine
1 tablespoon parsley flakes
1 teaspoon dry shredded green onions
  Thyme, paprika, seasoned salt, and pepper to taste
1 (14-oz.) can artichoke hearts, drained and
  halved or quartered
8 slices warm buttered toast, crusts removed
1 (3-oz.) can liver pâté
8 thin (but not *too* thin) sandwich-shaped slices
  boiled ham

Heat butter and oil in a large, heavy skillet; sauté chicken breasts, skin side down, just until golden. Turn chicken over; sauté just until meat is no longer pink. Remove chicken from skillet. Add flour to drippings and blend well; add chicken broth, liquid from mushrooms, and wine; cook, stirring, until mixture boils and thickens. Add parsley, onions, and seasonings. Return chicken to skillet with any juices that may have collected; cover; simmer gently for 30 to 45 minutes, or just until chicken is tender, turning and basting occasionally. Add mushrooms and artichoke hearts; heat thoroughly; taste and correct seasoning. To serve:

Spread each slice of toast with some of the pâté; place on heated dinner plates or in shallow individual baking dishes. Place a slice of ham, then a chicken breast on each piece of toast; spoon some of the artichoke hearts, mushrooms, and sauce over all. Serves 8. Wine choice: California Pinot Blanc.

Summer Squash Cups with Peas

Select 8 pattypan squashes, 3 to 3½ inches in diameter (1½ to 2 pounds). Scrub them; trim stem and blossom ends; cook whole in boiling salted water about 15 minutes, or just until tender. Drain, reserving liquid. When cool enough to handle, scoop out center of each squash to make a shell. (Save scooped-out portion for another meal; mash it with a fork, season to taste, and heat with a little cream or butter.) Shortly before serving, arrange squash shells in a single layer in a large skillet; moisten with a little of their cooking liquid; cover and reheat gently. (Or, reheat, covered, in a slow oven.) Cook 1 (10-oz.) package frozen petite peas as package directs; drain; add 1 tablespoon butter, 1 teaspoon dry shredded green onions, dash of thyme, and salt and pepper to taste. To serve, place squash shells on a platter or dinner plates; fill with peas. Serves 8.

Zabaglione Ring with Fruit

1 envelope (1 tablespoon) unflavored gelatin
⅓ cup cold water
4 eggs, yolks and whites separated
½ cup sugar
  Dash of salt
½ cup California Medium Sherry
2 teaspoons grated lemon peel
1 tablespoon lemon juice
  Fresh or well-drained canned fruit
  Berry pancake syrup
  Whipped cream

Soften gelatin in the cold water. Combine egg yolks, sugar, and salt in the top of a double boiler; beat with rotary beater until thick and lemon-colored. Gradually beat in Sherry. Cook, stirring, over hot (not boiling) water until mixture coats a metal spoon. Remove from heat. Add gelatin and stir until dissolved; add lemon peel and lemon juice. Chill, stirring occasionally, until mixture begins to thicken. Beat egg whites until stiff but not dry; fold in slightly thickened yolk mixture, blending gently

until no trace of egg white remains. Spoon into an oiled 8½-inch (5-cup) ring mold; chill until firm. Unmold on a platter; fill center and surround ring with fruit. Berries, sliced peaches or pears, diced pineapple...alone or in combination...are especially good. Pass a pitcher of berry syrup and a bowl of whipped cream to top the dessert. Serves 8. Wine choice: California Muscatel.

Timing Tips for the Hostess-Cook

Caviar Eggs in Aspic: Prepare molds and dressing early in the day or the day before. If refrigerator space permits, place molds on watercress or lettuce-lined plates shortly before guests arrive; dress and garnish just before serving. Otherwise, chill the plates ahead; assemble dish just before serving.

Breast of Chicken Sans Souci: Early in the day, sauté chicken breasts; make sauce; cook chicken until tender. Remove chicken from pan, cool, cover and refrigerate. Refrigerate cooled sauce. Prepare artichoke halves. Spread toast with liver pâté; arrange on a baking sheet; cover loosely with foil. Shortly before serving, place baking sheet, still loosely covered, in a slow oven for a few minutes to warm the toast. Reheat sauce, adding a little more chicken broth if it needs thinning; add chicken breasts, mushrooms, and artichokes.

Buttered Noodles: Cook noodles early in the day; drain, cover with cold water, refrigerate. Shortly before serving, drain noodles again. Melt butter, add noodles; toss over low heat until thoroughly hot.

Summer Squash Cups with Peas: Prepare and cook squash cups early in the day; cool, then cover and refrigerate. Reheat as directed in the recipe. If you cook the peas ahead, drain, reserving liquid; cover and chill. Just before serving, reheat with a little bit of their liquid, plus butter and seasonings.

Zabaglione Ring with Fruit: Prepare ring early in the day or the day before. Prepare fresh fruit as near to serving time as possible. Drain canned fruit early in the day; cover and refrigerate. Whip cream before guests arrive; cover and refrigerate.

DINNER

Hearts of Palm
with
Continental Dressing*
Roast Turkey Hickory Hill*
Creamed Chestnuts or Mushrooms*
in Spinach Mousse Ring*
Pickled Peaches   Cranberry Sauce
Frozen Date-Pecan Delight*

With this menu we enjoy the indicated
California Wines

Hearts of Palm with Continental Dressing

Chill 2 (14-oz.) cans hearts of palm thoroughly in the can. To assemble the salads, drain hearts of palm and cut lengthwise in strips or crosswise in ½-inch discs; arrange on 8 lettuce-lined salad plates. Garnish each salad with 2 peeled tomato quarters. Just before serving, spoon *Continental Dressing* (below) over all. Serves 8.

Continental Dressing: In a blender combine 1⅓ cups bottled Italian-style oil-vinegar dressing, 2 tablespoons California Dry Vermouth, 1 tablespoon lemon juice, 4 sliced green onions (white part only), several sprigs parsley, ¼ cup crumbled blue cheese, and 4 anchovy fillets, cut up. Blend until smooth. Pour into a pint jar; cover and chill. Shake well before using. Makes about 2 cups. This dressing is excellent with many mixed green and vegetable salads. Lacking a blender, you can chop the onions, parsley, and anchovies together *very* fine, crush the cheese with a little of the French dressing, and then combine all ingredients in a jar and shake well.

Roast Turkey Hickory Hill

1 (10 to 12-lb.) ready-to-cook turkey
  Melted butter or margarine
1 (4/5-qt.) bottle California White Table Wine

Rinse turkey with cold water; pat dry. Stuff the neck cavity lightly with *Hickory Hill Stuffing.* Pull neck skin over stuffing and skewer to back. Bring wing tips up and over back, shaping them "akimbo" fashion. Spoon stuffing *loosely* into body cavity. Shake bird to settle stuffing; do not pack it. (Leftover stuffing can be baked in the oven in a cov-ered 2-quart casserole.) Place skewers across body opening and lace shut with string. Tie drumsticks securely to tail. Place bird on a rack in a shallow pan, breast side up. If you're using a meat thermometer, insert it between thigh and body so that tip does not touch bone. Brush entire surface of bird with melted butter or margarine. Cover loosely with a clean piece of cheesecloth dipped in melted butter or margarine. Pour 1 cup of wine into pan. Roast in a slow oven (325°F.) about 4 to 4½ hours.

At the end of the first hour, add another ¾ cup wine to the pan and start basting the turkey. Continue basting every 15 or 20 minutes; add another ¾ cup wine at the end of the second hour, and the remaining wine at the end of the third hour. When turkey is about ⅔ done, cut away string holding drumsticks to tail, then continue roasting. For a browner bird, remove the cheesecloth ½ hour or so before end of cooking time. Turkey is done when meat thermometer registers 190°F.; fleshy part of drumstick should feel soft, and when drumstick is moved up and down, the joint should give readily. Remove skewers and string; place bird on a heated platter. Let stand at least 20 minutes before carving. Serve with *Giblet Gravy.* Serves approximately 10 to 12, with leftovers. Wine choice: California Dry Red or White Table Wine.

Hickory Hill Stuffing

1 (8-oz.) package *each:* herb-seasoned bread
  stuffing and corn bread stuffing
1½ cups water
1 cup (½ pound) butter or margarine
1 cup finely cut celery
¼ cup instant minced onion
1 cup pine nuts
2 tablespoons parsley flakes

Empty bags of stuffing into a large mixing bowl.
Heat water, butter, celery, and onion together until
butter melts; pour over stuffing; toss lightly with
fork until well mixed. Add pine nuts and parsley;
toss again. (*Note:* Stuffing may be made ahead, but
don't put it in the bird until just before roasting
time.)

Giblet Gravy: While turkey is cooking, place giz-
zard, heart, and neck in a saucepan; add 1 cup California White Table Wine, 3 cups boiling water,
1 stalk celery, 1 carrot, 2 or 3 slices onion, 1 bay
leaf, 3 or 4 peppercorns, dash of thyme, and 1 teaspoon salt. Cover and simmer about 2½ hours, or
until giblets are tender. Add liver, continue cooking
15 to 20 minutes. Drain, reserving liquid; chop giblets fine; discard neck.

When turkey is done, pour off drippings from roasting pan; let fat rise to the top, then skim it off. Add
liquid that remains to reserved giblet broth; add
water to make 4 cups liquid. Measure 6 tablespoons
of the fat into a saucepan; blend in 6 tablespoons
flour; add the reserved 4 cups liquid and cook, stirring constantly, until mixture boils and thickens.
Pour this gravy into the roasting pan; add chopped
giblets and salt and pepper to taste. Continue cooking gently for 5 minutes, stirring to capture any
little brown bits left in the roaster.

Creamed Chestnuts
or Mushrooms

¼ cup each: butter and flour
2 cups milk
2 chicken bouillon cubes
2 tablespoons California Dry or Medium Sherry
1 teaspoon dry shredded green onions
½ teaspoon Worcestershire sauce
  Dash of mace
  Seasoned salt and pepper to taste
1 (14-oz.) can water-packed chestnuts, drained
  and halved, *or* 2 (6-oz.) cans sliced broiled
  mushrooms, drained

Melt butter and stir in flour; add milk and bouillon
cubes; cook, stirring, until mixture is thickened
and smooth. Add Sherry and seasonings. Stir in
chestnuts or mushrooms; heat gently but thoroughly. Serve in center of *Spinach Mousse Ring*
(below). Serves 8.

Spinach Mousse Ring: Cook 2 (10-oz.) packages
frozen chopped spinach; drain *thoroughly.* Combine
with 2 cups (firmly packed) fine, soft bread crumbs,
2 cups milk, 4 slightly beaten eggs, ¼ cup melted
butter, 1 tablespoon grated onion, ¼ teaspoon nutmeg, and seasoned salt and pepper to taste; mix
well. Turn into a well-greased 9½-inch (1½-quart)
ring mold; set in a shallow pan of hot water. Bake
in a moderate oven (350°F.) 1 hour, or until firm.
Remove from water; let stand 5 minutes or so
before unmolding on a heated platter. Serves 8.

Frozen Date-Pecan Delight

Beat 2 eggs well; beat in ½ cup sugar, 3 tablespoons
flour, ¼ teaspoon salt, and 1 teaspoon vanilla; stir
in 1 cup finely cut dates and ½ cup chopped pecans.
Spread mixture in greased 9-inch square pan. Bake
in moderate oven (350°F.) 25 minutes. Cool thoroughly, then crumble with fingers. Place 1 quart
vanilla ice cream in a bowl; quickly stir in crumbled
mixture. Pour into refrigerator freezing tray, or pan
of similar size. Cover with foil; freeze until firm.
Serves 8. Wine choice: California Dry Champagne.

Timing Tips for the Hostess-Cook

Hearts of Palm with Continental Dressing: The
day before, put hearts of palm in refrigerator to
chill; prepare and chill dressing. Early on party day,
wash and chill lettuce; peel and chill tomatoes. If
there's refrigerator space, arrange salads on plates
shortly before guests arrive; chill. Otherwise, assemble them on chilled plates just before dinnertime.
Add dressing just before serving.

Roast Turkey Hickory Hill: Early in the day,
make giblet broth; prepare stuffing. Stuff bird just
before roasting. Time bird so it will be out of the
oven an hour or so before guests arrive, to give you
time to make gravy. Reheat gravy piping hot before
serving.

Creamed Chestnuts: Prepare early in the day;
reheat in double boiler.

Spinach Mousse Ring: Prepare mixture early in
the day. Just before baking, stir well and spoon into
mold.

Frozen Date-Pecan Delight: Prepare the day
before.

DINNER

Guacamole Molds*
Rolled Chicken Breasts
with
Mushroom Stuffing*
Risotto Rialto*
Buttered Asparagus Tips
Mincemeat Crêpes*

With this menu we enjoy the indicated
California Wines

Guacamole Molds

    2 (7¾-oz.) cans frozen guacamole (avocado dip)
    2 envelopes unflavored gelatin
    ½ cup cold water
    1 cup boiling water
    4 chicken bouillon cubes
    1 cup dairy sour cream
    ½ cup mayonnaise
    1 tablespoon lemon juice
    2 teaspoons dry shredded green onions
      Salt to taste
      Butter lettuce, washed and chilled
      Canned mandarin oranges and grapefruit
      sections for garnishing, or tomato quarters,
      if you prefer
      French dressing

Thaw guacamole according to directions on can. Soften gelatin in the cold water 5 minutes. Add boiling water and bouillon cubes; stir to dissolve gelatin and cubes; cool a bit. While gelatin mixture is cooling, blend guacamole, sour cream, and mayonnaise; stir in lemon juice, onions, and salt. Blend in gelatin mixture. Turn into 8 (½-cup) molds that have been rinsed with cold water; chill until firm. Unmold on lettuce-lined salad plates; garnish as desired. Spoon French dressing over each salad. Serves 8. P. S. For an excellent hors d'oeuvre, mold mixture in an 8½-inch (1¼-quart) ring mold; center with sprigs of parsley or watercress and surround with corn chips for spreading. For a small group, halve the recipe and use a 1-pint mold.

Rolled Chicken Breasts with Mushroom Stuffing

Have your meat dealer bone 8 good-sized chicken breasts. Remove skin; put each breast between two sheets of waxed paper; pound until flattened. Spread about ¼ cup *Mushroom Stuffing* (below) over each one; roll sides in toward center (to keep stuffing from escaping), then roll up from top to bottom. Place, seam down, in a shallow baking pan. Chill thoroughly (at least 1 hour). Brush chilled breasts with melted butter; sprinkle with salt, pepper, and paprika. Pour just enough white table wine into pan to cover bottom. Cover breasts loosely with aluminum foil. Bake in a moderate oven (350°F.) for 1 hour. To serve, place breasts on a heated platter or on dinner plates; spoon *Mushroom Sauce* over each; pass remainder of sauce. Serves 8. Wine choice: California Pinot Chardonnay.

Mushroom Stuffing:
    1 pound fresh mushrooms
    2 tablespoons butter
    2 green onions (white part only), finely cut
    4 teaspoons flour
    2 tablespoons *each:* California Sherry and
      canned condensed chicken broth
1½ small (2¼-oz.) cans deviled ham
    2 tablespoons grated Parmesan cheese
    1 teaspoon dry shredded green onions
    1 egg yolk, slightly beaten
      Dash of thyme
      Salt and pepper to taste

Scrub mushrooms gently; remove stems; chop mushrooms fine. Melt butter in a large skillet; sauté mushrooms and onions gently for 5 minutes, stirring frequently. Sprinkle with flour; mix well. Stir in Sherry and chicken broth; simmer a minute or two.

Add remaining ingredients; blend thoroughly. Cool, then chill thoroughly before spreading over chicken breasts.

Mushroom Sauce:

1 (6-oz.) can and 1 (3-oz.) can sliced
  broiled mushrooms
½ cup each: butter and flour
2 cups canned condensed chicken broth
1 cup California White Table Wine
¼ cup California Dry or Medium Sherry
1 tablespoon parsley flakes
1 teaspoon dry shredded green onions
½ teaspoon Worcestershire sauce
  Dash each of thyme and nutmeg
  Seasoned salt and pepper to taste

Drain mushrooms, reserving liquid. Melt butter and stir in flour; gradually add mushroom liquid, chicken broth, and wines; cook, stirring, until mixture is thickened and smooth. Simmer and stir for another minute or two. Add mushrooms and remaining ingredients. Serve piping hot.

Risotto Rialto

4 tablespoons butter
1½ cups uncooked long-grain white rice
1 medium-sized onion, finely chopped
⅛ teaspoon powdered saffron
½ cup California White Table Wine
2½ cups canned chicken broth
  Salt and pepper to taste
½ cup grated Parmesan cheese

Melt butter in a large, heavy skillet; add rice and onion; sauté *gently,* stirring *frequently,* until a light golden in color. Dissolve saffron in a little of the wine; add to rice along with the remaining wine and chicken broth; add salt and pepper. Bring to a boil, then cover tightly and cook over *very* low heat for 25 minutes, or until rice is tender and liquid absorbed. Stir in cheese. Correct seasoning. Serves 8.

Mincemeat Crêpes

1 cup sifted all-purpose flour
1 tablespoon sugar
½ teaspoon salt
3 eggs, well beaten
1½ cups milk
2 teaspoons grated lemon peel
1 tablespoon melted butter or salad oil
2 tablespoons each: California Sweet Sherry
  and Brandy
2 cups prepared mincemeat
2 tablespoons each: melted butter and sugar
  Sour cream

Mix flour, 1 tablespoon sugar, and salt in a bowl. Gradually add combined eggs and milk, beating until smooth. Stir in lemon peel and 1 tablespoon melted butter. Cook pancakes, one at a time, in a well-oiled skillet (measuring 6½ inches across the bottom), turning once. Use a scant ¼ cup batter per pancake, and tilt skillet as you pour in batter so that batter covers bottom evenly. (Makes 12 pancakes.) Add Sherry and Brandy to mincemeat; spread about 2 tablespoons of mixture on each pancake; roll up. Place side by side in 2 greased 12 by 8 by 2-inch baking dishes. Sprinkle with the 2 tablespoons melted butter, then the 2 tablespoons sugar. Cover loosely with aluminum foil. Bake in a moderate oven (350°F.) for 20 minutes. Serve warm. Pass sour cream. Serves 6. Wine choice: California Sec Champagne.

Timing Tips for the Hostess-Cook

Guacamole Molds: Prepare molds the day before. Early on party day, wash and chill salad greens. Also drain oranges and grapefruit sections, or peel and quarter tomatoes; cover and chill. If refrigerator space permits, assemble salads on plates shortly before guests arrive; spoon on dressing just before serving. Otherwise, assemble and dress salads on chilled plates just before serving.

Rolled Chicken Breasts with Mushroom Stuffing: Stuffing can be prepared the day before. Early on party day, pound, stuff, and roll chicken breasts; chill. Bake as directed; cool; refrigerate, covered with foil. Prepare sauce early in the day; cool, refrigerate. Fifteen or 20 minutes before serving, heat sauce in a large skillet; add chicken breasts; cover and reheat gently.

Risotto Rialto: Sauté rice and onion early in the day; set aside. About 30 minutes before dinnertime, add wine, broth, and seasonings; finish dish as directed; let stand in a warm place until time to serve. Or, prepare risotto early in the day; reheat in the oven in a covered casserole set in a shallow pan of hot water. Allow about 30 minutes at 350°F.

Buttered Asparagus Tips: Wash and trim fresh asparagus early in the day; refrigerate. Cook fresh or frozen asparagus (or heat canned asparagus) just before serving.

Mincemeat Crêpes: Crêpes can be made a day or two ahead; when cool, wrap snugly in foil; refrigerate. Early on party day, fill crêpes and place in casserole. Sprinkle with butter and sugar just before baking.

IX. Something to Nibble On

Delicious tidbits to serve before dinner

Some of my favorite foods are hors d'oeuvres and canapés. I welcome a chance to serve and savor them, and always hope I'll have enough strength of character to prevent their diminishing my appetite for dinner!

Here are recipes for some of the tempting morsels that we and our guests enjoy...all perfect companions to a pre-dinner glass of Champagne, Sherry, Vermouth, or whatever's your pleasure.

Chicken Liver Pâté

½ pound chicken livers
¼ pound lean bacon
1 small onion
1 clove garlic
1 tablespoon plus 1 teaspoon flour
½ cup canned consommé
1 large egg, slightly beaten
1 tablespoon California Brandy
½ inch anchovy paste, squeezed from tube
1 teaspoon parsley flakes
¼ teaspoon seasoned salt
   Dash each of nutmeg and pepper

With a sharp knife dice chicken livers, bacon, onion, and garlic. Combine all ingredients and mix well. Pour about ⅓ of mixture into blender container; run blender until mixture is smooth. Add and blend in remaining mixture, ⅓ at a time. Pour into buttered 1½-pint or 1-quart casserole. Cover casserole and set in a shallow pan of hot water. Bake in a moderate oven (350°F.) for 1¾ hours. Remove casserole from water; let stand a few minutes, then carefully pour off any liquid. Cool thoroughly before serving. Pâté can be kept covered in the refrigerator for a week or so, and can also be frozen successfully. Serve with melba toast or crackers. Slices of sweet midget pickle are a good companion. With this we enjoy California Dry Vermouth, Dry Sherry or Champagne.

Bacon Crisps

Wrap oblong or square saltine crackers with a single layer of bacon, covering crackers completely. Have the bacon at room temperature so it will be pliable. Place wrapped crackers on a rack in a shallow baking pan. Bake in a hot oven (400°F.) for 15 to 20 minutes, or until bacon is crisp and crackers are a toasty golden brown. Serve warm. These can be baked ahead and reheated very briefly in a slow oven. With these we enjoy California Champagne or Dry Sherry.

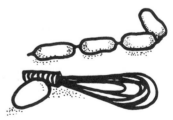

Vienna Bites

Drain canned Vienna sausages, reserving liquid. Cut sausages crosswise in halves; heat piping hot in the liquid. Serve on cocktail picks, accompanied by a bowl of *Mustard Mayonnaise* (equal parts of mayonnaise and Dijon-style mustard stirred together). One (4-oz.) can of sausages makes 14 "bites." With these we enjoy California Dry Vermouth or White Table Wine.

Savory Stuffed Mushrooms

Drain 2 (6-oz.) cans broiled whole mushroom crowns; with ball cutter or sharp knife, scoop out stems. Chop stems fine; add 1 (2¼-oz.) can deviled ham, 1 teaspoon *each* dry shredded green onions and parsley flakes, and 1 tablespoon California Sherry. Stuff mushrooms with mixture; place in a greased shallow baking dish. Sprinkle generously with grated Parmesan cheese. Bake in a hot oven (450°F.) for 10 minutes. Serve hot on cocktail picks. Makes about 40 appetizers. With these we enjoy California Champagne or Dry Sherry.

Shrimp Appetizer Mold

1 envelope (1 tablespoon) unflavored gelatin
¼ cup cold tomato juice
½ cup boiling tomato juice
1 cup dairy sour cream
2 tablespoons California Dry Vermouth
1 teaspoon each: dry shredded green onions, lemon juice, and drained capers
½ teaspoon each: dried dill weed, prepared horseradish, and Worcestershire sauce
¼ teaspoon seasoned salt
1 (4½ or 5-oz.) can shrimp, drained and rinsed

Soften gelatin in the cold tomato juice 5 minutes; dissolve in the hot tomato juice. Pour into blender container; add all ingredients except shrimp; run blender to mix ingredients well. Add shrimp; run blender until mixture is smooth. Pour into a 3-cup mold; chill until firm. Unmold and serve with crackers or melba toast for spreading. P.S. This also makes a very good molded salad, garnished with tomatoes and served with French dressing. With this we enjoy California Dry Sherry, Dry Vermouth or White Table Wine.

Caviar Cheesecake

Have 1 (3-oz.) package cream cheese at room temperature; blend with ¼ cup cottage cheese and ¼ teaspoon Worcestershire sauce. Shape mixture into a round, flat cake about ¾ inch thick on a small serving plate. Mix 1 (2-oz.) jar domestic caviar with 1 teaspoon *each* lemon juice and dry shredded green onions. Frost cheesecake with caviar mixture, covering it completely; chill thoroughly. Just before serving, sprinkle with grated or sieved hard-cooked egg. Serve with crackers or melba toast for spreading. Plenty for 6 to 8, if you're serving other hors d'oeuvres. Easily multiplied for a large party. With this we enjoy California Brut Champagne or White Table Wine.

Mini-Pizzas

With scissors, cut packaged refrigerator biscuits in quarters. Place on greased baking sheet; press each piece of dough into a 1-inch round. Spread each with catsup; sprinkle with oregano; cover with shredded Cheddar cheese; top with a tiny piece of anchovy fillet; drizzle a little olive oil over all. Bake in a hot oven (450°F.) for 10 minutes. Serve hot. One (8-oz.) package biscuits makes 40 mini-pizzas. With these we enjoy California Red Table Wine or Dry Vermouth.

Quiche Emily

Follow the recipe for *Ham and Cheese Pie* (page 72). Remove from oven and let cool 15 minutes or so, then cut in bite-sized squares and serve warm. Always a hit! P.S. If you're only serving 6 or 8 people, you can make just one pie for an hors d'oeuvre and then fill and bake the other shell for a main dish later. With this we enjoy California Dry Sherry or White Table Wine.

•••••••••••••••••••••••

Other good hors d'oeuvre recipes in this book: *Cheese Crisps* (page 106), good with California Red or White Table Wine; *Ann's Cheddar Fondue* (page 98), with California Dry Sherry or Dry Vermouth; *Herb Toasties* (page 108), with California Pink Chablis; *Trio Cheese* (page 109), with half-and-half California Dry and Sweet Vermouth or a glass of California Port; and *Guacamole Molds* (page 120), with California Chenin Blanc or Medium Sherry on the rocks.

X. The Pleasure of Wines with Dinner

Suggestions for serving and keeping

Though I have chosen one wine to complement most of the menus in this book, there is no reason why two or more wines can't be served, especially at parties or special family dinners. For instance, a glass of California Dry or Medium Sherry would be delicious with *Mushroom Consommé Imperial* or with an appetizer such as *Pâté Maison* or *Mushroom Canapé Belleview.*

For a fancy and formal meal, a small portion of one of the fish dishes, such as *Sole Angelique, Baked Sole in Oyster-Cheese Sauce,* or *Sole with Shrimp, Hollandaise,* could be served with a crisp, chilled California White Wine before a main course such as *Baked Stuffed Lamb Chops* or *Roast Prime Ribs of Beef* that are to be accompanied by a California Red Table Wine.

There are many desserts in the *Wine Cookbook of Dinner Menus* that would team happily with a glass of one of the rich, delicious California Dessert Wines, and of course there is always Champagne to end a dinner party on a really glamorous note. *Graham Cracker Torte, Pumpkin Chiffon Pie, Sabayon Pudding,* and *Coconut Bavarian Cream* ask for a glass of California Cream Sherry. When fresh fruit and cheese are served, California Port is the perfect companion, and with chocolate desserts try one of the California coffee or chocolate-flavored wines. With *Nectar-Glazed Strawberry Tarts* and *Orange Dessert Ring with Fruit* a glass of Muscatel would be delightful. Experiment and discover new pleasures for your palate!

A word about wine glasses: The ideal wine glass is one with a stem to keep the hand from warming the wine, of clear glass in order to be able to appreciate the wine's color and clarity, and large enough to permit a four-ounce serving with room enough in the bowl to capture aroma and bouquet. The diameter of the lip should be slightly less than the widest part of the bowl. All this can be accomplished with a single, all-purpose glass. But if a formal selection of wine glasses for parties is your heart's desire, here are the seven basic shapes correct for serving all wines.

White wines and rosés are at their best chilled, reds at cool room temperature. Many people like red wines chilled as well, but it should be remembered that the lower temperature can dull the full, big flavor of a fine red wine. Appetizer wines should be chilled and can also be served on the rocks. Dessert wines are at their smooth best served at room temperature, although here again some prefer a Muscatel, for instance, lightly chilled. Champagnes and sparkling wines should be placed in the refrigerator at least three hours before serving. Not only do these wines taste best well chilled, but they also retain their bubbles upon opening, instead of bursting forth in a shattering-to-the-host shower, as they will if too warm.

The one wine accessory that is essential is a good corkscrew, though when you buy one of the many good wines that are closed with an airtight, plastic-lined screw cap, you don't even need to worry about this.

A word about serving wine: The informal service of wine is easy and simple. The opened bottle may be passed around the table, the men pouring for the ladies before serving themselves. However for more formal occasions

All-purpose

White   Rhine

Red   Champagne

Port   Sherry

the host (or hostess) pours a bit of wine into his own glass first. He holds it up to the light to make sure of color and clarity, twirls the glass and holds it under his nose to sniff aroma and bouquet. Finally he takes a sip, rolls it around in his mouth and now, satisfied with the wine's flavor, body and texture, he starts around the table to his right, serving everyone in order. The glasses should be filled half full so that everyone can twirl the wine and enjoy its fragrance. (In a restaurant the waiter will usually adhere to this pleasant and practical custom by pouring a little wine in the host's glass to give him the opportunity to examine and approve the wine before his guests are served.)

In setting a table the correct position of the wine glass, or glasses, is shown in the sketch.

A question which very often worries a hostess in planning her party is "How many servings are there in a bottle of wine?" The following chart answers this question. The average serving of Dinner wine or Champagne is usually 4 to 6 ounces; of Appetizer or Dessert wine, 2 to 3 ounces.

Placement of wine glass is to the right of the water goblet. First wine served is farthest to the right.

Size	Ounces	Dinner Wines - Champagne	Appetizer-Dessert Wines
Split	6.4	2 servings	
Tenth (4/5 pt.)	12.8	2-3 servings	4-6 servings
Pint	16.	3-4 servings	5-7 servings
Fifth (4/5 qt.)	25.6	4-6 servings	8-12 servings
Quart	32.	6-8 servings	10-14 servings
½ Gallon	64.	12-16 servings	20-30 servings
Gallon	128.	24-30 servings	40-60 servings
Metric Size			
100 milliliters	3.4	1 serving	
187 milliliters	6.3	2 servings	
375 milliliters	12.7	2-3 servings	4-6 servings
750 milliliters	25.4	4-6 servings	8-12 servings
1 liter	33.8	6-8 servings	10-14 servings
1.5 liters	50.7	9-12 servings	16-25 servings
3 liters	101.4	16-25 servings	33-50 servings

A word on storing wine: If storing for a reasonably long period, choose a moderately cool place (50° is ideal, but the range between 60° and 70° is perfectly adequate), where there are no sudden temperature changes, away from furnace or radiator or sunny wall, and away from any source of vibration. Wines should always be kept out of direct sunlight. Corked wines should always rest on their sides or upside-down in their original fibre-board cases. Bottles with screw caps are airtight and should be stored upright, as should sparkling wines with plastic closures.

Store capped bottles upright, corked bottles on their sides.

Dessert Appetizer Wines

Red Table Wines

White Table & Sparkling Wines

In a broom closet

Table wines, with their low alcoholic content, are perishable after opening and should be consumed as soon as possible. Leftover table wine should be tightly corked or capped and kept in the refrigerator. Appetizer or dessert wines, because of their higher alcoholic content, will keep several months after opening, if closure is replaced. Refrigeration does not injure wines and many people keep a few bottles of white and rosé table wines and sparkling wines in the home refrigerator, ready to serve. No wine should be chilled lower than 35°, as temperatures lower than this damage the wine.

A simple home wine cellar can be located in a broom closet or cupboard, handy to the kitchen, or in a cool cellar if you have one. The illustration shows the best placement of wines, remembering that the coolest temperature is at floor level, the warmest nearest the ceiling, and pictures two different treatments of the home wine cellar. However a simple wine rack or the case the wines came in will provide satisfactory storage.

In a bookcase

You can start a real cellar of your own with a minimum of bottles: a California Red Table Wine, a White Table Wine, a Sherry or Vermouth, a Dessert Wine, a Sparkling Wine and one of the Special Natural Wines, and build from there. With your wine cellar and wine-cooked dishes from this book to choose from, you'll have the inspiration for many a happy meal!

XI. In Praise of California Wine

Some professional and knowledgeable opinion

California's wines are among the finest in the world, a fact which has become established and accepted by expert and amateur alike.

Not only are the higher priced wines recognized here and abroad for their excellence, but the lower priced wines have received the highest praise. Robert Balzer, in the *Los Angeles Times,* gave special praise to a bottle of California Burgundy which sold at the time of writing for 89 cents: "...its fine quality being testimonial to the advances made in the scientific art of enology in California in recent decades...a thirst-quenching dinner wine of remarkably reliable virtue."

And George Christy in an article in the *Los Angeles Magazine* stated: "Any Californian who bypasses California wines for European wines these days is only displaying abysmal ignorance. In fact, serving California wines at a dinner party is a double sign of style and taste: not only are you proud of your own backyard (which is what true status is all about) but if you... can introduce guests to surprises, they're delighted and enriched."

Finally, Henry Rubin in his column, "The Winemaster," in the *San Francisco Chronicle* says flatly, "...the best mass-produced wines in the world... wines selling for less than a dollar...without question beat those of Europe."

I have been drinking the fine wines of California and using them in cooking for many years and can only say amen to the above!

Several years ago the California wine producers decided to find out just how their wines would fare in "blind" tasting competition with comparable foreign wines. The average prices of the California wines tested ranged from $1.63 per bottle for table wines to $1.77 for dessert wines and $4.34 for Champagnes. Average prices of the foreign competitors of the same types were respectively $3.84, $4.34 and $8.34.

Of the 1,026 persons participating in the taste-test program, 269 were wine experts and the balance amateurs chosen from amongst newspapermen, advertising executives, theatrical and professional people. They were asked to determine two things: where they believed the wines came from and which wines they preferred.

Panelists were served California and foreign wines in numbered glasses, the bottles themselves of course being hidden from view.

The results of these contests over the six-year period were enlightening. Although the race was extremely close, California wines gradually asserted themselves and advanced to the leading place. Of the total preference points recorded the California contingent came out ahead by 675 votes.

It is no wonder that an article on wine quality syndicated in 17 U. S. newspapers had this to say recently, "...California vineyards have made such progress that their best wine compares favorably with...that imported from ...other great wine-growing countries." And in the November 1969 issue of *American Home,* in an article devoted to California wines, author Bob Thompson quoted wine authority, Hugh Johnson, as stating, "California's best red wines are great wines and California will ultimately become one of the finest vineyards in the world."

The California winemakers have good reason to believe that they have already achieved this shining goal.

A comprehensive index to all recipes in the series of six wine cookbooks is available in *Epicurean Recipes of California Winemakers.*

Recipe Index

The Wine Advisory Board Cookbooks
"The Classic Series on Cooking With Wine"

This series of six wine cookbooks is the largest collection of cooking with wine recipes available in the World. There is no duplication of features or recipes in the Wine Advisory Board Cookbooks. Specific wine types are recommended as table beverages for all main dishes. The present series represents over 2,800 different recipes of all types using wine. From wine cocktails, hors d'oeuvres, salads, soups, wild game, fish, eggs, many different main dishes to desserts and jellies; the magnitude of this collection of wine recipes is overwhelming. Who could possibly develop and test such a large number of recipes? These books are the result of the cooperation of over 400 people in the wine industry. In 1961 the Wine Advisory Board began collecting the favorite and best recipes of the various winemakers and their families. Most of the recipes are old family favorites, tested with time and then re-tested and proven in Wine Advisory Board test kitchens. We are particularly pleased with the recipes and wine choices from staff members of the Department of Viticulture and Enology and the Department of Food Science and Technology of University of California, Davis and Fresno.

So here is a series of the very best wine recipes; selected and developed by many of the most knowledgeable wine and food lovers of America.

#500 EPICUREAN RECIPES OF CALIFORNIA WINEMAKERS: Did you know that you can buy wild boar, cook it at home with Burgundy and produce a gourmet treat that your guests will rave about for years? Or, that you can make your reputation as an Epicurean cook by preparing and serving Boeuf ala Bourguignonne, according to the recipe of a famous wine authority? This book includes the most elaborate to simple recipes contributed by California Winemakers, their wives and associates; all selected for their unforgetable taste experiences. Another important feature of this book is it includes the comprehensive index of recipes for the entire six cookbook series. 128 pp, 8½'' x 11'', illustrated, 1978 Edition. $5.95@ ISBN 0-932664-00-8

#501 GOURMET WINE COOKING THE EASY WAY: All new recipes for memorable eating, prepared quickly and simply with wine. Most of the recipes specify convenience foods which can be delightfully flavored with wine, enabling the busy homemaker to set a gourmet table for family and friends with a minimum of time in the kitchen. More than 500 tested and proven recipes; used frequently by the first families of America's wine industry. 128pp, 8½'' x 11'', illustrated, 1978 edition. $4.95@ ISBN 0-932664-01-6

#502 ADVENTURES IN WINE COOKERY BY CALIFORNIA WINEMAKERS: The life work of the winemaker is to guide nature in the development in wine of beauty, aroma, bouquet and subtle flavors. Wine is part of their daily diet, leading to more flavorful dishes, comfortable living, merriment and goodfellowship. These recipes contributed by Winemakers, their families and colleagues represent this spirit of flavorful good living. A best selling cookbook with 500 exciting recipes including barbecue, wine drinks, salads and sauces. 128pp, illustrated 8½'' x 11''. $4.95@ ISBN 0-932664-02-4

#503 FAVORITE RECIPES OF CALIFORNIA WINEMAKERS: The original winemakers' cookbook and a bestseller for fifteen years. Over 200 dedicated winemakers, their wives and colleagues have shared with us their love of cooking. They are the authors of this book, which is dedicated to a simple truth known for thousands of years in countless countries: good food is even better with wine. Over 500 authentic recipes, many used for generations, are included in this "cookbook classic". 128pp, 8½'' x 11'', illustrated. $4.95@ ISBN 0-932664-03-2

#504 WINE COOKBOOK OF DINNER MENUS by Emily Chase and Wine Advisory Board. Over 100 complete dinner menus with recommended complimentary wines. This book will make your dinner planning easy and the results impressive to your family and most sophisticated guests. Emily Chase worked with the winemakers of California a number of years and was also the Home Economics Editor of Sunset Magazine. She tested recipes for six years and is the author of numerous articles and books on cooking. This edition contains 400 different recipes, suggestions for wines to accompany dinners and tips on serving, storing and enjoying wine. 128pp, illustrated, 8½'' x 11'', 1978 edition $4.95@ ISBN 0-932664-04-0

#640 THE CHAMPAGNE COOKBOOK: "Add Some Sparkle to Your Cooking and Your Life" by Malcolm R. Hebert. Cooking with Champagne is a glamorous yet easy way to liven up your cuisine. The recipes range from soup, salads, hors d'oeuvres, fish, fowl, red meat, vegetables and of course desserts—all using Champagne. Many new entertaining ideas with Champagne cocktails, drinks and Champagne lore are included along with simple rules on cooking with and serving Sparkling Wines. Recipes are provided by California, New York and European Champagne makers and their families. The author's 30 years of teaching and writing about food and wine makes this an elegant yet practical book. 128pp, illustrated, 8½" × 11" ppb, $6.95 @ ISBN 0-932664-07-5.

#641 THE POCKET ENCYCLOPEDIA OF CALIFORNIA WINE by William I. Kaufman. A convenient and thorough reference book that fits into your vest pocket and gives answers to all of your questions about California Wines. All the wineries, grape varieties, wines, geography and wine terms are covered briefly and authoritatively by one of America's foremost wine experts. Carry with you to restaurants and wine tastings to make you well informed on your choice of California Wines. 128 compact pages, 7¾" x 3½" with vinyl cover. $4.95 @ ISBN 0-932664-09-1, 1983 Edition.

#673 WINE IN EVERYDAY COOKING by Patti Ballard, The newest and freshest in our famous wine cookbook series. Patti is the popular wine consultant from Santa Cruz who has been impressing winery visitors and guests for years with her wine and food magic. Strong Italian heritage is evident in her recipes and the cooking tips from Patti's grandmother. Chapters range from soup and hors d'oeuvres through pasta, fish and desserts—all of course using wine. 128pp, illustrated, 8½"x 11" ppb, $5.95 @ ISBN 0-932664-20-2, Oct. 1981.

#671 CORKSCREWS, KEYS TO HIDDEN PLEASURES by Manfred Heckman. The first authoritative book on corkscrews, their history, science, design and enjoyment: for the connoisseur or the novice. Over 500 corkscrew models are covered with a multitude of photos and 10 full color pages. Essential for the collector and fascinating for anyone interested in wine. 124pp, color cover. English edition available 1983, $20.00 @ ISBN 0-032664-17-2.

#672 THE CALIFORNIA WINE DRINK BOOK by William I. Kaufman. Cocktails, hot drinks, punches and coolers all made with wine. Over 200 different drink recipes, using various wines along with mixing tips and wine entertaining suggestions. Today's accent on lighter drinks makes this a most useful handbook, and you'll save money too by using wine rather than higher taxed liquors! Pocket size, leatherette cover, 128 pp, $4.95. May 1982, ISBN 0-932664-10-9.

Each book includes its own index; however, **EPICUREAN RECIPES** includes a comprehensive index for the entire cookbook series. These books are available at bookstores, wine shops and wineries. If you have trouble finding them, they may be ordered direct from The Wine Appreciation Guild. Also, most other wine books and wine related items are available.

HOW TO ORDER BY MAIL: Indicate the number of copies and titles you wish on the order from below and include your check, money order, or Mastercard, or VISA card number. California residents include 6% sales tax. There is a $1.50 shipping and handling charge per order, regardless of how many books you order. (If no order form—any paper will do.) Orders shipped promptly via U.S. Mail—U.S. & Canada shipments ONLY.

ORDER FORM
WINE APPRECIATION GUILD
1377 Ninth Avenue
San Francisco, California 94122

SHIP TO: _____

Address_____

City_____ State_____ Zip_____

Please send the following:
_____ Copies #500 EPICUREAN RECIPES OF CALIFORNIA WINEMAKERS $6.95@ _____
_____ Copies #501 GOURMET WINE COOKING THE EASY WAY $5.95@ _____
_____ Copies #502 NEW ADVENTURES IN WINE COOKERY $5.95@ _____
_____ Copies #503 FAVORITE RECIPES OF CALIFORNIA WINEMAKERS $5.95@ _____
_____ Copies #504 DINNER MENUS WITH WINE $6.95@ _____
_____ Copies #505 EASY RECIPES OF CALIFORNIA WINEMAKERS $5.95@ _____
_____ Copies #640 THE CHAMPAGNE COOKBOOK $6.95@ _____
_____ Copies #527 IN CELEBRATION OF WINE & LIFE $20.00@ _____
_____ Copies #554 WINE CELLAR RECORD BOOK $32.50@ _____
_____ Copies #641 POCKET ENCYCLOPEDIA OF CALIFORNIA WINES $4.95@ _____
_____ Copies #671 CORKSCREWS $20.00@ _____
_____ Copies #672 CALIFORNIA WINE DRINK BOOK $4.95@ _____
_____ Copies #673 WINE IN EVERYDAY COOKING $5.95@ _____

Subtotal _____
California Residents 6% sales tax _____
plus $1.50 Shipping and handling (per order) $1.50 _____
TOTAL enclosed or charged to credit card _____

Please charge to my Mastercard or Visa card # _____
Expiration Date_____

Signature_____